The 15 most popular martial arts systems practiced in North America

Discipline	Country of Origin
Aikido	Japan
Arnis/Escrima	Philippines
Hapkido	Korea
Jiu-jitsu	Japan
Judo	Japan
Karate	Okinawa/Japan
Kendo	Japan
Kickboxing	USA
Kobudo	Okinawa/Japan
Kung Fu	China
Kyudo	Japan
Muay Thai	Thailand
Silat	Indonesia
Tae Kwon Do	Korea
Tai Chi Chuan	China

Martial Arts Ranking System

Popular Martial Arts Maxims

"A journey of a thousand miles begins with a first step."

"To know the road ahead, ask those coming back."

"The ultimate aim of Budo lies not in victory or defeat, but in the perfection of one's character."

"He who knows others is learned, he who knows himself is wise."

"To win one hundred victories in one hundred battles is not the greatest skill. To subdue the enemy without fighting is the highest skill."

Martial Arts Uniforms

Jiu-jitsu • Judo
Karate • Kobudo
Tae Kwon Do

Aikido • Kendo
Kyudo

Kung Fu • Silat
Tai Chi Chuan

Kickboxing
Muay Thai

Eclectic
Escrima

Most Common Karate Techniques

Oii-zuki	Lunge punch
Gyaku-zuki	Reverse punch
Shuto-uchi	Knife hand
Teisho-uchi	Palm heel strike
Hijiate	Elbow strike
Hiza-geri	Knee strike
Mae-geri	Front kick
Yoko-geri	Side kick
Mawashi-geri	Round kick
Ushiro-geri	Back kick

Most Common Judo Techniques

Osoto-gare	Big outside drop
Deashi-barrai	Forward foot sweep
Ippon-seionage	One-arm shoulder throw
Harai-goshi	Hip spring throw
Tai-toshi	Body drop throw
Taomoe-nage	Round throw
Kata-murana	Shoulder wheel
Uchi-mata	Inner leg throw
Oguruma	Big whirl throw
Osaekomi	Ground holding

Most Common Jiu-jitsu Techniques

Tate-zuki	Standing fist punch
Ippon-ken	One-knuckle punch
Haishu	Back hand strike
Ashi-barrai	Leg sweep
Ude-kansetsu	Arm bar
Kote-gaeshi	Wrist flex takedown
Kata-seionage	Shoulder throw
Goshi-guruma	Hip throw
Shime-waza	Neck restraints
Antachi-waza	Holding after takedown

Most Common Tae Kwon Do Techniques

Jirugi	Fore fist punch
Sonkal	Knife hand strike
Palkup	Elbow strike
Apchagi	Front kick
Yopchagi	Side kick
Dollyochagi	Turning kick
Dwitcha-jirugi	Back kick
Dwikumchichagi	Axe heel kick
Bandae-dollyochagi	Rear spin kick
Twimyo-dollyochagi	Jump turn kick

Top Ten Martial Movie Picks
In Alphabetical Order

Above the Law	Starring Steven Seagal
Enter the Dragon	Starring Bruce Lee
The Karate Kid	Starring Ralph Macchio
Once Upon a Time in the East I, II, III	Starring Jet Li
Samurai Trilogy I, II, III	Starring Various Artists
Seven Samurai	Starring Toshiro Mifune
The Shaolin Temple	Starring Jet Li
Super Cop	Starring Jackie Chan
The Yakuza	Starring Robert Mitchum
Yojimbo (The Bodyguard)	Starring Toshiro Mifune

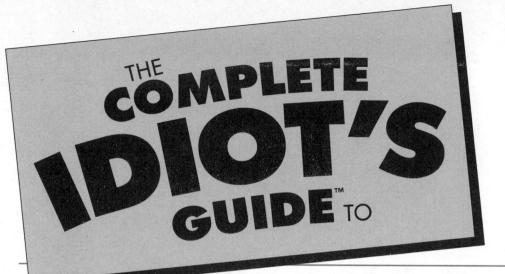

THE COMPLETE IDIOT'S GUIDE™ TO

Martial
Arts

♦ **Quick and easy facts**
   about 13 martial art disciplines

♦ **Valuable training tips** and
   suggestions for selecting the right
   martial art

♦ **Down-to-earth advice** about
   the physical and mental benefits
   of martial arts for children, teens,
   and adults

**Cezar Borkowski and
Marion Manzo**

An Alpha Books/Prentice Hall Canada
Copublication

With love and appreciation to our mothers, Alicja and Eileen, and to our "extended family"—the more than 2000 teachers, staff and students of Northern Karate Schools.

Cataloguing in Publication Data

Borkowski, Cezar
The complete idiot's guide to martial arts

Includes index.
ISBN Canada: 0-13-080937-3
ISBN United States: 0-02-862947-7

1. Martial arts.   I. Manzo, Marion.   II. Title.

GV1112.B67 1998   796.815   C98-932027-8

Macmillan Publishing books may be purchased for business or sales promotional use. For information, please write: Special Markets Department, Macmillan Publishing USA, 1633 Broadway, New York, NY 10019.

ISBN Canada: 0-13-080937-3
ISBN United States: 0-02-862947-7
Library of Contress Catalog Card Number: 98-87606

01 00 99   RRD 8 7 6 5 4 3 2 1

Printed in the United States of America

PRENTICE HALL DEVELOPMENT TEAM

Director, Trade Group
Robert Harris

Acquisitions Editor
Dean Hannaford

Copy Editor
Eileen Koyama

Assistant Editor
Joan Whitman

Production Editor
Lu Cormier

Production Coordinator
Shannon Potts

Art Direction
Mary Opper

Cover Design
Kyle Gell

Cover Photograph
Roy Morsch, The Stock Market

Page Layout
Gail Ferreira Ng-A-Kien

Contents

vii

Part 3: How You Can Get Started   97

9   Choosing the Right Martial Art   99

10   Finding the School That's Right for You   113

11   What to Expect in the First Month and Beyond   123

Foreword

As President of the World Kobudo Federation, the largest multidiscipline martial arts organization in the world, with membership in 42 countries, I travel around the world, propagating combative systems.

Historically, practitioners looked to the East for inspiration and technical know-how. Now, however, this has changed and more martial students are getting their education in the West, where there is an impressive array of experienced instructors teaching a broad spectrum of martial systems.

What's often the toughest part of a martial arts education is getting started. Understanding the differences between various types of martial arts and finding one that's going to appeal to you is difficult. What's even harder, sometimes, is locating a good teacher and school. Those are but a few of the key points addressed in *The Complete Idiot's Guide to Martial Arts*.

Another challenging aspect of training is staying motivated, and this book even addresses this issue—so it's a great resource for experienced martial artists as well.

Unlike lots of other textbooks, *The Complete Idiot's Guide to Martial Arts* is easy to understand. It's humorous without being insulting, and the language is simple but not condescending.

This book can help you begin studying martial arts, and that's something that can positively change your life forever.

Kyoshi John Therien,
Eighth Degree Black Belt,
President, World Kobudo Federation

Introduction

So you're thinking about studying martial arts. What prompted your interest? An action-packed demonstration at your health club or local mall? A well-intentioned, but relentlessly nagging, best friend who preaches (ad nauseum!) about the physical, mental and spiritual benefits of his or her martial arts training? Maybe it was the latest action film or a popular television program where the squeaky-clean protagonist saved all that is just and holy? Was it an enticing article in the latest issue of your favorite fitness magazine, or an intriguing ad in the telephone directory? Perhaps it's simply something you've wanted to do, or have your children do, for years.

Whatever the reason, you're now trying to develop a basic understanding of the words *martial arts*. That's where *The Complete Idiot's Guide to Martial Arts* comes in. This is an informative, occasionally humorous, sometimes irreverent look at this complex subject. (Don't think for a moment that just because we've presented some of the information in this book in a funny format we don't take our passionate devotion to this stuff *seriously.*)

This guide is designed to be educational and entertaining. It's also reader friendly. We used the most common spellings for martial arts terms and provided simple translations where necessary so you'll be able to figure out even the most complex information quickly and easily. Most importantly, you'll be taken, step by step, through the seeming maze that surrounds the martial arts. You'll discover how and why they originated, how the major types differ and what benefits you can expect as a practitioner.

How to Use This Book

To make things even easier, we've divided this book into five parts.

Part 1: The Basics   This section explains how martial arts developed in response to one of our most basic needs: survival. It also provides common sense personal protection advice and practical safety checklists. You'll discover some of the physical and nonphysical benefits martial arts training can provide children, teens and adults. You'll explore the combative systems of ancient Egypt, Greece, Rome and India and begin to understand the basic categories of martial arts systems taught today. You'll also examine essential information about finding a good instructor and an appropriate school.

Part 2: Stepping Up to the Mat   This part debunks martial myths and misconceptions, outlines essential beginner do's and don'ts, and offers key safety tips for novice, intermediate and even advanced practitioners. This section will walk you through the various stages of martial arts training. It reinforces the importance of finding an instructor who takes a balanced approach to teaching. You'll get practical information regarding basic nutrition for martial artists, and learn about the importance of cross-training and using special training equipment. Additionally, you'll get some sensible advice on establishing and adhering to a goal plan. As you explore the mental and spiritual side of your study, you'll learn some Zen lessons that can be applied to daily life and discover the ultimate goal of martial artists.

Part 3: How You Can Get Started   This section gets right down to the nitty-gritty of finding, and enrolling in, a martial arts school. It includes checklists that will assist you in comparison shopping for different disciplines and styles, screening prospective instructors, deciphering advertisements, inspecting schools, participating in introductory or trial programs and calculating the real cost of uniforms, equipment and tuition. Furthermore, you'll pick up some tips on surviving your first day and month of training, and preparing for your first advancement examination. Assuming you've achieved some of your preliminary martial arts goals, this part will discuss the importance of establishing new objectives and will delve into more complex areas of training, such as fending off several opponents, facing armed attackers, competing in tournaments, breaking bricks, boards and other inanimate objects, and learning to teach.

Part 4: Major Martial Arts in Detail   Whereas Part 1 provides an overview of major martial arts, this section discusses each discipline in greater detail. You'll learn how various armed and unarmed systems and styles originated and evolved, and gain greater insight into the differences between the major combative arts of Kung Fu, Jiu-jitsu, Karate, Judo, Aikido, Muay Thai, Silat, Escrima, Tae Kwon Do, Kendo, Kyudo, Kobudo and Tai Chi Chuan. You'll also discover something about the eclectic (out-of-class) approach to training, which includes surfing the Net, using videotapes and CD-ROMs, reading books and magazines, and attending seminars and workshops. Furthermore, this part contains information about lesser known styles like Jeet Kune Do, Capoeira, Shootboxing and Shootwrestling, Trapfighting, Sambo, Vale Tudo, Mu Tau, as well as military based systems including Kravmaga, Spetnats and one that's based on U.S. Navy Seals training.

Part 5: Making Your Journey with Confidence   The final section sums it all up. It will assist you in assessing the body-mind-spirit value of your training. This section will explain how you can take inventory of your achievements and determine the influence the martial arts have had on your life. Most importantly, it will educate you about how you can use your martial arts experience to make your community—and perhaps, even the world—a better place.

Extras   As you embark on your martial arts journey and begin reading this book, you'll notice a few "signposts" that provide additional information.

Martial Smarts

Quotes and anecdotes that are inspirational, intriguing and humorous.

Warrior Words

Definitions and explanations for martial arts and related terminology.

Risky Moves

Warnings and cautions about things to avoid.

Master Speaks

Advice on a variety of martial arts and other relevant topics.

And because we believe a "picture is worth a thousand words," we also included dozens of photographs that illustrate some basic techniques taught by the major martial arts covered in this guide.

Acknowledgments

Many thanks to our colleagues and friends Claire and Dominic Moscone, Steve Ouslis and Michael Walsh for their editorial and research assistance and, most of all, for their support and love. Also thanks to Grace Braga for doing a superhuman job on the administrative front and to the many instructors who filled in for us while we were in the grips of "book madness." We'd like to express our appreciation to the martial artists who patiently posed for the photographs in this book: Mike D'Acenzo, Rob D'Amata, Vito Brancaccio, Antonio Coelho, Pablo Grossi, Rafael Holody, Joanna Loon, Claire and Peter Moscone, Walter Morocco, Steve Ouslis and Michael Walsh. Huge thanks to Antonius Lo for the incredible snaps. We'd also like to express our gratitude to Kevin Blok, Aikido-*ka* extraordinare, William Adams for lending us his Tai Chi Chuan expertise and Antonius Lo for additional background information on the martial arts of Southeast Asia.

Finally, we wouldn't sleep if we didn't acknowledge the superb efforts of the Prentice Hall crew: Dean Hannaford for his wonderful quarterbacking performance, Karen Alliston, Lu Cormier and Jody Schaeffer for pulling together the words and images that make up this book, Imogen Brian for cleaning up all our typos and spelling mistakes, and Eileen Koyama for making sense of each and every chapter. Final and heartfelt thanks to Hart Hillman for coming up with the idea for this guide in the first place.

If we've missed anyone, we apologize and we'll make it up to you in our next book!

Part 1
The Basics

You're probably eager to tie on a martial arts uniform and take your first class. But hold on! Before you come out swinging like a pro, you should read this section because one of the first lessons you'll learn about training is how important it is to learn the basics. Let's begin by taking some baby steps, like understanding why martial arts came about in the first place, discovering how they evolved and examining the physical and nonphysical benefits of practicing. Then, you can begin your infancy as a martial artist.

Chapter 1

Why Martial Arts?

In This Chapter

➤ How combative systems help people continue to "survive"

➤ Tips for personal protection

➤ Martial arts and physical fitness

➤ Other benefits for the young and young at heart

➤ Traveling the path to self-awareness

Throughout history, in addition to battling the elements, humankind has had to defeat any number of attackers, both animal and human. Our cave-dwelling ancestors simply used clubs and rocks to break each other's bones. The advent of simple, even crude, weapons and the debut of unarmed fighting skills marked the birth of martial arts.

Today, it's unlikely you'll need to fight a woolly mammoth. Why, then, would *you* want to study combative systems?

While martial arts will teach you how to protect yourself in the event of physical confrontation, this is the most modest of their benefits. In addition to helping you get and stay physically fit, martial arts can help you minimize stress, develop better focus and self-discipline, and move you along the road to self-discovery. That's why you should study martial arts, and, after reading *The Complete Idiot's Guide to Martial Arts,* you'll know more about these and other reasons you should enroll in a school.

Martial Smarts

One ought never to turn one's back on a threatened danger and try to run away from it. If you do that, you will double the danger. But if you meet it promptly and without flinching, you will reduce the danger in half. Never run away from anything. Never!

—*Winston Churchill*

Warrior Words

Feeling gutsy? Military strategist John S. Roosma described *guts* as "the ability to take it." He went on to explain that this meant the discipline to stand fast when your body wants to run. Martial arts training can help imprint this message onto your brain and into your heart, enabling you to face the myriad of challenges life may bring.

Our Most Basic Need

"Sticks and stones may break my bones…" This nursery rhyme has a painfully familiar ring, doesn't it? It also illustrates the fact that since the dawn of humanity, survival has been the cornerstone of our hierarchy of needs.

Nothing to Fear but Fear Itself

Whether accurate or inaccurate, the stereotypical image of an intimidating thug is some oversized, burly, venom-spewing, prehistoric type crushing our bodies and egos as we attempt to withdraw our weekly earnings from the corner bank machine. We fear what's real, but more often than not we fear what's unreal. Our worst nightmares are often far more terrifying than someone of superior size and strength, even if these ruffians do have our worst interests at heart.

As a martial arts student, you'll learn how to triumph over this kind of individual, not just physically, as your ancient ancestors did, but mentally and spiritually as well. You see, the *real* lesson of martial arts is to face and conquer your fears.

Leveling the Playing Field

In each martial arts class, you'll learn how to harness your natural strength. Not just the muscular variety, but the power that lies in your spirit and mind. As a martial arts practitioner, each drop of perspiration you shed will help wash away your fears, and each passing year can leave you feeling more confident.

At a very basic level, you'll learn how to better manage physically threatening situations. It doesn't matter if your opponent is the size of a defensive linesman. Speed, the element of surprise, and knowing where, when and how to strike will "shrink" any opponent down to size.

At a more advanced level, you'll discover how to anticipate and avoid these situations. Be forewarned—there are no quick fixes. This level of awareness can take you years, decades, perhaps even a lifetime to achieve. But if you stick around, you'll probably find it's well worth the effort.

Security Check

There are two basic types of personal defense:

1. defending yourself

2. defending others

You'll notice that we don't include "defending your possessions." We're pretty certain that, even though this is an *Idiot's Guide*, you're smart enough to know that you shouldn't struggle with an attacker to hang onto your purse, wallet or car.

The following checklists will help you determine your and your family's safety status. These are by no means comprehensive, but they should give your some ideas about developing your own checklists.

Safety inside the Home

Like charity, the need for personal protection often begins at home:

➤ Our home is a safe place. It is childproofed and has fire or smoke detectors and extinguishers, safety locks, flashlights, storm provisions and so on.

➤ Our family members have constructed and practiced emergency plans. We have discussed fire and storm escape routes, summoning police, medical and backup caregiver aid, handling burglaries and home invasions, and contacting children's crisis centers.

➤ Our family members never let strangers know they're home alone unless the caller or visitor is familiar with our special password or is a "safeface" person (such as a police officer or firefighter) with proper identification.

➤ Our family members know basic first-aid techniques.

Safety outside the Home

The great outdoors are not always so great. Therefore, we've provided some recommendations that you can use in crafting your own safety plan to prepare for what lies beyond your front door.

➤ Our family members carry identification that is not visible to strangers. We all know our first and last name, address and telephone number with area code but we never give this information to strangers unless our parents or caregivers say it's okay.

➤ Our family members know how to behave like good "defenders." That is, we stay alert and know our surroundings.

➤ Our family members know how to find "safeplaces" and "safefaces".

➤ Our family members know there is safety in numbers, so we avoid traveling alone.

➤ Our family members have practiced emergency role playing and route rehearsals. For example, we have reviewed the route from school to home, noting safe places, well-lit and densely populated streets, and locations of Block Parent homes or stores where we regularly shop. We also know how to ask the operator to interrupt a telephone call. We have discussed contingency plans, such as what to do if no one arrives to pick us up or we get lost in the mall.

➤ Our family members know how to use equipment—from gardening tools and lawnmowers to sports gear (hockey sticks, cycling helmets)—safely. We are also very careful about learning the necessary skills for all our extracurricular activities (such as swimming and skiing).

➤ Our family members travel safely. We obey traffic signals, wear seat belts, know about car-jackings and are familiar with airport, bus depot, subway and train station regulations. We carry and know how to use an "emergency" travel fund (bus and cab fare, coins for pay telephones and so on).

➤ Our family members never get into a stranger's car or, for that matter, enter a stranger's home.

➤ Our family members know to yell, run away and go to a safe place to get away from strangers who follow us. If someone tries to pull us into his or her home or car, we know how to attract attention and scatter our belongings on the ground.

➤ Our family members never touch strange animals.

➤ Our family members always let each other know where we're going and when we will return. If we're late or our plans have changed, we call to report in.

➤ Our family members report all the important details about any unusual activity in our neighborhood to the authorities.

➤ Our family members are familiar with a variety of street-proofing techniques.

General Safety

Because knowledge is power, we've provided some basic tips that can help both children and adults construct their own general checklist.

➤ Our family members have identification files, which include recent photographs, hair and nail clippings and fingerprints, and which list blood type and distinguishing physical characteristics.

➤ Our family members have identification cards that give last and first name, address, telephone numbers or contact information, and note health issues (such as allergies and special medication requirements). These cards are *never* visible to strangers.

➤ Our family members keep an updated activity chart including all pertinent information (telephone numbers, addresses, contact names). If we do not report for any activity, our home is called immediately.

➤ Our family members have regular group conferences to discuss things that might be making us feel unsafe (for instance, bullies or media reports of catastrophes).

➤ Our family members have discussed safe social behavior regarding drugs and alcohol, sex, weapons, truancy and crime. We also say no if someone tries to make us do something uncomfortable or touch us in an inappropriate way, and we tell our parents or caregivers if this happens.

➤ Our family members don't take gifts, food, candy or beverages from strangers without our parents' or caregivers' approval.

➤ Our family members have reviewed special safety needs (those that concern people with physical or mental disabilities).

➤ Our family members have carefully screened our caregivers, teachers, counselors and other people who play an important role in our lives.

➤ Our family members know how and when to use self-defense skills.

Again, these are general checklists and you should construct lists that are specific to your family's needs. Additionally, your and your family's martial arts program should include practical safety training that addresses these kinds of emergencies. Furthermore, in addition to helping you and your family prepare for physical confrontations, your martial arts training should help all of you develop a positive sense of self that will enable you and your children to withstand peer pressure and say no to negative influences.

The Shape of Things to Come

Now that we've reviewed one essential aspect of the martial arts, personal protection, let's examine some of the physical benefits you can expect as a practitioner.

Martial arts training can help you become stronger, more flexible and more cardiovascularly fit as you learn self-defense skills. It can help you get or stay in shape. Whereas Chapter 5 explains how you can incorporate other physical activities to heighten your strength, flexibility and cardiovascular gains, this section is devoted to the physical improvements you can look forward to as a result of your martial arts training.

Don't Succumb to "Too-ism"

Too many people come up with countless excuses for why they can't enroll in a martial arts program: *I'm too old, too out of shape, too busy.* But the moment they realize the physical rewards of this type of training, most of them will be hooked for life because, in addition to fortifying your spirit and strengthening your mind, the martial arts can help you cultivate a powerful, pliable, energy-charged body.

Aerobic Conditioning

Although martial arts training is, for the most part, "anaerobic" (without air), if you practice certain drills for a sustained period (20 minutes) and at a moderate to high level of intensity, it can have an "aerobic" (with air) benefit. That's the kind of activity you need to strengthen your heart.

For example, performing "basics" (fundamental drills) using your arms and legs as you move across the length of the martial arts classroom is very physically demanding. Not only must your brain be engaged, but your heart has to pump vigorously and your breathing has to quicken to match your pace.

Similarly, practicing several "forms" (routines that resemble dance) back to back can make the same demands on your heart and lungs as would running a mile or two.

> **Warrior Words**
>
> *Aerobic* means "with air" and *cardiovascular* means "heart and blood vessels." These two terms are commonly used to describe activities that raise your heart rate, resulting in, among other things, increased expenditure of calories, improved endurance and more efficient use of oxygen.

Additionally, sparring (offensive and defensive movements with partners) and target drills (striking heavy bags and pads), when performed nonstop, can raise your heart rate to a level that has aerobic benefits.

Additional information about supplementary cardiovascular training for martial artists is provided in Chapter 5 of this book.

Anaerobic Conditioning

Short rounds of martial arts activity like striking bags and targets, performing basics and forms, and sparring for brief, intense periods represent anaerobic exercises. These are to aerobic activities what sprinting is to running. That is, they are performed in energy-exhausting short bursts, which may last a minute or two.

Strength Training

As we explain in Chapter 5, weight training can help you develop even greater strength for performing martial arts techniques. But many martial arts drills, like push-ups, tricep dips, partner resistance routines and bag and target exercises, on their own, go a long way in helping you construct a powerful, sculpted physique. A strong, healthy body is better equipped to meet the demands of not only a martial arts program, but life in general. Additionally, if you don't use it, you'll lose it. By age 65, men and women who don't engage in any kind of power training can expect a reduction of 30 to 40 percent in their strength levels.

Martial Smarts

"The person who has lived the most is not the one with the most years but the one with the richest experiences," said Jean-Jacques Rousseau, the great philosopher. If you're among the "seasoned set," don't use your age as an excuse not to train. A competent teacher will work with you to help ease you back into the physical fitness "swim" of things. Additionally, martial arts students are taught to respect those of advanced age, so you'll probably fit right in. Furthermore, in addition to getting back in touch with your body, you'll learn some practical skills and make new friends. Put down the remote control, get out of your plush recliner and get kicking. It beats the heck out of bingo!

Benefits outside the Classroom

Beyond self-defense skills, the rewards of a more physically fit body and the chance to have fun, a martial arts education can offer you and your children other important dividends.

Benefits for Children

As a society, we are becoming better educated about the needs of children who suffer from a seeming alphabet soup of maladies like ADD (Attention Deficit Disorder) and ODD (Oppositional Defiant Disorder). And all too often, we read newspaper and magazine reports or catch a glimpse of the evening news, peppered with stories about increased episodes of violence at the hands of our alienated youth.

Additionally, now more than ever before, we are aware of the serious health problems, like increased risk of heart attacks, arthritis and cancer, that being overweight can bring, and we are bombarded daily with frightening statistics about the rising rate of obesity among young children and teens.

A well-rounded martial arts curriculum can help your child cope with these problems and develop essential physical, motor, linguistic, perceptual and social skills. Children as young as three years of age learn fundamental movements that can improve their sense of balance and coordination. As boys and girls advance through their training, they'll be introduced to more complex drills that will challenge and improve their ability to concentrate, which in turn can elevate their self-esteem.

Martial arts training can teach your son or daughter to learn to function individually, as well as part of a group, as they make friends and share positive growth experiences with teachers and classmates.

They'll develop a deeper understanding of positive values while polishing their social skills. These values include self-respect and respect for others, teamwork and cooperation, honesty, perseverance and patience. They'll also cultivate a strong work ethic, develop a sense of pride in their accomplishments and acquire key self-protection skills. Martial arts training will help them become stronger and more flexible as they build a healthy body.

The result is boys and girls better equipped to face the physical, mental and spiritual challenges of modern life. In fact, child and health care professionals often recommend martial arts training as a way of helping children realize their potential. As kids reach for the coveted Black Belt, they'll begin to understand their greater place in society as a role model for other children and for adults.

Benefits for Teens

Adolescence, that tumultuous stage of life between childhood and adulthood, is fraught with difficulty. As the cocoon of childhood slips away, youngsters enter a period where they become increasingly independent of their parents. Their physical growth is readily apparent but their intellectual and emotional development cannot be as easily measured. Lines of communication can become crossed, tangled, strained and, in some cases, completely disconnected.

Master Speaks

"And the winner is . . ." In too many sports activities there are clear winners and losers. While competition can have value, it may not be an appropriate learning tool for all youngsters. In martial arts programs, if 20 children begin training, most instructors look forward to the day when all 20 will receive their next belt. In a good martial arts institution, everyone's a winner.

What role can martial arts play in helping teens and their parents make this transition less traumatic? These systems can help young men and women test their bodies, minds and spirits in a supportive environment.

Unlike organized, team sports, which often fail to nurture the individual, Karate, Judo, Jiu-jitsu, Kung Fu, Tae Kwon Do and other martial arts can provide your son and daughter with the chance to become stronger and more flexible and to improve their overall health and self-image. They'll come to recognize the rewards of hard work and discipline, which often lead to improved academic performance. They'll make friends who share a healthy interest and they'll fortify themselves against negative peer pressure. Youngsters who have been taught to respect their bodies and minds are less likely to fall prey to using life-endangering substances or engaging in activities that can destroy their health.

Your son or daughter's martial arts school can be a haven in an increasingly confusing world. Given the important role this institution will play in your child's or teenager's life, it only makes sense to choose your school wisely.

Benefits for Adults

On the surface, it may seem that many adults practice martial arts to learn self-defense techniques. But they are learning on a much deeper level—to confront and combat their fears. Fear, whether it's rooted in the dangers of everyday life or in imagined horrors, can result in a host of emotional, mental and physical ailments. These include depression, paranoia, inability to concentrate, muscle tension, high blood pressure, insomnia and gastrointestinal maladies.

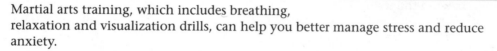

Risky Moves

Practitioners who never learn how to deal with stressful situations may not possess the confidence and clarity of mind to address life-threatening confrontations or even face the challenges of daily life. While martial arts training can help reduce stress and assist you in understanding and controlling your fears, it does not eliminate them. Therefore, it's imprudent not to train for worst-case scenarios.

Martial arts training, which includes breathing, relaxation and visualization drills, can help you better manage stress and reduce anxiety.

Maybe you're anxious about riding the subway during off-peak hours. Perhaps you're frightened at the prospect of addressing your company's sales force at your international meeting. Knowing that you possess the ability to defend yourself and that you have achieved your martial arts goals can help you meet these types of challenges with a greater sense of personal confidence.

Your Road to Personal Discovery

From the first day you wear your uniform, you'll begin to reap the benefits of a martial arts education. You'll learn new skills while reshaping your body, mind and spirit. You'll enjoy the assurance of knowing that you're capable of overcoming whatever obstacles—physical, emotional or mental—you face.

Martial Smarts

Life is either a daring adventure or nothing.

—Helen Keller

The real value of martial arts training is not the ability to smash bricks or boards. It's not in wearing a psychedelic array of belts or uniforms. It's not about bragging rights, titles or trophies.

11

The real value of the study of martial arts is the ability to begin to recognize who you are. Martial arts can also help you become who you want to be: someone who is strong, disciplined, patient, cooperative, focused and confident. Once this revelation hits, you'll realize that martial arts can help you continue to "raise the bar" and assist you in achieving physical, mental and spiritual goals you might have thought were impossible to reach.

The Least You Need to Know

➤ Survival is one of our most basic needs.

➤ Martial artists learn to confront and combat real and imagined fears.

➤ Personal protection involves defending yourself, and those you love, inside and outside your home.

➤ Constructing checklists can help you manage personal safety emergencies.

➤ In addition to teaching essential self-defense techniques, a martial arts program can help practitioners of all ages achieve impressive physical gains.

➤ Martial arts training can help you develop a sense of self-confidence that extends beyond the training area.

Chapter 2

Combat in the Ancient World

> **In This Chapter**
>
> ➤ How organized systems of martial arts evolved
>
> ➤ Exploring Egyptian combative systems
>
> ➤ Investigating the fighting arts of ancient Greece
>
> ➤ Beholding gladiator contests in Rome
>
> ➤ Understanding ancient India's defensive systems

The gifts bestowed upon us by ancient cultures include language, literature, science and religion. As if all this weren't enough, ancient Egypt, Greece, Rome and India also gave us the precious knowledge of how to deal—effectively and quickly—with adversaries, in the form of combative systems.

In this chapter you will learn about the origin and evolution of these martial arts and their impact on modern combative methods.

What's Mine is Mine, and What's Yours is Mine, Too!

For our ancient ancestors, hunting and gathering were means of acquiring goods. In a more sophisticated sense, this remains true. As a cave dweller, you would have hunted your "cold cuts" on the open plains. Today, with a wobbly shopping cart as your only weapon, you have to do likewise at your local supermarket. Whether your

Master Speaks

One major difference between our ancestors and us is the acceptance of hunting as a sport. In the interest of remaining politically correct, we will avoid judging the appropriateness of this activity!

Warrior Words

The word *martial*, as in *martial arts*, is derived from the name of the ancient Roman god of war, *Mars*.

"possessions" take the form of a mate, offspring, land, precious metals and stones, food or shelter, once acquired, protecting and defending your family and property still is of paramount importance.

As a skilled hunter armed with a spear, you could definitely make your "point" felt—whether the target was of the four-legged or two-legged variety. Several millennia later, you could use farming tools and weapons intended for tracking and slaughtering animals to protect yourself against an individual or group of attackers. In modern times, your average garden hoe could be used with equal effectiveness to groom a field or bring an abrupt halt to a heated "discussion."

What if, however, these implements were not within reach? You would likely have had to rely on your brain and body to protect you and your belongings. This is, quite simply, the raison d'être of all martial arts.

In the opinion of many people, combat is the true "universal language." It transcends all boundaries: time, geography, language, religion, politics, gender, age and socioeconomic class.

Most, or perhaps all, cultures have, and continue to have, armed and unarmed fighting traditions. An overview of four ancient cultures—Egypt, Greece, Rome and India—and their respective personal defense systems follows.

And in This Corner, King Tut!

The walls of some Egyptian tombs dating as far back as 4000 B.C. portray images that could have served as the inspiration for many modern action movies. Fading figures depict military training exercises that appear to resemble prizefighting! In fact, the illustrations include combatants wearing glovelike hand protectors, just as you would as a modern martial arts practitioner.

Other visuals, "subtitled" with hieroglyphics, picture a variety of weapons, like spears, short swords and throwing projectiles, coupled with training and combat scenes.

Artifacts dating back to 3000 B.C. reveal that hand-to-hand sports, early cousins of boxing and wrestling, enjoyed a measure of popularity in the Sumerian Kingdom of Mesopotamia—although, perhaps, not to the same degree as today's bouts on pay television. Additionally, murals in the Beni-assan Tomb, believed to be more than two thousand years old, show combatants engaged in pugilistic activities. In addition to hand-striking techniques, kicking maneuvers are also depicted. Transport these guys into the twentieth century and you've got a modern martial arts tournament.

Despite these visual images, little is known about the combative arts practiced by ancient Egyptians. In the chronicles of Ramses II, the victory of the Battle of Kadesh against the Hittites is credited to the Egyptian army's superior weapons skills. If this report is accurate, these warriors had unparalleled proficiency with the lance and sword. Furthermore, they were highly skilled in unarmed combative techniques. Sadly, these chronicles don't include any technical information that might shed light on the training regimen of ancient Egyptian soldiers.

In addition to sharing information regarding martial arts, as well as fine art(!), this highly evolved culture left an impressive legacy of sports and physical fitness. For example, if you were a barbarian nomad, or a native inhabitant living in Sudan (which was then called Nubia), you would likely have practiced wrestling for both its recreational and defensive value. In addition, you would probably have learned to use several exotic weapons like a *kat* (curved single-edged dagger), a *seft* (long curved sword) and a *khopish* (axelike implement).

From Eye Gouging to Olympic Sport

Like modern televised sparring matches, the Greek martial art of *Pankration* (meaning "complete strength") featured brutal free-for-all bouts. In a sweat-spraying tribute to Zeus (Supreme God of Olympus), the Ted Turner of his day, wrestlers squared off against boxers. In all likelihood, these were the first recorded no-rules combative contests and, obviously, few of these bouts ended in a cheery finish of the Disney variety. Predictably, the level of violence was astronomical and so, too, was the body count at the end of the day, resulting in, in modern media terms, a genuine ratings booster.

If you were practicing *Pankration* and other Greek combative systems during this period, you would have trained at an *akademos* (school). The common layout of these training facilities included one room or gymnasium called a *palestra* that had a soft clay surface. This is where you would have practiced wrestling. In another room, called a *korykos,* which was equipped with kicking and punching apparatus, you would have boxed or studied *Pankration*.

In the following sections, you will learn about these three principal combative systems of ancient Greece.

Wrestling

Competitive wrestling is old—really old! It dates back to 708 B.C., when it debuted at the Eighteenth Olympiad. The throws, grappling and restraining techniques used in this sport closely resemble those employed by Judo-*ka* (practitioners of Judo).

Martial Smarts

Olympic boxing debuted at the Twenty-Third Olympiad in 688 B.C. Ancient Greek boxers could use any part of their hands, feet or head to achieve victory. In a legendary bout, a champion by the name of Damoxenus defeated his opponent, Crvegas, by means of a straight-fingered strike that pierced his body. Yikes, that had to hurt!

Risky Moves

In ancient boxing contests, taking your time in finishing a match could be painful – literally! If a bout lasted too long, both fighters mutually agreed to trade punches. No blocking or evading techniques were permitted. Competitors simply went at it until one of them fell down. This adds painful meaning to the phrase *tit for tat*, doesn't it?

Additionally, if you were a wrestler in ancient Greece, you would have had at your disposal all manner of leg, shoulder and hip throws, as well as an assortment of foot sweeps (off-balancing maneuvers) and neck restraints.

To make it difficult for your opponent to "get a handle" on you, you would have stripped down to your birthday suit and greased your body from head to toe. (Pass the olive oil, please!)

There were few rules governing competitive bouts. In fact, one popular way of intimidating and incapacitating opponents was to break their fingers at the beginning of a match, leaving them in pain—and unable to phone home!

Boxing

Boxing matches in ancient Greece bore little resemblance to those held today. No glitz. No glam. No tuxedoed, cigar-chewing promoters escorting satin-outfitted million dollar bad boys (and girls!) into a spot-lit ring in some big-buck Las Vegas casino.

What's more, these ancient bouts were technically different. Competitors were free to use open-hand strikes and blocks, as well as closed-hand techniques like a hammer fist to the top of an opponent's head.

Leg strikes like kicking with your knees, shins and foot were permitted and were often used to set up a hand technique. As a result, many of these bouts probably looked more like modern Kickboxing than boxing.

If you were training for an upcoming bout, you would have practiced shadow (solo) boxing and sparring with opponents. You also would have lifted and hit sand-filled bags, stretched and ran for hours to increase your strength, flexibility and endurance.

Contrary to today's standards, in ancient times there were few, if any, rules governing boxing matches. For example, there were no weight divisions, no time limits, no scoring—there wasn't even a ring! Oh, there was one simple rule: the person left standing at the end of the match won!

Pankration

Although the first recorded date of a *Pankration* match was 648 B.C., at the Thirty-Third Olympiad, a no-name version of this type of martial art was practiced by Greeks and Spartans since the birth of civilization. The country that gave us philosophy and medicine also shared what might be deemed barbaric combative techniques like hair pulling and eye gouging. Think about it: guys modeling togas and debating ethics while on the other side of town contestants wearing—well, *nothing*—and pummeling the heck out of one another. As they say in the tabloids, weird but true.

If you were a *Pankration* competitor, you'd probably launch your attack with a barrage of kicks aimed at your opponents' knees, groin and stomach, and finally, when they were too weak to block or defend themselves, toward their head. You'd then strike with an open hand or a closed fist before grabbing their legs, torso or hair to throw them off balance. These tactics were called *krocheirismos* (opening moves).

Eventually, you and other combatants would force each other to the ground, where grappling and restraining techniques would take over until a submission hold would bring the bout to a close.

Today, most practitioners work out in a martial arts school, boxing gym or wrestling class. Historically however, these combat sports were often practiced al fresco, in the unforgiving sunlight. With matches lasting for hours and without the benefit of sun protection products, this was undoubtedly an exhausting (and blistering) way to spend the day.

All Roads Lead to Rome

Greek combat methods attracted the interest of the ancient Romans, whose aim became producing the ultimate soldier by having competitors engage in a host of testosterone-elevating contests!

With life and death hanging in the balance, gladiatorial contests of the period were far more

Master Speaks

There are remarkable similarities between the martial practices of ancient Greece and those of Asian disciplines. The Greeks used a yell of spirit or power, similar to the *kiai* of Japanese martial arts practitioners or the *kihap* of students of Korean disciplines. Additionally, the Greeks called your body's energy *pneuma* (air, breath or spirit) and Asians name this life force *chi* or *ki*.

Warrior Words

A *supplex* is a Greco-Roman wrestling technique involving bending your opponent's spine into a pretzel. It is derived from the Roman and Latin words *supples* or *sup* (easily bent, pliable) and *plicis* (to bend, also implying submission).

dangerous than sport-oriented Greco-Roman wrestling events. This difference was probably not readily apparent to the unfortunate wrestlers who found themselves dangling upside down while locked in a painful, spine-restraining supplex.

Your Gladiator Training Program

If you were preparing for these events, your training plan would have included—

1. basic drills
   - ➤ penetrating your opponent's defense
   - ➤ holding and off-balancing an opponent
   - ➤ using your arms to lift your opponent

2. takedowns
   - ➤ fake attempts (methods of deceiving your opponent)
   - ➤ tripping an opponent with your feet
   - ➤ tripping an opponent using your hands
   - ➤ arm drags (pulling your opponent with your arms)
   - ➤ ankle and knee picks (off-balancing your opponent by pulling the ankle or knee)
   - ➤ bear hugs (not the "teddy" kind!)
   - ➤ head locks (methods of restraining your opponent's head)

3. escapes and reversals (evading an opponent's attack and applying a counter-hold)
   - ➤ stand-ups (standing up quickly to release an opponent's hold)
   - ➤ rolls (not the bakery version) and sacrifices (techniques for removing an opponent's hold)
   - ➤ counterholds (counterrestraining techniques)

4. pinning (holding an opponent on the ground)
   - ➤ nelson series (techniques for locking an opponent's shoulder and head together)
   - ➤ arm bars (restraining an opponent by locking one or both arms)
   - ➤ wrist control (restraining an opponent by locking the wrists)
   - ➤ shoulder restraints
   - ➤ cradles (raising your hips to throw off an opponent)
   - ➤ using your legs to restrain your opponent

5. free-style or spontaneous practice

This is a typical training plan for practitioners of ancient Greco-Roman wrestling. Some, but not all, techniques are now part of the curriculum of modern free-style students of this combative sport.

Clash of the Titans at the Great Coliseum

While some participants engaged in the lower-risk sport of Greco-Roman wrestling, others found themselves, often unwillingly, competing in the Gladiator Games at the Great Coliseum. In this arena, the phrase *risk management* would likely have taken on an entirely new meaning.

A wide range of armaments were featured at these wildly popular extravaganzas, including swords for slashing and stabbing, shields to strike and parry, tridents to hook and thrust, and nets, which were employed to ensnare and unbalance your opponent. If, as a gladiator, you had the misfortune to find yourself disarmed, you would have had to resort to the "scratch your eyes out" method of defense: gouging eyes, pulling hair or biting an opponent à la Mike Tyson.

A Roman boxing match might have preceded the main event. If you were a participant in this match, you would have worn the *cestus*, a leather glove that was decorated with metal studs. You would have used this accessory to maim, or even kill, your opponents. This match would have been followed by battle reenactments, chariot races and wrestling with lions and bears.

> **Martial Smarts**
>
> The great gladiators of ancient Rome employed a multitude of training drills, some of which could be classified as unusual. For example, there's a popular tale about a contestant who would hoist a calf (that's right, a baby cow) above his head every day. As the calf grew, its weight increased. Understandably, then, it was a true moment, or *moo–ment*, of personal best when the gladiator was able to carry the fully grown cow around the Coliseum. Sadly, after his impressive stroll, he promptly placed the animal on the ground and killed it with one blow!

Strike, Grapple and Easy on the Curry

The first records of martial arts activity in India appear around 500 B.C. They included combat techniques in which you seize or reverse holds on an opponent's joints, strike with your fists or grapple and throw your adversary. These three activities developed in conjunction with, as well as independently of, each other.

One thousand years later, during the fifth century, classic epics such as *The Mahabharata*, which paints a colorful picture of military struggle and martial virtues, were written. Additionally, great religious texts like *Buddharata Sutra,* also penned during this period, provide an overview of an Indian martial art called *Vajaramusti*.

Master Speaks

The striking similarity in the postures of both yoga and Indian martial arts is a clear indication of their close relationship. Additionally, both focus on the lower abdominal region as the center of all human energy, and their common purpose is to help you develop a healthy body, increase your lifespan and achieve a state of bliss (without a year's supply of Prozac).

Vajaramusti incorporated wrestling, striking arts and weapons practice with a study of vital pressure points (or *marman).*

The origins of the more modern martial art, *Kalaridpayattu,* can be traced back to India's southern provinces in the twelfth century A.D. *Kalaridpayattu* is characterized by defensive postures (to protect your vital points), low stances, long strides, high kicks and jumps. More advanced training methods include breathing exercises, a study of economy of movement and energy, and development of a strong life force or intrinsic energy called *pranavayu* (*chi,* in Chinese, and *ki,* in Japanese).

As in many other cultures, Indian martial arts are closely linked to native religious practices. Hindus, Muslims and Buddhists have their own "unofficial" defensive systems.

Two of India's most well-received exports—its religions and martial arts—were enthusiastically embraced in other parts of Asia.

The Least You Need to Know

➤ Some form of combative system existed, and in most cases, continues to exist, in virtually every culture.

➤ Evidence of the presence of martial arts in ancient Egypt appears in murals on the walls of tombs.

➤ The ancient Greeks competed in no-holds-barred bouts in honor of Zeus.

➤ The Romans embraced the combat methods, including boxing, wrestling and other martial arts, of the ancient Greeks.

➤ The combative systems of India, like its religions, made their way to other countries across Asia and, later, the world.

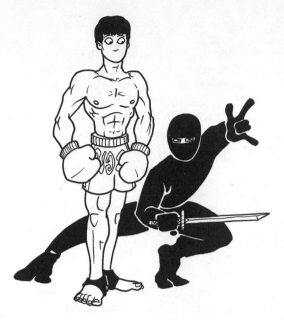

Chapter 3

Martial Arts Overview

In This Chapter

➤ Comparing "old" and "new" martial arts

➤ Examining "hard" and "soft" systems

➤ The difference between striking and grappling arts

➤ Taking a quick tour of some popular martial arts

You channel surf while sitting in your comfy chair, munch popcorn at your neighborhood movie theater or multiplex, or thumb through glossy magazines while relaxing at a local café. You shift impatiently as you wait your turn in the supermarket checkout line, or read the latest subway advertisements hawking a dizzying array of products—from soft drinks to antiperspirants. And all the while, you are bombarded with images of people who represent every race, ethnic group and age. They're average Joes and Janes, as well as the rich 'n' famous. Diverse though they might be, they all have one thing in common: they're all punching and kicking! So you ask yourself, *What's the deal with all this martial arts stuff?* And the answer is, these self-protection or self-perfection programs, although hundreds and in some cases thousands of years old, are *hot.* They offer families from the heartland and folks on the cutting edge a way to get and stay in shape, learn important skills and have lots of fun!

Martial artists run the gamut from traditional practitioners in white uniforms moving to the strains of Japanese folk music, to youngsters in combat boots and jeans whirling dervishlike to bass-loaded techno!

Martial Smarts

Speak of moderns without contempt and of the ancients without idolatry; judge them by their merits, but not by their age.

—*Lord Chesterfield*

Warrior Words

Hybrid, composite and *eclectic* are the new "in" words in the world of combative systems. These terms refer to a blend or mix of various martial arts. See Chapter 23 for more information about eclectic combative systems.

So now that you've decided that you may be interested in joining these men and women and boys and girls, you're doing your homework to figure out what martial arts style or system might best fulfill your needs. That's where this chapter comes in. Read on and you'll learn something about basic martial arts categories and take a quick tour of some popular styles and systems.

Classical versus Modern Martial Arts

The line dividing martial arts falls between traditional and modern systems. The former group, which includes combative arts like Kung Fu, Karate, Judo, Tae Kwon Do, Jiu-jitsu and Aikido, enable practitioners to develop their body, mind and spirit. The latter category, in which you find newer martial arts like Kickboxing and Shootfighting, is primarily physical.

This dividing line does not separate the martial arts into "good" or "bad" systems. It's simply a demarcation to assist you in selecting a martial art that is compatible with your goals.

Trends come and go. The same is true in the warrior's world, where Kung Fu was the rage in the 1970s, Ninjitsu (the art of stealth) dominated the 1980s and Brazilian grappling is the current hot ticket.

What doesn't change is the fact that, if what you're looking for is an activity designed to improve cardiovascular fitness, increase strength and flexibility, reduce stress and provide important self-defense skills, then martial arts can fit the bill. The style or system you study doesn't matter much. Finding one that matches *your* needs and then locating the right teacher and school are far more important.

Regardless of whether you pursue a classical or modern discipline, you should plan to practice at least twice a week if you want to make any measurable gains. After a few months, you should see a difference in the way you look and feel.

Hard and Soft Systems

On the surface, it's easy to classify various fighting systems as either "hard" or "soft." Kickboxing, for example, would belong to the hard category, while Tai Chi Chuan fits into soft martial arts. In reality, most systems contain both hard *and* soft elements.

There are some clearly defined types of martial arts. For example, Kyokushin-kai is easily classified as a hard style of Karate. If you were a Kyokushin-kai practitioner, you'd demolish stacks of bricks, splinter baseball bats and slice beer bottles using only your bare hands and feet. As a Kyokushin-kai competitor, you would participate in full contact tournaments around the world.

On the other hand, if you were studying Shotokai, a system of Karate developed by a famous Japanese teacher, Shigeru Egami, you'd lean more toward avoiding contact with your partner.

As noted, one martial art that readily fits into the soft category is Tai Chi Chuan, but even in this combative art there are variations. Some schools stress pair exercises like "pushing hands" (continuous, flowing block and counter drills) and self-defense. Others take the holistic approach and concentrate on improving your physical and spiritual health through individual training like "forms" (routines that resemble dance).

The *hard* and *soft* labels are not confined to styles. You can take a hard(core) approach to your training, attending classes 7 days a week, coupled with at-home practice. Or, you might use the nice-and-easy method, popping in for one or two sessions a week. Herculean effort applied to training and pushing full-steam ahead toward Destination Black Belt may work for you, or you may be the type of person who gains greater benefit from a more relaxed attitude, enjoying the journey as much as the destination.

Risky Moves

Reality check: although the concept of harmony is an essential part of martial arts training, a cooperative partner's willingness to fall can make you believe that you are invincible and, perhaps, cause you to overestimate your skills. Remember, the *dojo* (school) is a friendly environment—the street is not! When assessing your self-defense abilities and shortcomings, be realistic.

Master Speaks

Regardless of which martial system you study, regular attendance is the secret to success. On average, you should attend two to three classes per week, and if you plan to be away for an extended period, advise your instructor, perhaps practice while you're away and schedule refresher classes when you return.

Kicking and Striking, or Grappling and Throwing

As you shop around for a martial arts school, you'll undoubtedly encounter lots of new terminology. What you should determine is whether a "kicking and striking" art like Tae Kwon Do and Kung Fu will satisfy your needs, or whether a "grappling and throwing" system like Judo or Aikido would be more appropriate.

Martial Smarts

Seventeenth-century poet Baltasar Gracián said, "There is none that cannot teach somebody something, and there is none so excellent that cannot be excelled." Most novice practitioners focus on the *differences* between martial arts and think their discipline is unique and superior to all others. Conversely, a seasoned practitioner looks for the *similarities* between various forms of combat, recognizing and respecting each one.

Risky Moves

A common self-defense scenario involves confrontations that end up on the ground. But before you grapple an opponent to the floor, be certain there are no additional attackers. Once on the ground, you are placed in a vulnerable position if you need to defend yourself against several people.

Both these categories offer the same basic benefits: improved physical, mental and spiritual fitness. Both offer you unique life-affirming experiences and the opportunity to achieve personal awareness as you confront and battle your fears. Additionally, as previously noted, most progressive schools incorporate elements of other systems. What that means is many modern Karate schools include grappling training, and a goodly number of Jiu-jitsu schools have added kicking and striking techniques to their curriculum. Nearly all systems feature sweeps (techniques for off-balancing your partner), throws and takedowns.

Martial arts that stress kicking and striking techniques are designed to prepare practitioners for middle- to long-distance defensive situations. Those that focus on grappling and throwing educate practitioners for closer activity. Ideally, you'd want to be skilled in both areas. Furthermore, your repertoire should include:

➤ one-to-one standing defense

➤ one-to-one ground defense

➤ one-to-one sitting or kneeling defense

➤ defense against several unarmed opponents

➤ defense against one or more armed opponents

This well-rounded approach, generally featured in all martial arts, can ensure you will have honed your self-defense skills. And, should you be faced with a physical confrontation, you will be capable of protecting yourself.

Your Quick Tour of the Martial Arts

Chapters 13 to 23 of this book provide detailed information about some of the more popular martial arts practiced today. In this section, we have summarized the essential information you'll need to know in order to recognize different kinds of martial arts and select one (or more) that may offer you what you're looking for. This is by no means a comprehensive list and, in an effort to keep things simple, we've provided only fundamental information, so you might want to refer to later chapters, contact schools or associations listed in Appendix E or do some additional reading to obtain more details. Furthermore, this general overview does not allow for stylistic and school differences.

➤ **Aikido (the way of harmonious spirit)**   This Japanese martial art relies on redirecting and controlling an attacker's force using unbalancing and joint manipulating techniques. Fitness demands are moderate but, as an Aikido practitioner, you can expect tremendous spiritual rewards. It's a great "stress buster"!

➤ **Escrima (art of fencing)**   Escrima is a Filipino martial art that centers around the use of short sticks, called *bastons* or *mutons,* and other weapons that are employed individually or in pairs. Escrima is unusual in that, as an *escrimador* (practitioner), you would begin by learning armed combat and progress to unarmed fighting skills, including boxing, grappling and trapping.

➤ **Jiu-jitsu (the soft/pliable method)**   This highly practical combat system was developed in feudal Japan when self-defense skills were of paramount importance. As a practitioner of this martial art, you would use strikes coupled with throwing and grappling techniques. Little emphasis is placed on cultivating flexibility, and cardiovascular conditioning is more prevalent in modern, sport-oriented schools.

➤ **Judo (gentle, soft way)**   The Olympic sport of Judo, which originated in Japan, teaches you how to use leverage to throw an opponent of any size. It's a highly combative system, so you'll have to defeat fellow students in order to advance in rank. Judo can provide you with a workout that varies in intensity from light to moderate, or intense if you are preparing for competition.

➤ **Karate (empty hand)**   Originating in seventeenth-century Okinawa, this martial art offers a balance of upper and lower body defensive techniques, coupled with cardiovascular, strength and flexibility training. Like in other martial arts, as a Karate-*ka* (student) you may elect to participate in competitions or take a more recreational approach to your study. Training at most Karate schools includes a spiritual component.

➤ **Kendo (way of the sword)**   Kendo is a Japanese martial sport based on ancient samurai sword skills called *Ken-jitsu.* As a Kendo practitioner, you would wear protective armor called *bogu* and attempt to strike your partner with a bamboo sword called a *shinai.*

Master Speaks

Many martial artists engage in some form of cross-training as an adjunct to their combative studies. Aerobic activities like running, cycling or swimming, coupled with resistance exercises (such as weight training) can improve your martial arts skills (and vice versa).

➤ **Kobudo (ancient martial way)**   The term *Kobudo* is used to describe Okinawan weapons disciplines that include use of more than 30 armaments. The most popular among these are the *bo* (long wood staff), *sai* (three-pronged metal truncheon), *tonfa* (wood-handled baton), *nunchaku* (small wood flail) and *kama* (sickle).

➤ **Kung Fu (skill or art)**   Kung Fu is a Chinese martial art that can be traced back 2000 years. As a Kung Fu student, in addition to practicing strikes and kicks, you can rely on this martial art to develop balance and speed, improving your overall health and cultivating self-discipline. Fitness demands can be moderate to high, depending upon the type of Kung Fu you practice and the school in which you enroll.

➤ **Kyudo (way of archery)**   Kyudo is a Japanese martial discipline whose students use a *yumi* (long bow) and *ya* (arrow). As a Kyudo practitioner, the bulk of your training would revolve around the spiritual aspect.

➤ **Muay Thai (Thai Boxing or Kickboxing)**   This full-contact sport originated in Thailand and can offer you a very intense workout, which will include skipping rope, kicking and punching heavy bags, shadow boxing and sparring with partners. Kinder, gentler versions of this lethal combative art are sweeping the nation and can likely be found at your local gym or fitness facility. Well-heeled execs and waif-thin models, as well as stars of stage and screen, practice these PG-rated renditions.

➤ **Silat (to fend off)**   Hailing from Indonesia and Malaysia, this mysterious and exotic combative system was developed by a peasant woman. Silat's staples include striking, kicking and evasive movements. As a student of this martial art, you will learn to take your opponent to the ground by grabbing their legs or entwining your limbs around theirs. As the real emphasis of this martial art is self-defense, fitness demands are classified as low to moderate. Furthermore, this is a relatively obscure martial art. As such, locating an authentic Silat instructor in your neighborhood may be difficult.

Martial Smarts

It's safer than golf! Did you know that fewer injuries are reported among martial artists than among golfers? Furthermore, martial arts training is a safe alternative to many other forms of physical fitness. It is essential, however, that you practice under the supervision of a qualified, professional instructor in order to minimize your risk of injury.

➤ **Tae Kwon Do (foot hand way)**   As a practitioner of this Korean martial art, you would rely on hand strikes and kicks, with emphasis on the latter. Tae Kwon Do was originally intended as a form of self-defense. However, since gaining acceptance as an Olympic sport, many Tae Kwon Do practitioners and teachers prefer to focus strictly on its value as a competitive activity. Tae Kwon Do promotes good cardiovascular fitness, flexibility and strength development. Some schools still stress this martial art's value as a means of improving one's behavior.

➤ **Tai Chi Chuan (grand ultimate fist)**   An ancient Taoist combative system, Tai Chi Chuan is based on circular, flowing defensive movements. As a student of this martial art, you will practice techniques slowly. For this reason, it is an ideal choice for people seeking a low-impact activity and a way to reduce stress. Fitness demands are relatively low and little emphasis is placed on developing flexibility.

The Big Picture

For easy access, we have developed a chart that will assist you as you embark on your search for an appropriate martial arts school (see page 28). Again, it's hardly comprehensive but it summarizes much of the information noted above and includes additional details to aid—and simplify—your research.

We remind you that these descriptions are fairly general. Schools and instructors vary, as do the level of physical intensity, self-defense training and spiritual focus of each discipline.

In conclusion, when it comes to finding a martial arts school that's right for you, it's impossible to generalize about the kind of instruction you can expect to receive in a given institution. Every instructor has different preferences, strengths and frailties, and no two schools are alike. Read this book from cover to cover, wear your good-consumer hat and remain open-minded as you shop around, and you'll undoubtedly find a school where you'll fit in.

Warrior Words

Expert or not? An *expert* is a person who has special skills or knowledge. When it comes to martial arts, an expert may not, however, necessarily be a good teacher. Look for an instructor who can impart information and guide you on the road to achieving personal martial arts excellence.

An Overview of Popular Martial Arts

Martial Art	Availability of Schools	Fitness Demands	Estimated Time to Learn Basic Self-Defense Skills	Spiritual Component
Aikido	High	Low	8–10 months	High
Escrima	Low	Moderate	4–8 months	Low
Jiu–jitsu	Moderate	Moderate[1]	4–8 months	Moderate
Judo	High	High	6–10 months	Moderate
Karate	High	High	4–8 months	Moderate
Kendo	Low	Moderate	Limited use[2]	Moderate
Kobudo	Low	Moderate	Limited use[3]	Moderate
Kung Fu	Moderate	Moderate	8–10 months	Moderate
Kyudo	Low	Low	Limited use[4]	High
Muay Thai	Low	High	3–4 months	Low
Silat	Low	Moderate	8–10 months	Moderate
Tae Kwon Do	High	High	4–8 months	Low–Mod
Tai Chi Chuan	Moderate	Moderate	One year+	High

1. *Classical Jiu-jitsu can be classified as "moderate," while modern Jiu-jitsu can be more physically demanding.*
2. *Defense practice is limited to partner exchange drills, such as attacks by another Kendo-ka.*
3. *Due to the fact that weapons are required, the practical defense value is somewhat limited.*
4. *Due to the fact that weapons (bow and arrow) are required, practical defense value is somewhat limited.*

The Least You Need to Know

➤ There are numerous martial arts styles and systems, but basically they're categorized as classical or modern, hard or soft, and kicking and striking or grappling and throwing.

➤ There is a fair degree of crossover when it comes to martial arts systems and styles, and most contain some elements of other forms of combat.

➤ Different martial arts styles require varying degrees of physical fitness, strength and flexibility. Some are more sport-oriented, while others include a greater spiritual component. All can provide a wealth of personal rewards.

➤ While you'll want to find a martial art that is compatible with your personality and fulfills your needs, it is more important to locate a good instructor and a school where you'll fit in.

Part 2
Stepping Up to the Mat

Once, people believed that the world was flat and that we'd never set foot on the moon—bunk! Misinformation and half-truths distort how you view a variety of things, including the martial arts. In this section, we give myths and misconceptions that surround combative systems the "one-two" punch. You'll obtain real *information—answers to questions, safety suggestions, advice about nutrition and cross-training. You'll even get direction on martial arts goal setting and suggestions for modern living that come from 1000-year-old teachings, to stimulate your personal growth.*

Chapter 4

Myths and Realities of Martial Arts Training

In This Chapter

➤ Dispelling myths about martial arts training

➤ Why all instructors are *not* created equal

➤ Figuring out food fiction and fact

➤ Weighing the importance of supplements

➤ How a game plan improves your odds of martial arts success

You search for a martial arts school while scenes from your local movie screen or television set swirl inside your head: you brand yourself with tattoos of dragons and tigers and enter "death" fights on your next trip to Hong Kong. You imagine yourself using ancient training devices, like large pots of beans, wood logs and concrete jars to build rippling muscles, or crushing bricks and wood with your bare hands and feet. Then, you envision rushing down to your local police station to register your body as a "lethal weapon." Scary stuff!

Will you come upon schools that require prospective students to carry out an array of menial tasks, like washing floors for months, maybe even years, before being granted permission to take their class? Will you face gigantic tattooed instructors barking commands at beginners who, if they fail to perform an infinite number of push-ups and other exercises, will be banished?

What is martial fact and what is martial fiction? Is the real picture one of knowledgeable consumers like you shopping around to find the right martial arts school,

Martial Smarts

To question a wise man is the beginning of wisdom.

—*German proverb*

screening instructors as you scan ads and solicit the advice of your friends and family? Does it include novice students who are eased gently into their training, receiving positive reinforcement as they take their first tentative steps into the martial arts classroom?

What's real and what's not? This chapter will help you answer these questions. In the following pages, you will learn what to expect, and in some cases, avoid, as you continue your martial arts research. This chapter also addresses three often overlooked areas that can improve your chances of achieving your martial arts objectives: finding a suitable instructor, maintaining good nutrition and setting goals.

Inquiring Minds

Let's look at some of the myths and misconceptions about martial arts study.

➤ *I'll have to be in good shape before I begin practicing martial arts.* Although some people believe they have to be in top physical form before enrolling in a martial arts course, this simply isn't true. A competent instructor will factor in your age and fitness level in constructing your martial arts program. If you have concerns about the state of your health or you haven't engaged in any physical activity for many years, it's advisable to consult your health care provider before beginning any exercise program, martial arts or otherwise.

➤ *I'll be expected to perform dozens of push-ups and other conditioning exercises my first day.* Absolutely not. If you observe a class where students are doing these and other seemingly challenging drills, these individuals are probably intermediate or advanced level members. In beginner classes, on the other hand, teachers focus on helping students develop proper form and, although the training session should be physically demanding, you should have the opportunity to work up to an acceptable level of participation. Challenge yourself. Strive to improve the quality of your movement while you safely and gradually increase the number of repetitions you're able to complete.

➤ *It will take a long time before I'll be physically fit and capable of performing basic exercises.* This time period depends on a variety of factors: your current level of physical fitness, genetics, your overall health and the consistency and frequency of your training. If you attend two to three classes weekly, supplement them with practice at home and engage in complementary exercise (see Chapter 5), you'll probably achieve dramatic results in less time than your less fit, less committed training partner. Typically, students see physical improvements in 2 to 3 months.

➤ *It will take many, many years before I can defend myself.* It's difficult to estimate the time required for you to get to the point where you'll be capable of defending yourself. This will vary from student to student. Some folks are very aggressive, while others shy away from confrontation. Furthermore, while you can expect to learn basic blocking, striking and kicking drills in 3 to 6 months, developing the capability to defend yourself transcends simply learning techniques. Self-defense ability is tied into a web of complex psychological issues. While you may learn the physical skills necessary to protect yourself in a matter of months, being able to perform them reflexively and, more importantly, possessing the mental ability required could take longer.

Warrior Words

Are you afraid of commitment? *Commitment* is defined as "a sense of moral dedication or adherence to a course of action." If there is *one* quality you need to develop early on in your martial arts training, it's commitment.

➤ *I'll need to maintain a special diet to train.* While in the initial stages of your martial arts study a customized nutritional program may not be necessary, it's always a good idea to adhere to a sensible diet in order to ensure you have the "fuel" necessary to meet the physical and nonphysical demands of training and daily life. As you become more serious about your martial arts practice, what you feed your body will become increasingly important, and you should plan to do research to ensure this essential component of your program is appropriately addressed. Consulting *The Complete Idiot's Guide to Eating Smart*, a nutritionist or your health care provider may give you more "food for thought" on the issue of a suitable eating program.

➤ *Martial arts training will help me lose weight.* Maybe, and maybe not. While a martial arts program will definitely make you look and feel better, you also have to consider what you put into your mouth—by this, we don't mean your training partner's fists or feet! Even the most challenging, balanced fitness program, whether it's martial arts or not, can be undermined by a diet that is based on high-fat, salt- or sugar-loaded, chemically processed foods. Quite simply, if you eat large quantities of the wrong foods and you don't use the calories you consume, you will become, or stay, overweight—or more precisely over-*fat*. Most people are scale-obsessed. They don't consider how much of the number that registers on the bathroom or health

Risky Moves

"Quick" weight loss programs rarely produce the kind of long-term results people desire. More importantly, they can be *dangerous*—they're called "crash" diets for a reason! Instead of relying on these diets, aim to increase your lean mass. One pound of muscle burns 50 calories per day, versus 2 calories burned by each pound of fat. And engage in activities, like martial arts, that raise your metabolic rate.

35

Warrior Words

The Japanese word *tamashiwara* refers to the martial arts practice of breaking solid objects with your hands and feet. Translated, it means "to test one's spirit."

Master Speaks

In well-established schools, it is not uncommon to see men and women who have been practicing martial arts for 10, 15, 20 or more years routinely taking a class. The more time these dedicated individuals spend pursuing their objectives and achieving their goals, the more they realize they've only scraped the surface of combative systems.

club scale is lean mass and how much is fat. Before deciding you need to lose "weight," you'll have to determine which type you're talking about. Consult your martial arts instructor, nutritionist or health care provider for more information on how you can calculate the amount of lean mass versus fat in your body.

➤ *I'll have to break boards and bricks.* Not when your training begins. While breaking boards, bricks, concrete blocks or—brrrrr—giant slabs of ice is the kind of exciting activity generally performed by experts, it has little to do with daily practice. After perhaps a year of training, some martial arts schools may ask you to break one-inch pine boards with a hand strike or kick. Like other aspects of martial arts practice, the aim of this exercise is not to demonstrate your prowess, but rather to help you face and conquer your fears and boost your confidence.

➤ *It will take years or decades to earn my Black Belt.* The length of time it can take to attain your Black Belt or a comparable rank will vary from practitioner to practitioner, and discipline to discipline, but on average you can expect to reach this level in 3 to 5 years if you train regularly.

➤ *Receiving my Black Belt means I am an expert and have reached the end of the road.* False. The First Degree Black Belt is viewed by most martial arts experts as an intermediate level. While you should be proud of the hard work and dedication this rank symbolizes, you should also recognize that there is much, much more to be learned.

➤ *There's one martial art that's superior to all others.* Every martial arts system and style can offer innumerable benefits. It is essential, however, that you find one compatible with your needs and that you select an instructor who will help you achieve your goals.

➤ *I'll have to meditate and chant because it's a religious thing.* Although martial arts training can provide practitioners with spiritual sustenance (see Chapter 7), it is not—repeat, *not*—a religious pastime. Seated meditation at the beginning of class is simply a way for you to clarify your mind and quiet your spirit as you mentally prepare for training. At the end of each session, many students and teachers take a few moments to reflect on in-class performance and to make some mental notes. These are usually brief relaxation periods lasting a few minutes. Some practitioners regard martial arts training itself as "moving meditation."

➤ *I'll have to be subservient and bow to everybody.* In most martial arts schools, teachers and students bow. This is a greeting, much like a handshake. It's not a display of idolatry or an indication of subservience. Students bow to one another as well as to their teachers. Teachers bow to students. This action symbolizes their mutual respect.

➤ *I won't be able to practice if I am pregnant or injured or have any physical limitations.* Yes and no. Even if you have physical limitations or injuries or you're pregnant, an experienced instructor can construct a martial arts program that will enable you to train. Individualized programs can also be created for students with special physical needs. Many women practice (minus contact activity) throughout their pregnancies. Most health care providers believe that a healthy body makes for a healthy pregnancy and delivery. Students who have been injured or who have chronic health problems practice martial arts successfully by modifying their training programs. In fact, the type of well-rounded conditioning martial arts practice represents can actually aid students in recovering from an injury or help them improve their health.

It is essential, however, that you find a special instructor, one who is competent and open to customizing a course for you, a teacher capable of addressing your individual needs. You can expect many of the same benefits as students who do not face your challenges: a stronger, more flexible body, improved vitality and self-image, and the ability to defend yourself or others, should the need arise. If you have concerns about practicing martial arts due to any health or physical problems, consult your health care provider before beginning or continuing a program.

➤ *I'm too old (or young) to enroll in a martial arts program.* Most well-established schools with experienced, competent instructors offer programs for preschoolers, older children and teenagers, as well as adults. Students of all ages can benefit from martial arts study.

Martial Smarts

Is the glass half empty or half full? This ia a popular brainteaser used by Zen devotees. It illustrates the role individual perspective plays in how we view and embrace or reject life. How an individual perceives physical, mental or emotional challenges can make his or her existence one of limitation or limitless achievement. A martial arts classroom is a place of optimism, where students learn to meet and master their fears. It's a place where anything can happen.

Martial Smarts

Tell me, and I'll forget. Show me, and I may not remember. Involve me, and I'll understand.

—*Native American Saying*

➤ *It's expensive.* Tuition at most schools is competitively priced, and when you divide the cost of the program by the number of classes you'll attend weekly, it probably works out to just a few dollars per class. Furthermore, it's difficult, and in some cases impossible, to assign a dollar figure to what you'll gain from martial arts training. For more information about how much it might cost to enroll in a martial arts course, refer to Chapter 10.

➤ *My son or daughter will become more violent if he or she practices martial arts.* For the most part, through their study of martial arts, youngsters learn self-respect and respect for others, two characteristics that can discourage bullying and other forms of negative social behavior. They learn that cooperation is one of the best ways to achieve their objectives. They'll also have the opportunity to use their energy more constructively and to reduce stress (in much the same way as do adult practitioners).

➤ *Women and girls can't take martial arts.* False, false and false again! Although practice of combative arts was once the exclusive domain of the male of the species, today, many schools boast highly ranked female instructors and school directors. Additionally, parents are enrolling their daughters at an unprecedented rate in these programs, where they'll develop physically, mentally and spiritually as they learn essential self-defense skills. It is imperative, however, that you find a martial arts school that is not gender biased. How can you tell? Look for girls and women training at every level and female instructors leading classes.

➤ *There's a relatively high risk of injury.* False. Statistically speaking, more people are injured playing golf than practicing martial arts. However, it's important to locate a school that emphasizes safe training. That is, instructors should ensure that students wear protective equipment and are adequately prepared prior to engaging in sparring activities. They should also closely monitor exchange drills (drills with partners) and use a cushioned floor or padding when teaching ground techniques.

Instructor Profiles

Martial arts teachers come in all shapes and sizes. Like their students, they represent a varied cross section of our society. So when hunting for a martial arts instructor for you, your family or friends, what should you look for? As noted throughout *The Complete Idiot's Guide to Martial Arts,* a few "givens" apply. This person should be proficient at his or her discipline. He or she should be a good communicator and motivator, with a teaching style that is compatible with your learning style.

In addition, there are a few general teacher "profiles" we'd like to share with you in the hope that they may help you simplify your search.

➤ **The Samurai Executive**   This individual cares less about your martial arts experience than making sure you sign on the dotted line. The presence of the Samurai Executive doesn't mean that a professionally run martial arts school, one that requires you to put your John or Jane Hancock on an agreement and adhere to the rules of the institution, won't deliver on the promise. Quite the contrary. Just be certain your teacher-student interaction isn't limited to collecting payments.

➤ **The Benevolent Buddha**   The yin to the Samurai Executive's yang, this instructor teaches for little or no money. Simply bring him or her a box of chamomile tea or a votive candle, and you're a student for life. Generally, these teachers don't offer the same professional scope of instruction you'll find in more commercial schools. This limitation doesn't mean they're not competent martial arts teachers, but, because they probably have to do something else to make a living, don't expect to find more than a handful of classes on their weekly calendar.

➤ **The Social Worker**   This instructor wants to be everyone's buddy. He or she generally devotes more time to listening to students' confessions than to teaching martial technique. While you want your teacher to lend a sympathetic ear as you grapple with the challenges of your training (and, in some cases, daily life), if you're seeking deep counseling, then your dollars are probably better invested in a psychologist's couch.

➤ **The Drill Sergeant**   This instructor offers few, if any, words of encouragement. He or she will rely on negative motivators, like assigning an infinite number of push-ups to terrified students or refusing to allow you to drink water, rather than resorting to positive motivation techniques. If "extreme boot camp" is your style, visit your local martial arts Drill Sergeant or check your telephone book under Pain-for-a-Price!

➤ **The Wise Philosopher**   This individual's idea of a demanding workout is flipping pages of the latest Zen text. He or she is generally too busy sharing the good word to kick or punch, but if you like your martial arts in a lecture format, then you've found your guru.

➤ **The Champion**   Somewhere deep inside, this individual regards your and other students' presence as an intrusion. He or she would rather prepare for the next tournament or world championship, or spend the day waxing nostalgic on former competition victories. Again, this approach doesn't mean that this type of teacher won't occasionally get off his or her laurels long enough to teach a stimulating class.

➤ **The "Wired" Warrior**   This individual is usually wild and reckless, hovering on the border between sane and screwy! He or she may make seemingly inhuman demands on the training floor without any regard for your health or safety. If you

like your training severe and your life insurance premiums are up to date, then
this may be the right teacher for you.

➤ **The Party Master**   This instructor frequently socializes with his or her school
members, often crossing the line between instructor and student. Training sessions are merely a prelude to all-night drinking and dancing binges. So if you're
looking for megadoses of debauchery and some martial arts training, call 1-800-
555-BURP!

So what's a good consumer to do? It's imperative you find a teacher who is balanced.
Most good martial arts instructors will be disciplined and nurturing, may share a motivational message at the beginning or end of class, and take a personal—but not intru-
sive—interest in what's going on in your life. They might even share a beer or two with
you and other students on special occasions. The most important thing to do is shop
around until you find a teacher who's right for you.

Fighting Fuel

If the popular saying "You are what you eat" were true, then many martial arts
beginner classes would be made up of neat rows of pepperoni pizza, french fries and
milk shakes! If you plan to train for years, however, you'll have to decide if a sensible
diet is your foe or friend. By this we mean committing to a nutritional program that
includes proteins, carbohydrates, fats, supplements and fluids in appropriate
proportions. Since the conventional "food pyramid" may prove inadequate for martial
artists, if you're really interested in developing an eating plan that can provide
optimum results, you should consult books on this topic like *The Complete Idiot's Guide
to Eating Smart*, a nutritionist or other health care professionals.

In the meantime, we've provided a few guidelines that can help you get started on the
path to better nutrition for martial arts training. These suggestions are very general and
will vary from person to person. For example, someone who is interested in increasing
his or her muscle mass may require higher levels of
protein than the 20 to 25 percent recommended by
most nutritional specialists. At least these guidelines
will give you some idea about the kinds of food you
might want to eat, fluids you might want to drink
and vitamins, minerals and other supplements you
might consider taking as a martial arts student.

One basic recommendation is to reduce your con-
sumption of junk and processed foods, as well as
foods that are high in fat or loaded with sugar or salt.
Learn to read labels and understand what's in the
foods and beverages you're putting into your body.
Reeducate yourself to live "clean." Many nutritionists recommend drinking only pure bottled or

Warrior Words

Protein (of Greek origin, meaning
"of prime importance") is an
essential nutritional element for
martial artists and other athletes,
as well as for the general
population.

distilled water. Others strongly suggest eating organically grown produce and free-range meat and poultry exclusively. As a general rule, avoid contaminating your body with unnecessary chemicals and pollutants.

The following section addresses the important role proteins, carbohydrates, fats and water play in a healthy eating plan.

Protein Power

One of the most important components of your cells, protein is involved in the formation of muscles, enzymes, antibodies, blood—well, you name it! The primary function of protein is to provide amino acids (your body's building blocks) to maintain an anabolic or muscle-growing state.

So how much protein does the martial artist need? Most nutritionists follow standard guidelines, which encourage people to consume 0.8 grams of protein daily for every 2.2 pounds (1 kilogram) of body weight. This amount may be adequate for a sedentary person whose most physically demanding activity of the day is channel surfing or re-moving tabs from soda pop cans. Martial artists, on the other hand, who are interested in packing on some lean, mean mass, should consider eating 1.5 to 2.0 grams of protein per day for every 2.2 pounds (1 kilogram) of body weight.

Some of the best natural sources of protein are—

➤ eggs

➤ milk

➤ fish

➤ beef

➤ poultry

➤ soy

➤ nuts

Most experts agree that protein should represent 20 to 25 percent of your caloric intake.

Cashing In with Carbohydrates

"Carbs" are energy-producing organic compounds (starch, sugar and glucose) that are made up of carbon with oxygen and hydrogen. Carbohydrates are stored in your body as "glycogen" and used for fuel.

Master Speaks

Good things come in small packages. Eat small amounts of protein (15 to 30 grams, roughly the amount that fits in the palm of your hand) with every one of your five to six small meals (instead of three big meals) throughout the day. Doing this can result in improved muscle growth and better endurance while aiding digestion. If you opt for fish, meat or poultry as sources of protein, explore the feasibility of buying organically produced, free-range varieties.

There are two types of carbohydrates:

1. complex — pasta, breads, vegetables and legumes

2. simple — candy, cake, soda pop, other sugary sweets

Fruits can fall into both categories. For example, apples are generally classified as "complex" and bananas as "simple." Fruits are also chock full of vitamins and are a terrific source of fiber, which also plays an important role in maintaining good health.

Complex carbohydrates are loaded with good stuff that can aid your martial arts progress. Simple carbohydrates pump you up with empty calories that provide a quick rush, often followed by a sharp reduction in energy levels.

Foods like whole-grain pasta, sweet potatoes and brown or wild rice can serve as excellent, low-fat sources of carbohydrates.

Many sports, nutrition and health specialists believe the bulk of your diet, between 60 to 65 percent, should be composed of carbohydrates.

Risky Moves

Moving into the "fast" lane? While some practitioners of various disciplines advocate fasting, which involves abstaining from eating some or all foods, this is a rather controversial method for cleansing your system. Before engaging in this kind of activity, consult your health care provider or a nutritionist.

Fat Facts

Consuming some fat is necessary if you want to ensure proper nerve function, as well as have healthy skin, hair and teeth. How much and what type of fat you consume are the real issues when it comes to constructing a sound eating plan.

Generally speaking, there are three types of fats. Polyunsaturated and monounsaturated fats are considered "good," while saturated fats are classified as "bad."

Good fats can be sourced from foods like walnuts, almonds, peanut butter, olive oil and avocados. They can actually clean clogging cholesterol from your arteries. Although classified as good fats, they should still be used sparingly.

Bad fats can contribute to buildup in your arteries, which in turn can lead to strokes and other serious health problems. Sources of saturated fat include marbled beef, butter and cheese. These fats are pretty easy to spot, as they stay solid at room temperature.

Many experts recommend that your total daily caloric intake be limited to no more than 20 percent fat.

The Watering Hole

Sports nutrition specialists describe water as "the most important nutrient." It's everywhere: in your bones, your brain, your lungs and your breath. It's in your blood, sweat and tears. In fact, approximately 60 percent of your total body weight comes from this stuff.

Drinking pure, clean water before, during and after working out isn't a sign of weakness—it's smart! Depriving yourself of this essential fluid is, at the very least, stupid and, at the very worst, dangerous. Dehydration can reduce your ability to perform and, more frighteningly, result in serious health risks, even death.

Some athletes and sports medicine professionals recommend consuming "isotonic" beverages. If you opt for these sports drinks, choose ones that are low in sugar and citric acid, as high levels of both can impede absorption of water.

Risky Moves

Water in, water out! When young children are given water breaks during training sessions, they should also be given washroom breaks. If not, their martial arts instructor would be well advised to keep a mop and bucket nearby!

Supplementing with Supplements

As a martial arts practitioner, your body will experience physical demands uncommon to sedentary folks. As a result, you might consider taking vitamins, minerals and other supplements in order to replace nutrients lost through exercise. In conjunction with a sound diet (one that is made up of 60 percent carbohydrates, 20 percent protein and 20 percent fat), they can prove advantageous. Again, we recommend you consult your health care provider or a nutritionist to determine which vitamins, minerals and other supplements can best round out your personal "fuel" plan.

Other dietary aids come in the form of meal replacement or enhancement drinks, bars and pills. These include things like ginseng and yohimbine root (for mental alertness and increased energy) and creatine monohydrate (for endurance and heightened muscle growth). These products are gaining popularity among martial artists and other athletes, as well as people who engage in a variety of physical activities.

While use of supplements can complement your eating plan, they are not a replacement for a balanced diet of wholesome foods. Additionally, some people have special needs (for example, pregnant and nursing women, vegetarians and those with chronic health problems). Some prefer to ingest these nutrients in one shot, as a multivitamin. Others insist on taking them individually.

So, do your homework! Obtain relevant literature, consult sources like *The Complete Idiot's Guide to Eating Smart* or see your health care provider or nutritionist. Be certain you understand both the benefits *and* risks of taking these products before incorporating them into your regimen.

In the meantime, we have provided some basic information and general recommendations to get you started. All vitamins and minerals can be obtained from supplements, as well as from food.

Vitamins and Minerals for Martial Artists

Vitamin	Functions	Sources
Thiamine	Converts carbohydrates into usable forms of energy, giving martial artists fuel for aerobic activity.	Yeast, mushrooms, whole-grain and enriched breads and cereals.
Riboflavin	Assists in energy release during martial arts activity.	Dairy products, liver and whole-grain and enriched breads.
Niacin	Converts carbohydrates, fats and proteins into usable forms of energy needed for aerobic and anaerobic activity.	Eggs, poultry, fish and milk.
Vitamin B_6	Aids martial artists in the reactions responsible for converting mostly protein into usable energy.	Liver, lean meats, fish and poultry.
Vitamin B_{12}	Assists in the production of red and white blood cells, which keep the immune system healthy and combat disease.	Liver, meat, eggs and milk.
Folate	Same function as vitamin B_{12}	Liver, leafy vegetables, oranges, and whole grains.
Biotin	Metabolizes fat, proteins and carbohydrates so as to extract energy to use when training.	Cauliflower, egg yolks, nuts and cheese.
Pantothenic Acid	Same as biotin.	Most foods.
Vitamin A	Aids in maintaining the immune system.	Liver, milk, butter, cheese and carrots.
Vitamin C	Promotes wound healing and repair of connective tissue, which aids in the recovery of injuries.	Peppers, broccoli and brussels sprouts.
Vitamin D	Develops and maintains bones, enabling martial artists to better withstand bone-to-bone impact and to protect vital organs.	Fortified milk, fish and liver oils.

Vitamin	Functions	Sources
Vitamin E	Maintains cell membranes, allowing the martial artist to function effectively and efficiently.	Vegetable oils, whole grains and leafy vegetables.
Vitamin K	Aids in blood clotting after a cut and protection from infectious cuts caused by scrapes.	Liver, green leafy vegetables and milk.

Mineral	Functions	Sources
Calcium	Maintains bones, assists in blood clotting and protects martial artists' vital organs and bones by reducing brittleness.	Milk and milk products, tofu and fortified oranges.
Phosphorous	Aids in bone growth and maintenance and helps martial artists maintain bone density.	Nearly all foods, especially milk.
Magnesium	Helps transmission of nerve impulses, allowing martial artists to maintain reaction time, and inhibits nerve degeneration.	Widespread in foods and bottled and tap water.
Iron	Makes up one component of blood, carries oxygen to tissues, assists in oxygen uptake and allows martial artists to perform aerobic and anaerobic activity.	Liver, lean meats, legumes and enriched flour.
Iodide	Aids in metabolism regulation and assists martial artists in extracting energy for performing exercise.	Iodized salt and seafood.
Zinc	Assists in the synthesis of protein to energy, which martial artists use during training.	Meat, eggs, liver and seafood.
Copper	Participates in red blood cell formation and allows the blood to deliver more oxygen, thereby supplying the body with energy while training.	Liver, shellfish, nuts and dried beans.

Risky Moves

Not reading or understanding labels can find you paying 50¢ for a vitamin when a 5¢ one will do the job equally well! Be certain you're getting your money's worth.

Are You Committed?

When it comes to martial arts practice, attending class regularly, engaging in cross-training activities where necessary and maintaining a sound nutritional program are some ways to stay on track. Another important element is developing and following a goal plan—just as you would for other aspects of your life.

In most professionally run martial arts institutions, students are encouraged to set timelines for their belt exams. For example, let's say you're currently a White Belt or beginner. You're following your school's curriculum (which should be explained to you in detail, either by the instructor or in a student manual). You're training consistently and eating and drinking healthfully. In consultation with your instructor, you should set a target date for your first color belt exam. This process should continue to and beyond the Black Belt, or an equivalent, level. Following this route won't guarantee your continued progress in the martial arts, but it will make your chances of success far more likely.

Additionally, you might want to reexamine your lifestyle. Is it productive or destructive? A few examples follow.

Is Your Health Going Up in Smoke?

Do you smoke or take recreational drugs? People who get their kicks from using illegal substances or who light up daily are putting themselves at risk for a barrage of health problems. In addition, smokers and other people who abuse their bodies rarely have the kind of energy, strength and discipline necessary to be a martial artist. Furthermore, they often smell bad—and that's not good when it comes to sweating alongside a training partner.

Espresso Anyone?

While moderate caffeine use (one to two cups of coffee or tea per day) is generally acceptable, ingesting large quantities in the hopes of enhancing your performance in class or on the day of a tournament or an exam can have disastrous effects. Besides acting as a diuretic, which can rob your body of essential fluids, excessive caffeine can deplete your energy stores and prevent the absorption of calcium, impeding your training. Drinking one too many cappuccinos, gulping gallons of soft drinks or chowing down on chocolate can leave you feeling indefatigable initially, then nervous and agitated, and finally exhausted because of rapid energy loss. Too much caffeine can also distort your ability to sense pain—not a good idea when you're engaging in drills with a partner or even when you're performing individual techniques. It's also not advisable to be too "hyped up" on caffeine, or any substance for that matter, if what you really want is to enjoy the stress-reducing benefits of a martial arts program.

Warrior Words

In ancient Arabic, the word for coffee *(qahweh)* means "gives strength." While caffeine in moderation *can* give you a boost, too much of a good thing can leave you feeling fidgety and, later, fatigued.

Another Round?

Like caffeine, alcohol in moderation can be part of some martial artists' balanced nutritional program. Sometimes, after (not before!) a strenuous class, nothing's better than an ice cold beer or a relaxing glass of wine. Additionally, while we're not advocating regular use or overuse of alcoholic products, small quantities can actually bolster your immunity to heart disease. Some experts contend that a glass or two of wine per day can increase longevity. Knowing when to stop drinking is the key. Several brewskies a day can fill your body with unnecessary calories—maybe that's why people say "belly up to the bar"! Furthermore, the statistics regarding alcohol abuse that cite impaired judgment, diminished health and so on are well documented. Finally, mixing excessive drinking and martial arts can be a lethal "cocktail," resulting in men and women behaving in a violent manner that is not appropriate for serious practitioners.

In most modern martial arts schools, students recite a creed wherein they promise to become the best possible person they can be. This won't happen if you get stoned or drunk or abuse your body in any way. This doesn't mean you'll *never* encounter martial artists who smoke, use drugs or are dependent on caffeine and alcohol. It simply means you should ask yourself if that's the kind of practitioner you want to be.

The Least You Need to Know

➤ Myths and misconceptions about martial arts abound. It's important to ask questions and obtain answers about aspects of training that concern you.

➤ Finding an instructor who takes a balanced approach to teaching martial arts can help improve your chances of achieving your goals.

➤ Nutrition can play an important role in your martial arts training program. A balance of carbohydrates, protein, fats and water, and, when necessary, vitamins, minerals and other supplements, can improve your progress.

➤ Establishing and adhering to a goal plan can keep you motivated and help you progress.

➤ Substances that can impede your martial arts progress should be avoided.

Chapter 5

Physical Assets

In This Chapter

➤ Important tips for improving your flexibility

➤ Weight training for martial arts

➤ The correct way to use heavy bags and targets

➤ Enhancing your cardiovascular ability

➤ How training with a partner can benefit you

Boredom is the number one reason people drop out of physical exercise programs. As exciting as cycling, running or stair climbing may be at first, these activities can rapidly lose their luster. Once the romance is over, folks seeking innovative and stimulating ways to challenge their bodies trek off to find the next fitness flavor-of-the-month.

Martial arts, on the other hand, have longevity. Two thousand years ago, they provided Buddhist monks with a means of fortifying their bodies. Today, they serve as the ultimate body-mind-spirit fitness programs for men and women at martial arts schools and cutting-edge gyms and health clubs. As noted in Chapter 1, Karate, Kung Fu, Tae Kwon Do, Judo and other martial arts can also help children get fit and learn self-discipline.

While martial arts can serve as a stand-alone physical regimen, they can also represent an important component in a more broadly based fitness program. This chapter will help you discover how this type of program, based on martial arts along with comple-

Martial Smarts

Those who think they have no time for bodily exercise will sooner or later have to find time for illness.

—*Edward Stanley, Earl of Derby*

mentary physical activities, can change your humdrum fitness regimen, help you improve your cardiovascular health and lead to increased levels of strength and flexibility.

Let's Be Flexible about This

Flexibility is defined as "the range of motion or distance a joint can move." If you become inactive as you age, your muscles and connective tissues stiffen, shorten and tighten. Martial arts training will twist, flex, extend and elongate every part of your body. This type of rigorous physical training can help you not only *see* your toes, but perhaps *touch* them as well!

These 10 tips for stretching can help improve your flexibility:

1. Now and later! Stretch before *and* after a workout or class. After class, when your muscles are warm and your joints are adequately prepared, is the best time to increase your flexibility, while preclass stretching can help you avoid injuries during training.

2. Hold it! While holding a stretch for 20 seconds may be adequate for a warm-up, if your goal is to improve your flexibility, generally you should maintain each position for a minimum of 60 seconds.

3. Bouncers need not apply! Avoid bouncing or forcing yourself into a stretch, both of which can lead to serious injury.

4. Tiny increments are safer than gains-by-the-yard. Work slowly to achieve small, gradual improvements in your flexibility.

5. Breathe naturally. Holding your breath as you stretch will tell your muscles to tighten rather than relax.

6. Give them equal time. Ensure you stretch all muscle groups equally.

7. Maintain proper form. Distance has to take a back seat to quality of movement. Learn how to perform each stretching movement correctly, with the guidance of an experienced instructor.

8. Don't forget to listen to your body. Some days your body may feel tighter or more fatigued than other days, and you may want to limit your range of motion.

9. Consistency is key. Stretch regularly in order to ensure you maintain or increase your flexibility.

10. This is not a contest. One of the nicest things about martial arts training is the fact that you work to your own ability rather than that of others. So never

force a stretch or attempt to overextend yourself. If you tear a hamstring, it'll be you, not your partner, who'll feel it!

Like most sports specialists, the vast majority of martial artists agree that regular stretching performed properly can minimize your risk of injury, reduce muscle soreness and improve your overall performance. Besides, stretching feels good and it's the perfect "prescription" for treating not just a tired body, but an exhausted mind and spirit.

While you should consult your martial arts instructor in creating your stretching program, a sample follows:

Sample Stretching Exercises for Martial Artists

Body Part	Sample Stretching Exercises
Neck	Lean your left ear toward your left shoulder, then your right ear toward your right shoulder. Lower your head gently toward your chest and then look toward the ceiling (maximum 45 degrees above eye level). Next, simply look all the way to your left, then to your right.
Shoulders	Squatting, place your hands on your knees and slowly rotate your right shoulder in the direction of the floor. Repeat this movement with your left shoulder. With feet parallel, shoulder width apart, roll your shoulders toward the rear of the room and then toward the front.
Upper Back	With feet parallel, shoulder width apart, reach both hands around your back as if to give yourself a big hug while bending forward.
Triceps	Reach one arm behind your head, your elbow pointing to the ceiling, as if to touch your shoulder blades. Place your opposite hand on the bent elbow and gently press the palm of the bent arm between your shoulder blades. You should feel a stretch at the back of the bent arm. Repeat with other arm.
Biceps	While sitting cross-legged, place your palms on the floor in front of you with your fingertips rotated to the rear. Attempt to flatten your palms on the floor to ensure you feel the stretch in your bicep.
Lower Back and Hips	Lie on your back and hug both knees to your chest. Keeping your right knee bent, extend your left leg to the floor. Gently drop your right knee toward your left side as your head turns in the opposite direction. Repeat this stretch with your left leg.

Abdominals	This is a modified "cobra" stretch (from yoga). Lie face-down. Supported by your arms and keeping your hips and legs on the floor, raise your torso slowly upwards. This move also stretches the lower back and must be done with extreme care. You should feel no strain or pain. Move slowly, working within your range of flexibility.
Hamstrings	Lie on the floor. Extend one foot toward the ceiling and hold it there while the other leg remains straight on the floor. You should feel a stretch at the back of the thigh. Repeat this stretch with your other leg. Alternatively, try a modified "hurdler's stretch": Sit on the floor, with one leg extended and the other foot resting against the inner thigh of the extended leg. Reach your upper body toward the foot of the extended leg. Repeat this stretch with the other leg.
Quadriceps	While standing or reclining on your side, bend one leg and grab your foot from behind. Gently press the heel of your foot toward your behind, feeling the stretch in the front of the thigh. Repeat this stretch with your other leg.
Inner Thigh (Groin)	While sitting on the floor, extend your legs in a *V* shape and lean your chest forward (don't round or bend your back). (In this position, you can also stretch each hamstring by simply extending your trunk in the direction of one foot. Stretch both sides.)
Calves	Stand with feet together. Extend one leg as if to take a big step, bending it at a 90-degree angle and transferring your weight to that leg. Leave your rear leg straight, or slightly bent, as you press your back heel into the floor. For added support, you can perform this stretch with your hands resting against a wall in front of you.
Lower Body (advanced)	A challenging lower body stretch geared to experienced students is the front and side split (toes pointing upward) with your legs fully extended at a 180-degree angle.

These stretches can be performed on your own or with a partner. Remember to hold each position for 20 to 60 seconds without forcing the stretch and breathe naturally throughout. Maintain the mind-muscle connection (translation: concentrate on the muscle or muscles you are elongating and stay in touch with your body as you perform each stretch). These exercises represent but a brief sampling of dozens of stretches appropriate for martial arts training. For more detailed information, consult your martial arts instructor or books and magazines that address this topic.

"Weighing" the Importance of Strength Training

Martial arts superstar Bruce Lee had one of the best physiques in the business. While he was not, by any "stretch" of the imagination, big and beefy, he had to-die-for striation—the kind of muscle definition that would make even hard-core bodybuilders green (or at least chartreuse) with envy!

But Bruce didn't get buffed simply by meditating and eating tofu burgers. He worked at it. In addition to practicing martial arts, he cross-trained, using resistance programs that included weight lifting or strength training. This means using equipment (such as barbells, dumbbells, cable machines and elastic bands) to gain more strength for performing powerful martial arts techniques like blocking, striking and kicking.

Master Speaks

Some martial arts schools provide basic weight training equipment, but if you're really keen to develop your strength and improve your endurance, joining your local gym may not be a bad idea. Weight training, as little as twice a week and as a part of a comprehensive fitness program that includes martial arts, cardiovascular activity and stretching, can add power to your punch and maximum force to your kicks.

The misconception that this kind of training will make you "muscle bound" went out in the 1960s—like the mountains of trash left after Woodstock. Thirty years ago, magazine ads featured 98-pound weaklings using weights or vibrating belt machines to help them put on 100 pounds of mass (often resulting in the Pillsbury Doughboy look!). Faster than you could say "Surf's up," supernerds were magically transformed into amazing hulks who easily defeated evil, sand-kicking bad guys.

Today, progressive martial artists recognize the important role strength training can play in a well-rounded fitness program.

Muscling In with a Basic Martial Arts Weight Training Program

Looking the part is not as important as developing real strength. Colossal pecs and biceps may get you lots of attention on the beach, but they won't necessarily translate into martial arts power. What will? Basic weight training exercises that can serve as an adjunct to your martial arts program.

Regardless of the discipline you are practicing, resistance training can help you develop additional strength and improved body awareness. This, in turn, can help you enhance your martial arts technique. It can also help you better meet the demands of daily life, like hoisting heavy shopping bags or stuffed briefcases. Furthermore, weight training

Master Speaks

Commune with nature. Training outdoors can give you an entirely new perspective on your martial arts practice. If you head down to the beach or neighborhood swimming pool, you can perform kicking drills in water or dig your feet into the sand and attempt to move, using long strides. In addition to adding a new dimension to your routine, both are great ways to let nature help you strengthen your legs!

can help prepare your body for other sports like tennis and golf.

The amount of weight you lift and the number of repetitions and sets you perform must be customized to your needs. For example, if your primary goal is to develop mass and maximum power, you'll probably lift heavy weights with fewer repetitions. Conversely, if your aim is to tone and improve speed and, to a lesser degree, increase your power, you'll likely use lighter weights with a higher number of repetitions. To develop a suitable resistance program, consult your martial arts instructor, a personal trainer or books or magazines on this topic.

As with stretching, it is important to take a balanced approach when performing resistance exercises. Work all opposing muscle groups evenly. Additionally, maintain that mind-muscle connection and focus on good form. That is, take each movement through its full range of motion without locking the joint or swinging the weight. Furthermore, allow ample time to rest and recover, and be sure to warm up, stretch and use proper form.

A more detailed description of your muscles follows. Understanding your body's muscle components and how they work when you are performing martial arts can help you or a trainer design an appropriate resistance program.

Your Back

Your back has three principal muscle groups. In daily life, they help you lift, pull and carry things. In martial arts training, they play an important role in blocking, punching and throwing your partner.

1. trapezius – the triangular muscle that extends from your neck to your shoulders and mid-back

2. latissimi dorsi – the largest muscles of your upper body, extending from your armpits along both sides of the small of your back

3. spinal erectors – several muscles along the lower back that protect your nerves and, as their name implies, help keep your back straight

Your Chest

Your chest helps you push things, whether you're closing a door, moving furniture or shoving an opponent off balance. It also provides protective padding against strikes.

This area consists primarily of three principal muscles:

1. pectorals – the clavicular or upper portion and the sternal or lower portion, which spread out fanlike to protect the upper rib cage

2. subclavicus – a small, cylindrical muscle that rests between the clavicle (collarbone) and your first rib

3. serratus (anterior) – a small, thin muscle sheet located between the ribs and the scapula (shoulder blades)

Your Shoulders

The two main muscles that make up your shoulders are the deltoids and the trapezius. In daily life, they help you carry things. In martial arts training, they play an important role in blocking, striking and grabbing your partner.

1. deltoids – thick, large, three-headed triangular muscles that originate at your clavicle (the top of the shoulder and shoulder blades) and insert into your upper arm

2. trapezius – the triangular muscle that extends from your neck to your shoulders and mid-back

Your Legs

Legs not only help move us but play an important role in martial arts practice as the foundation for all techniques, whether performed with the upper or lower body. How well you'll punch, block, strike and kick is rooted in your stances (leg positions). In addition to maintaining good form, your stances can be improved through strengthening exercises targeting the lower body. Let's look at the six main muscles that make up your legs.

Risky Moves

You're only as strong as your weakest link. The neck is an often neglected part of an otherwise strong body. From a martial arts standpoint, not strengthening this area can leave you vulnerable to neck restraints and strikes to the head. A simple, isometric resistance exercise for safely strengthening this area is to place your palm against the front of your head and push. Repeat with your palm on the side and then on the back of your head.

Master Speaks

To be the best, rest! If you are lifting heavy weights, you'll have to rest between sets and stations and ensure your body has ample time to recover. Additionally, you shouldn't work the same muscle groups two days in a row. Your muscles grow during the rest phase, not while you're working out. This recommendation also applies to your martial arts class schedule.

1. quadriceps – These four muscles make up the front of your thigh and enable you to extend your knee and flex your hip.

2. hip flexors – These two muscles flex your hip joint. This muscle group plays an important part in helping to "chamber" your leg (placing it in a ready position) before and after executing many martial arts kicks.

3. hamstrings – These three muscles at the rear of your leg help you flex your knee and extend your hip. Along with the quadriceps and hip flexors, these muscles play an important part in helping you chamber your leg.

4. gluteals – The gluteus maximus and minimus (your buttocks) aid the extension of your hip and knee when you kick, and help you maintain certain stances.

5. gastrocnemius – This muscle consists of two heads that lie over the soleus and are joined to the Achilles tendon (which inserts into your heel bone). The "gastroc" (part of your calf) helps you form the correct foot position for martial arts kicks.

6. soleus – This is the larger of your two calf muscles, which together with the "gastroc" helps you jump, as well as shift forward, back and laterally.

Your Arms

Your arms enable you to hold, pull and strike things, whether in daily life, or when practicing martial arts techniques like blocking, punching or takedowns. There are three main muscle groups of the arms:

1. biceps – This is a two-headed muscle that originates under the deltoid (top of the shoulder) and ends slightly below the elbow. It lifts and flexes your arm and plays an important part in enabling you to rechamber for striking and blocking techniques.

2. triceps – This three-headed muscle opposes the biceps and extends from the deltoid to the elbow. This muscle enables you to extend your arm to deliver a punch.

3. forearms – Your forearm flexors help you curl your hand toward your

Warrior Words

Get "set" to get strong. A "set" is a group of continuously performed repetitions (complete movements of an exercise). The number of sets and repetitions you perform are related to your goal (for instance, to build size and power or to tone and improve speed).

forearm, while your extensors enable you to curl your hand away from your forearm. Strong forearms help stabilize your wrist.

Your Abdominals

Your abdominal muscles help protect vital organs and stabilize your body for many daily and martial arts activities, so you should plan to devote time to conditioning this area. Your abdominals include three primary muscles:

1. rectus abdominis – Although most people refer to the "lower" and "upper" abs when discussing exercises that target this area, the reality is that there is one long muscle that extends the length of your abdomen.

2. internal and external obliques – These muscles run along the sides of your torso.

3. intercostals – These two thin planes of muscle and tendon connect the ribs.

This chart can help you, your instructor or your personal trainer develop a customized weight training regimen that is appropriate for the martial arts.

Sample Strengthening Exercises for Martial Artists

Area	Muscle	Common Strengthening Exercises
Back	Latissimus	Lat pull-downs, seated cable rows, pull-ups.
	Erectors	Facedown reclines with leg and arm lifts.
Chest	Pectorals	Flat, incline and decline bench presses, push-ups.
Shoulders	Deltoids	Front military presses, lateral and front raises.
	Trapezius	Upright rows, shrugs (which also work part of your back).
Legs	Quadriceps	Squats, leg presses, leg extensions.
	Hamstrings	Leg curls, lunges (which also strengthen your gluteals).
	Calves	Standing and seated calf raises.
Arms	Biceps	Barbell and dumbbell curls, bicep pull-ups.
	Triceps	Barbell and dumbbell extensions, kickbacks, dips.
	Forearms	Barbell and dumbbell wrist curls.
Abdominals	Rectus abdominis, obliques and intercostals	Crunches, hanging leg raises, oblique twists.

Master Speaks

Some strengthening exercises are "isolation" techniques. This means they require a single muscle to do the work. Others, like push-ups and squats, are "compound" exercises, which incorporate several muscles and joints. Compound exercises that mimic the movements you would perform when doing combative techniques are most advantageous for martial artists.

Another method for improving the form of your martial arts technique while cultivating power is to perform slow blocks, punches and kicks while wearing light wraparound ankle and wrist weights. Ensure you use a weight that is appropriate to your size, and never lock your joint completely, whether you're practicing with or without weights. Overextension can result in serious injury.

One final tip about weight training: your body is an interesting machine. Just as you begin to feel really comfortable performing resistance exercises (approximately 4 to 6 weeks), you'll probably need to revise your program. This change will ensure you continue to challenge your muscles. Just as with your martial arts training, you'll need to set new goals in order to avoid becoming complacent.

It's in the Bag

Heavy bags and target pads are essential tools that can help you develop strong striking and kicking skills. Regular practice with these implements can also improve your ability to aim your techniques and boost your

self-esteem. Each time you strike or kick these targets properly, you receive audible affirmation (a.k.a. a loud "whacking" sound) that your techniques work—or, as martial artists say, "connect."

Martial Smarts

"It's more important to look good than to feel good...and you look mahh-velous!" says Billy Crystal. While this humorous advice may ring true for supermodels and bodybuilders, the opposite is the case for martial artists. Rather than focusing on the aesthetic results of years of strength work, it's more important to understand the real value this activity provides. While you will undoubtedly enjoy the cosmetic benefits of a more toned body, strengthening your arms and legs will make your defensive and offensive techniques more effective. So, before you shave your body from head to toe, slather on self-tanning cream and begin practicing poses in your bedroom mirror, remind yourself that your weight training program is only *part* of a comprehensive fitness regimen.

These striking apparatus fall into the following categories.

➤ **Heavy Bags**   These are generally large vinyl, leather or canvas sacks filled with foam, water or sand. They can weigh anywhere from 50 to 150 pounds (23 to 68 kilograms) and extend from 3 to 6.5 feet (1 to 2 meters) in length. More often than not, they are suspended from metal supports in the ceiling, but they may be freestanding. Martial artists use heavy bags much like boxers do, to test and increase the power of hand strikes. Unlike boxers, they also elbow, knee and kick this bag.

➤ **Light Bags**   Also constructed of canvas, leather or vinyl and filled with foam, water or sand, these bags are smaller and lighter than their heavier counterpart. They are generally suspended from the ceiling, and double-ended versions also attach to the floor. They weigh 5 to 50 pounds (2 to 23 kilograms), measure 18 to 36 inches (45 to 90 centimeters) in length and are usually positioned at head level. While, for the most part, martial artists use the light bag when punching, this is also an excellent target for high stationary and jump kicks.

➤ **Speed Bags**   Constructed of leather or vinyl, these small pear-shaped bags contain an air-filled bladder. They are suspended by a swivel mount, supported by a circular base that is secured to the ceiling. Martial artists and boxers strike this device to develop speed and timing, and improve their reflexes.

➤ **Focus Pads**   These hand-held targets are usually constructed of vinyl-covered foam with handles on the top, side and rear. They may measure from 10 to 48 inches (25 to 120 centimeters). As you become more skillful, your partner will gradually increase the height and distance of these targets. Striking focus pads can help you improve your speed, power, timing and coordination.

Master Speaks

Some martial arts schools include classes that use a "circuit" format. Students move from pad to pad, or bag to bag, using a variety of hand and leg strikes continuously, without rest between techniques. This type of training can assist you in developing speed, power, more focused techniques and improved cardiovascular ability. As this exercise relies on interaction between partners, as well as within a large group, it also cultivates teamwork.

Risky Moves

Hit with caution. To minimize your risk of injury, it is essential you learn the proper way to both hold and strike bags and targets before you begin using them. Additionally, because the bones of their hands are still developing, young children should be monitored carefully when hitting heavy bags. Some schools use softer, children's versions of these training tools.

Hit the Ground Running

For the most part, martial arts training is anaerobic. This means most of the physical activity is performed in quick, short bursts of concentrated energy. But it is the aerobic component that can improve your overall health and lead to increased vitality. Therefore, in order to complement your martial arts training and round out your fitness program, it is essential to include some aerobic activity.

Some of the more popular forms of aerobic exercise used by martial artists include—

➤ skipping rope – This activity also involves use of the upper body. In fact, some people prefer to use weighted ropes to heighten the strength-training component of this form of exercise. Increase your "jumping" time gradually.

➤ running, jogging and walking – These activities can be done indoors and outdoors, on city streets and country roads, and on tracks and treadmills.

➤ aerobic classes and videotapes – Your local gym probably offers a varied menu of aerobic classes. If you prefer to train solo, videotapes can provide cardiovascular conditioning in the comfort of your own home. Some of these activities require special equipment (slides, steps).

➤ stair climbing – This activity can be done indoors on a machine designed for this purpose, or outdoors in stadiums or arenas (or even, for those with charge cards in hand, in shopping malls!).

➤ Versaclimbing – Your local gym or fitness facility may have machinery that mimics mountain climbing. This equipment allows you to exercise the muscles of the upper and lower body simultaneously.

➤ cycling – This is another activity that can be performed in the comfort of your home or gym or while outdoors as you enjoy city or country scenery.

➤ swimming – Whether you're swimming indoors or outdoors, be certain you do a sufficient number of laps at adequate intensity to make this activity an aerobic workout (a dead man's float doesn't count). Some martial artists use flotation devices, placing them either between their legs (resulting in increased demands on their upper body) or between their arms (requiring their lower body to perform most of the work). These devices can add an interesting strengthening component to your pool training.

➤ cross-country skiing – This is another activity that can be done indoors on specially constructed machines or outdoors.

➤ elliptical machines – This equipment combines the movements of a treadmill, stair climber and ski machine with reduced stress on the joints of the lower body.

Although most of your martial arts training may be done in bare feet, be sure you have appropriate sports shoes for these cross-training activities.

The following chart lists the aerobic activities discussed, notes whether equipment is required and indicates levels of cardiovascular benefit and potential risk of injury. Initially, these activities should be performed at minimal to moderate intensity for a minimum of 20 minutes, two to three times per week. As your body adapts, you can gradually increase the intensity, duration and frequency of these exercises. Your long-term goal may be to do 30 to 40 minutes of continuous aerobic exercise, three to four times each week. Couple this exercise with martial arts training and strengthening and stretching exercises for a comprehensive fitness program.

Sample Aerobic Exercises for Martial Artists

Exercise	Equipment	Benefits	Risk of Injury
Skipping Rope	Required	High	Minimal-Moderate
Running/Jogging	Optional	High	Moderate-High
Walking	Optional	Moderate-High	Low
Aerobic Classes	Optional	Moderate-High	Low-High
Aerobic Videos	Required	Moderate-High	Low-High
Stair Climbing	Optional	High	Moderate-High
Versaclimbing	Required	High	Moderate
Cycling	Required	Moderate-High	Moderate
Swimming	Required	Moderate-High	Low
Cross-country Skiing	Required	Moderate-High	Low
Elliptical Machines	Required	High	Low

As with the stretching and strengthening exercises mentioned, these guidelines are designed as samples and, depending on your fitness level and intensity and duration of exercise, your benefits and risk of injury will vary. These guidelines are general and require the input of your instructor, a personal trainer or additional individual research in order to customize a plan that's right for you.

Your Most Valuable Training "Tool"

Doing things alone can get, well, lonely! Human beings are, by nature, social animals. We crave interplay with other people and, among other things, seek their support, respect, attention and admiration.

That's where your most valuable training "tool"—good partners—comes in. From the day you step foot into your martial arts classroom, you will begin developing relationships with other students who share a common interest.

Cooperative interaction with fellow students will, obviously, include exchange activities inside the martial arts classroom. These can encompass assisted stretching, target, self-defense and sparring drills. This kind of teamwork can help you progress more quickly and better enjoy the learning process. Furthermore, the support of training partners can help you clear hurdles that will, undoubtedly, block your martial arts "path" as you train for months and years.

Student interaction may extend to areas outside classes, such as carpooling, sharing a beer or a pizza, and attending extracurricular events. Before you participate in these activities, be certain you understand your school's policy and be mindful of etiquette and possible pitfalls if you socialize with students and instructors outside your school.

The Least You Need to Know

➤ A comprehensive fitness program should include martial arts, stretching, strength training and cardiovascular activity.

➤ Stretching can help you avoid injury, reduce muscle soreness, improve the form of your martial arts technique and decrease overall body tension.

➤ In addition to preparing you to better address the physical challenges of daily life, strength training can help you increase the power of your strikes, blocks and kicks.

➤ Use of heavy bags and focus pads can help you improve your speed, coordination, power and accuracy. They can also help you feel more confident about the effectiveness of your techniques.

➤ Cardiovascular activities like running, swimming, skipping rope and skiing can help you strengthen the muscle that drives your body: your heart. These activities also enable you to feel more energetic when performing ordinary tasks and martial arts drills.

➤ Cooperative training partners can aid your progress and make martial arts practice more enjoyable.

Chapter 6

Better Safe Than Sorry

In This Chapter

➤ Avoiding some common training mistakes

➤ Learning how to warm up and prepare for class

➤ Safe sparring and self-defense practice

➤ How to ensure steady progress

➤ The importance of supervision

When properly instructed by a competent teacher, martial arts training is a safe, challenging and enjoyable activity for the entire family. Despite this fact, minor injuries can occur, so it's important to do what you can to minimize your risk.

By following the simple suggestions included in this chapter, you will greatly improve your odds of experiencing a long, rewarding and safe martial arts journey.

Essential Beginner Tips

The following are some basic do's and don'ts that apply generally to novice practitioners, but they also hold true for seasoned martial artists.

Obeying the Rules

Every martial arts school has a list of rules. These guidelines can help you figure out what's expected of you and avoid minor or major faux pas. Typically, they'll address everything from student dress, behavior and grooming, to more detailed aspects of practice, like use of school equipment. If you don't adhere to these regulations, you may not have a productive and enjoyable martial arts experience.

Overtrain = Drain and Strain

As you begin your martial arts study, you will undoubtedly be swept along by a strong wave of enthusiasm that is common among most newcomers. When you realize how much there is to learn and how greatly you're going to benefit from your training, it's difficult to avoid becoming overzealous.

Master Speaks

When planning your martial arts schedule, don't forget to factor in your travel time, as well as the fact that you'll have to change and prepare before and after class.

Some beginners attend one or several classes every day. Within a short while, however, muscle soreness, fatigue and injuries, coupled with an overwhelming sense of burnout, develop—clear signals that they're overdoing it.

So don't ignore the sage advice of instructors who recommend that as a new student you limit your training to two to three times per week. Setting such a limit will give your body a chance to recover while ensuring you stay on track with respect to learning required material.

Building the Comfort Zone

Attend classes that are appropriate to your level of experience. Some smaller martial arts schools conduct mixed classes, where beginners train with intermediate or advanced students. While these classes can serve as a source of motivation, inspiration and perspiration, for students at lower belt levels, they can be frustrating and dangerous. So in order to ensure you have ample opportunity to progress at your rate, don't attend mixed level classes unless advised by your instructor.

Family Class

"The family that kicks together, sticks together" is a popular martial arts maxim and certainly there are a number of martial arts schools that offer a mixed age, mixed rank class, where family members can train side by side. While sharing your martial arts experience with your family and friends can bring immeasurable benefits, you should weigh the pros and cons of participating in this type of class. For example, the convenience of driving the entire family to your local martial arts school to take a class at the same time will probably simplify your life. One disadvantage to this format, as noted, is that with a mixed class, it's extremely difficult to ensure that beginner, intermediate and advanced students cover their required curriculum. Furthermore, in this setting, there is a tendency both for moms and dads to continue to play the parental role and for children to be distracted by the presence of an authority figure other than the instructor. So don't attend a family class until you weigh the pluses and minuses.

Don't Touch Other People's Toys

Before a class begins, it's fairly common to see novice students saunter over to the heavy bag or pads and begin striking them. They may also pick up a skipping rope and, even if they haven't seen one since they were in nursery school, begin jumping wildly as they gasp for air. Remember the old saying "Curiosity killed the cat" before you start playing with unfamiliar equipment. While these kinds of equipment can greatly aid you in developing your martial arts skills, don't use them until you've consulted your teacher. This is a courteous—and safe—approach.

Testing the Waters

A belt exam is one way you can measure your progress. Most beginners are in a rush to reach their first advancement in rank. As a martial arts rookie, you should remember that it could take anywhere from 3 to 6 months to reach your first color belt level. While these moments of celebration are important in the life of every practitioner, don't let them take precedence over regular attendance, acquiring new skills and embracing the learning process.

Risky Moves

As a novice (or even advanced) student, you are expected to do your best. But when you're performing conditioning and stretching exercises, don't try to pump out more push-ups than other students or attempt to twist your legs into the shape of a pretzel. Trying to keep up with the Joneses can be hazardous to your health. Simply focus on improving the quality and quantity of your own movements.

Master Speaks

In most martial arts schools that teach kicking and punching, you'll find various striking implements, including heavy and light bags and targets. It is advisable to "wrap" your hands with appropriate materials and wear "bag" gloves to protect yourself before using these training tools.

Cultivating Skill or Collecting Trophies?

Posters and flyers announcing upcoming competitions are frequently displayed at martial arts schools. While most tournaments include divisions for beginners, don't try your hand at competing until you have a good grasp of your particular discipline. This might require several months or more of training. Furthermore, don't enter these events until you have obtained your instructor's advice and prepared accordingly (that is, you know the rules, you have selected the categories in which you'll compete and you have practiced the material required for each division). It's also a good idea to observe a few of these events before actually participating, so you'll know what lies ahead, and to make sure your instructor agrees that you're ready to compete.

Saving Pennies

Relative to other activities like scuba diving, golf or tennis, martial arts are a very economical pastime. When you divide tuition fees by the number of classes you'll take, it probably works out to a few dollars per session. So, investing in top-quality protective equipment is not out of the question. For example, a pair of inexpensive, vinyl, heavy-bag gloves will cost about $20. If you purchase a leather pair, you'll probably have to spend at least twice that much, but, like most other things you buy, you'll probably get what you pay for. The cheaper pair will likely split, tear and become useless well before the more expensive gloves, which may last several years. The same holds true when you're shopping around for quality martial arts instruction. Paying less for your classes doesn't necessarily mean you will be buying substandard instruction. But if one school is charging $20 per month for classes and another expects you to pay $50 or more, don't sign on the dotted line until you've figured out why there's such a discrepancy in the price.

Nicky Narcissism

After training a few months, you'll begin to realize you know some very cool stuff! The temptation to boast about your skills or test them on the street is real—and foolhardy! Furthermore, it is not uncommon for beginners to think of themselves as "teachers," all too ready to dole out advice to less, and even *more,* experienced students. While your enthusiasm is to be applauded, don't give in to this kind of ego-driven energy until you have trained for a little longer.

Next to Godliness

There are no two ways about it. Martial arts training is physically demanding and with it comes buckets and buckets of sweat, so it's important to keep your practice outfit, safety equipment and body immaculate. If not the first, than one of the most important, commandments of all martial arts is "Thou Shalt Not Wear a Dirty

Uniform"! You should adhere unswervingly to this cleanliness rule if for no other reason than it's difficult for your partner to train with one hand holding his or her nose! A clean uniform in good repair is an essential training detail. Besides being unsightly, tears in tops or pant legs can lead to injuries in grappling sports like Judo and Jiu-jitsu. Furthermore, if you don't show enough respect to keep your uniform clean, you probably won't respect yourself, training partners, instructor or martial art.

Warming Up to Your Training

Performing elaborate throws or soaring effortlessly through the air while executing a perfect "flying" kick are some of the physical rewards of years of martial arts study.

But you will never master these advanced skills without carefully warming up and striving to perform even basic techniques with the greatest attention to form. Let's start by learning how to warm up properly.

Turning Up the Heat

How long you need to warm up depends largely on several components: genetics, your age, your level of physical fitness and environmental factors. Some people are naturally flexible and require very little time to warm up and stretch out their muscles. Children, too, are generally quite pliable. People in the 40-plus age bracket who are physically fit usually require less time to stretch adequately than do their contemporaries who are out of shape. In addition, if the temperature of your training area is fairly high, you may be able to limber up more easily.

It's becoming more and more common to see men and women in their 40s, 50s and 60s participating in martial arts classes. As an adult, perhaps one who hasn't exercised for quite some time, you should pay special attention to preparing for every training session by warming up and stretching properly.

A good warm-up is just that—a warm-up, not a workout. At the beginning of an hour-long class, 15 to 20 minutes should be devoted to cardiovascular activity, calisthenics and stretching to help your body prepare for your martial arts class. Devoting less time than this may not be sufficient. Conversely, an extended version may eat into your class time, preventing you from covering required martial arts material.

Master Speaks

Pump up the volume? In many modern martial arts schools, warm-ups and series of activities (for instance, circuit drills) are performed to music. Moving to a beat might help you train for longer periods and with greater intensity. But check with your instructor before popping a cassette into your school's sound system because more traditional martial arts institutions frown on this practice.

Start Your Engines

A comprehensive warm-up will generally include—

➤ brief preliminary stretch

➤ several minutes of cardiovascular activity like running, jumping rope or shadow boxing to elevate your heart rate

➤ calisthenics, such as push-ups, tricep dips and abdominal exercises, done in sufficient repetitions and at a rate to ensure your body temperature remains elevated

➤ full body stretch

After a good warm-up you shouldn't feel exhausted. Rather, you should be invigorated and ready for action!

Martial Smarts

Baltasar Gracián, in offering sage counsel about the need for courtesy in life, says that we are born as barbarians and only raise ourselves "above the beast by culture." His advice holds true for martial arts practice as well. At the beginning and end of each sparring session, always display proper sporting conduct. A respectful bow and handshake go a long way toward maintaining an atmosphere of civility.

Tag, You're It!

Kumite in Karate, *daeryon* in Tae Kwon Do and *randori* in Judo all refer to sparring practice. Quite simply, sparring allows you to test your offensive and defensive skills with a partner.

This activity is a training method and should not be confused with "fighting." It's human nature to lose your temper when you're sparring but doing so is risky and counterproductive. Instead of focusing on winning each match, view each exchange as an opportunity to polish your blocking, striking, kicking, movement, distance and timing skills.

When many neophytes begin to spar, they look forward to scoring points (tagging parts of a partner's body) or, in schools that teach full contact, exerting maximum force. More experienced practitioners generally aim to improve their skills and demonstrate the utmost respect for their partner throughout each match.

For many people, sparring, like other things, is an acquired taste. As you become more adept, you may develop a real appreciation for this aspect of training. Although most beginners approach this activity with some trepidation, intermediate and advanced students, when properly coached, find it an enjoyable and productive exercise.

Typically, this type of practice is either—

1. one-step sparring, where one student advances an attack and the other blocks or shifts out of the way and counterattacks, or

2. free sparring, where both students exchange offensive and defensive techniques spontaneously

Most progressive schools encourage or require students to wear protective equipment for all exchange drills (drills with partners) including sparring and self-defense training. If you have concerns about this activity, discuss them in advance with your instructor.

Walk Before You Run

There is an old joke that goes something like this: "I went to a fight last night and a hockey game broke out!" The fact that you're more likely to get a shiner or a chipped tooth playing hockey, football, soccer or other sports has something to do with the philosophy of the martial arts. It also has a great deal to do with the kind of supervision you receive from your school's teaching staff.

Master Speaks

In better schools, properly trained advanced students will demonstrate optimum control over their techniques when sparring with lower belts. This is an essential martial arts legacy passed from student to student as each climbs the rank ladder. Don't forget to demonstrate to novice students the same courtesy that you received when you were a mere martial arts tadpole.

Often, the most dangerous person in the classroom is *you*. While accidents do happen, the likelihood of someone pummeling your proboscis is remote. Most injuries occur when students "walk into a technique" (a nice way of saying they use their face to block a punch or kick) or when students who fail to properly warm up pull a muscle. So be certain you prepare your body, mind and spirit properly, use suitable techniques with good control and train under the supervision of competent instructors. Following these precautions will help minimize your risk of injury.

Adhering to your school's rules and being careful when practicing as a White Belt can

Risky Moves

Don't be a copycat. Trying to imitate the movements of advanced students while you are still a beginner can lead to injury and frustration. While seasoned practitioners can make even the most complex combinations look easy, remember it may have taken them years, even decades, to get to the point where they are now. Attempting these moves before you're ready can leave you watching from the sidelines.

Risky Moves

After an injury, RICE is in order. No, not that white, starchy stuff, but *rest, ice, compression* and *elevation*. Rest your sore muscles, apply ice, wrap up the injured area and elevate it. If you don't allow yourself time to recover, and fail to follow your instructor's or health care professional's advice on the best way to resume your training, you may be faced with a growing number of injuries.

greatly improve your chances of achieving your martial arts goals. Stay safe and follow your teacher's instructions.

Big Brother Is Watching You!

In a professionally run martial arts school, an acceptable student-teacher ratio is approximately 8 to 1. When a group of 20 or 30 students are training, there should be at least one senior instructor supervising the class, with the help of several instructors or assistants. In addition to possessing sufficient martial arts knowledge to conduct and supervise the class, these teachers should have a basic understanding of first-aid procedures in the event a minor injury occurs.

These well-trained individuals are your tour guides on the road to martial arts success. They're your mentors, coaches and big brothers and sisters. Given the important role they'll play in your life, be certain you entrust your martial arts future to the right team.

Satisfying their egos should be secondary to improving your skills. They should be vigilant when it comes to your safety and progress. And their tone should be one of discipline, respect and encouragement.

In addition, advanced students are usually more than willing to help beginners learn the ropes. Take advantage of this valuable resource and remember to extend the same helping hand when it's your turn.

Master Speaks

Frequently, parents enroll their children in martial arts programs, only to find themselves signing up for classes shortly after. Mom, dad, sister and brother might all practice side by side. But because martial arts rank is generally based on experience and merit rather than age, some adults find it difficult—and somewhat humbling—to follow the instructions of a more advanced child!

The Least You Need to Know

➤ Avoid beginner don'ts like overtraining, performing complex techniques or using school equipment before you're ready, and engaging in competition prematurely.

➤ The importance of a safe, thorough warm-up that includes cardiovascular activity, calisthenics and stretching cannot be overestimated.

➤ Sparring with proper preparation and supervision can be a safe, productive and fun martial arts activity.

➤ Injuries among martial arts practitioners are, for the most part, rare and generally minor. Following the advice of your instructor can minimize your risk of injury and keep you from being sidelined.

➤ Make sure you entrust your martial arts education to a professional, experienced team consisting of senior instructors, instructors and assistants, as well as advanced students.

Chapter 7

In the Spirit of Things

In This Chapter

➤ Cultivating a sixth sense with martial arts mental training

➤ Combative arts from the inside out

➤ Notes on meditation

➤ How Zen teachings can positively affect your daily life

The body-mind-spirit connection in martial arts training is undeniable.

Genetic factors, your age, fitness level and approach to training often dictate, and occasionally limit, the advances you can make from a physical standpoint. Mental and spiritual gains, on the other hand, can be boundless but difficult to achieve—and almost as difficult to explain in one chapter. There have been countless texts of encyclopedic proportions written on the mental and spiritual side of the martial arts. If this aspect of training is your primary area of interest, we encourage you to compile a reading list with your instructor, and to purchase these books or borrow them from your local library.

In the meantime, this chapter is intended simply to acquaint you with these less tangible benefits of martial arts study and provide you with a rudimentary understanding of the mental and spiritual gains you can hope to enjoy as a practitioner. It will touch on the positive effect these gains can have on your life and on the lives of those around you. And while this chapter will give you some idea of how to achieve a "highly evolved intuitive state," don't confuse this with the psychic ability required to predict next week's winning lottery numbers.

Your Mind as the Ultimate Weapon

It may come as a surprise to you that martial artists strive to *defuse* conflict and *avoid* physical confrontation, rather than duking it out at the drop of a hat. Trading kicks and punches or grappling in the dirt is considered by most practitioners to be the lowest form of martial strategy.

Learning self-defense skills, becoming stronger and more flexible, and developing greater cardiovascular fitness are daunting tasks. They pale by comparison, however, when it comes to cultivating mental and spiritual fitness—perhaps the most formidable undertaking.

One way to get closer to achieving this aim is to listen to your martial arts instructor. A good teacher will share tidbits of wisdom and provide lessons that will challenge your mind's "muscle" and nourish your spirit.

The mental and spiritual side of training doesn't usually play a major role in the life of a novice or intermediate student, and in some schools it doesn't fit into the curriculum at all. Generally speaking, at the rookie stage of your martial arts study, you'll focus on the physical aspect of your education. But bit by bit, inch by inch, your instructor will begin to introduce material of a nonphysical nature, which can help you realize why

some martial artists are always able to face even the most intimidating situations head on.

As the months and years pass, your body will become stronger and respond more quickly to your mind's commands, leaving you feeling more confident. As your training progresses and you continue to confront and combat your fears, you'll come to celebrate a mental strength that you once may have thought impossible. It may occur to you one day, like those pesky lightbulbs positioned over the heads of cartoon characters, or perhaps it will be a revelation that is gradual in coming: You're not just physically powerful. You're *mentally* powerful.

Your martial arts training has taught you how to react in the event of physical confrontation. You've honed your self-defense skills to the point where they've become reflexive. But more importantly, as an advanced student, you've developed a sixth sense that may help you anticipate and thus pre-empt an attack.

This is why martial arts practitioners know that your mind—and the mental strength you achieve as a result of your training—is your most mighty weapon.

Zen and Now

Before we get into the spiritual aspect of martial arts training and you encounter terms like *religio-philosophical schools,* it's essential for you to understand that we're not suggesting this component is a *religious* thing. Your martial arts classroom is not meant to take the place of your house of worship. Martial spirituality and philosophy is not mysterious or magical. This training element is generally intended to provide simple guideposts, pointing you in the direction of a life that is better balanced and more blissful. Now that we've cleared any "mystical" misconceptions out of the way, let's begin.

Some martial arts schools include a strong spiritual, meditative or philosophical component in their curriculum. Others offer none. But most are somewhere in the middle and include a brief relaxation period at the beginning and end of each class. This provides you with the opportunity to prepare yourself in advance of every session and to reflect on your performance afterwards, as you strive to nurture the body-mind-spirit connection.

You Gotta Have Faith

Several religio-philosophical schools influenced martial arts. For example, the principles of Taoism or Daoism (based on the teachings of the celebrated philosopher Lao Tsu), Confucianism and Buddhism influenced ancient Chinese, Japanese and Korean martial traditions. Taoists are generally carefree and yielding, and they embrace the metaphysical. Confucianists, on the other hand, are usually more pragmatic, focusing their interest on morality and a political system that molds their society. But these two groups share many beliefs that revolve around community and the universe. Hindu and Islamic teachings influenced martial arts of Southeast Asia like Silat, an indigenous Indonesian system of self-defense. Early Tagalog religions, as well as Catholicism and Islam, participated in the evolution of Filipino combative systems like Escrima (short-stick combat). Buddhism's influence on Muay Thai (Kickboxing) is still readily apparent in the rituals of this martial art. Furthermore, combative experts contend there is a relationship between the religions of Brazil and Africa (like Candomble) and combative systems like Capoeira.

Although these religio-philosophical movements contributed to the development of martial arts and Asian culture in general, the simplicity and emphasis on action of Zen made it an ideal doctrine for the warrior classes. Therefore, we'll focus primarily on Zen in examining the spiritual side of the martial arts. Furthermore, while the language of Zen is Japanese, the concepts and precepts noted in this section transcend language and apply to most martial arts disciplines.

You've probably heard about Zen from popular books like Robert M. Pirsig's *Zen and the*

Art of Motorcycle Maintenance, which lies on nearly every baby boomer's bookshelf. But just what is Zen?

Quite simply, Zen is a blending of Taoism and Mahayana Buddhism, which was introduced to China in A.D. 520 by the Indian Buddhist monk Bodhidharma (you'll learn more about him in Chapter 13). Individuals who adhere to the principles of Zen strive to achieve *satori,* also called nirvana. This can be explained as "enlightenment" or a breakthrough that transports you to the ultimate level of consciousness. *Satori* is generally reached through meditation called *zazen,* which leads you to a state of *mushin* (no-mind). "No-mind" doesn't mean you're mindless. On the contrary, it means that you're able to see things more clearly in your head. Your judgment isn't clouded with any pre- or misconceptions. You're able to see the big picture. Modern athletes and coaches call this state of mental clarity "the zone."

Entering the Zen Zone

It doesn't matter if you're a robed, shaved-head Zen master, a dedicated martial artist, an elite marathon runner, a world-class tennis player or a top-ranked golfer. *Mushin* connects you, in an indescribable manner, to whatever activity you're performing.

Risky Moves

Don't confuse verbal gymnastics with spiritual guidance. Many teachers talk "a blue streak." But instructors can speak volumes by relying more on their actions than on their words to communicate with students. If you're pursuing a well-rounded martial arts education, be certain you balance words and silence with action. Don't be preoccupied with achieving a Zen state. It could take you months, years or even a lifetime to get there, and some practitioners *never* make it. Pontification is no substitute for perspiration.

Your hand and calligraphy brush become one. Your sword or bow and arrow are simply extensions of your arm. You run mile after mile as your feet and the road seem umbilically linked. You can no longer discern the boundary between your hand and your tennis racket or golf club. The action and you are one and the same. It sounds mystical and weird but this concept will become a little clearer as you read on.

There are two main Zen sects. The Buddhist monk Eisai brought one sect, called Rinzai, from China to Japan in the twelfth century. The other, Soto, was introduced by the monk Dogen in the thirteenth century.

In feudal Japan, Zen philosophy helped warriors transport themselves, mentally speaking, to a state of battlefield readiness. More recently, after the Second World War, many European and American artists and philosophers became interested in Zen, embracing the beauty of simplicity.

Zen has had a profound influence on numerous aspects of Japanese culture—from tea drinking to the martial arts—because it is a philosophy of action rather than theory.

As previously noted, there are martial arts schools that spend a great deal of time on the spiritual aspect of training and others that prefer to focus exclusively on punching, kicking and grappling. Most schools are somewhere in the middle when it comes to the issue of meditation and the metaphysical side of combative arts.

Martial Smarts

I was thrown out of college for cheating on a metaphysics exam. I looked into the soul of the boy next to me.

—*Woody Allen*

The Mechanics of Meditation

There are numerous ways to meditate. Martial arts practice is often viewed as "moving meditation" because certain exercises, like "forms" (routines resembling dance), require your body, mind and spirit to work together toward a common purpose. As with seated meditation, your breathing pattern is extremely important.

Another method of meditation involves remaining motionless and is performed as follows:

1. Sit in a lotus, half-lotus or kneeling position or, if your joints are painfully uncooperative, in a chair. Keep your spine in a neutral position to facilitate proper breathing.

2. Cup your palms together just below your navel or join your thumb and index finger and rest the backs of your hands on your knees.

3. Close your eyes partially or completely (no power-napping, please).

4. Clear your mind of any distractions. If you are a beginner, your instructor may give you a riddle to contemplate. This *koan,* which is similar to a mantra (an incantation or instrument of thought), can help focus your mind while you meditate. When you're more experienced, using a *koan* will probably not be necessary.

5. Breathe slowly, inhaling through your nose and filling your lungs to capacity. Hold your breath before releasing it through your mouth, emptying

Master Speaks

Some practitioners rely on visual or audio cues to aid meditation, including Zen calligraphy, called *bokuseki,* simple flower arrangements, soft music (*not* Barry Manilow) or recorded nature sounds. Other practitioners prefer to simply close their eyes, releasing themselves from the image-cluttered world, and bask in the joy of silence—a rare commodity in today's noise-polluted society.

Risky Moves

If you meditate for an extended period of time, for example, 15 minutes or more, you may feel light-headed, as blood is directed to your stomach and away from other parts of your body. After you've finished meditating, move carefully and slowly until this feeling subsides.

your lungs completely. You might experience a heightened sense of awareness. Ordinary sounds like the ticking of a clock or the breathing of those around you may seem amplified.

In addition to helping you achieve clarity of mind, meditation can provide you with numerous health benefits, such as reduced tension and lowered blood pressure. The duration of this practice and any additional information specific to your needs should be discussed with your martial arts teacher.

Following extended meditation periods, you'll probably need a Zen "seventh inning stretch":

1. Slowly stand up.

2. Rub your legs.

3. Rotate your shoulders and arms.

4. Massage your head and face vigorously.

These post-meditation exercises can help you stimulate blood flow.

Zen's Life Lessons

As we mentioned before, martial arts practitioners agree that certain training exercises, like forms, also called *kata* (in Japanese), *kune* (in Chinese) and *hyung* (in Korean), are moving meditation. By repeating movements over and over again and focusing outside as well as inside your being, you can ascend to a higher level of awareness. Interestingly, many people are of the opinion that enlightenment can be achieved through simple actions in daily life, like brushing your teeth or washing dishes. Furthermore, they believe you can use Zen lessons as tools for self-improvement. This concept is described in the following sections.

➤ **Learning by Making Mistakes**   *Nana karobi ya okii,* a Zen expression that means "Fall seven times, get up eight times," is attributed to the fifteenth-century monk Bokuden. Translation: it's okay to make mistakes as long as you learn from them.

➤ **Forging Ahead**   *Seishin tanren* means to "forge" or "fortify" your spirit. When repeated 1000 or 10 000 times, correctly performed martial movements, like the strikes of a blacksmith's hammer, forge your body, fortify your mind and strengthen your spirit. This exterior and interior strength is not limited to the martial arts classroom, but can benefit other aspects of your personal and professional life.

➤ **Mind of No-Mind** *Mushin* (no-mind) is a meditative state. It refers to a mind that is undistracted and untroubled. In a state of *mushin,* you are able to remain focused, single-mindedly accomplishing any task, whether it's performing a martial arts drill, preparing a report for work, doing your homework or even cleaning the house. This advanced martial arts Zen concept was explained by the swordmaster Yagyu Tajima as follows: "Students often ask me how they should prepare for combat and I say 'do not prepare, simply forget what you are doing and strike the enemy.' "

➤ **It's the Little Things That Matter** *Zensho* can be explained as living every moment to its fullest. Ancient samurai were acutely aware of the fact that, during times of war, each day might be their last. With the prospect of death looming large, they came to appreciate life's minute details and take nothing for granted. Shouldn't we all?

➤ **Dedication and Commitment** *Nyumon no kokoro* means "the heart of a beginner." *Nyumon* (entering the gate), which refers to the ancient practice of dedicating yourself to martial arts, is combined with *kokoro,* meaning heart or spirit. Regardless of rank, physical ability and years of training, martial arts students make a promise to maintain the "heart of a beginner." Throughout years of martial arts study, this was a simple way of encouraging practitioners to retain the zealous and humble approach to training characteristic of a new student. Imagine if you applied this same enthusiasm and modesty to your career, home or school life.

Warrior Words

In the Western world, athletes are judged by the "tale of the tape," or the list of their accomplishments. In the East, however, merit is not measured by whether individuals have won or lost, but whether they've tried their best. What is admired is a person's *kokoro* (spirit or heart).

Martial Smarts

Ignorant men [and women] don't know what good they hold in their hands until they've flung it away.

—*Sophocles*

Don't it always seem to go that you don't know what you've got 'til it's gone.

—*Joni Mitchell*

➤ **Observation Deck** *Fuden no den* (transmitting the untransmittable) is an advanced concept wherein students learn by observing more experienced practitioners. It's a lot like an academic or corporate mentoring program. As a quiet observer, you're encouraged to pay special attention to the most minute details of the more seasoned student's performance, as if you were examining amoebas

Master Speaks

A gun used by a criminal is a tool of fear, violence and destruction. In the hands of a police officer, this weapon can be an instrument of peace. The same concept applies to martial arts. The techniques you'll learn as a practitioner can be employed positively—to defend yourself—or irresponsibly to willingly hurt others. Be mindful of the power you as a martial artist can wield.

under your high school microscope. This observation also provides you with an opportunity to study not simply with your eyes and brain, but with your heart and soul. In the martial arts classroom, and in life in general, actions speak louder than words.

➤ **Quality of Life** *Satsujinken kara katsu-jinken made* can be translated as "going from the sword that takes life to the sword that gives life." This concept refers to a shift in focus that occurs as you mature as a martial artist. In the early stages of your training, you'll concentrate on striking or grappling to overcome an opponent. At a more advanced level of study, you'll come to realize that the real value of martial arts training is not in knowing how to defeat another human being, but rather in improving the quality of life of everyone around you.

More Martial Wisdom for Everyday Life

People hunger for knowledge. They thirst for wisdom. Folks will spend countless hours tuned in to morning talk shows, or break out their credit card and ring up any number of psychic chat lines in search of sage advice. What many of them may not have tried, however, is finding a good martial arts teacher.

One of the greatest benefits of a martial arts education is the opportunity to acquire wisdom. Not the sitting-on-a-rock-contemplating-the-meaning-of-life variety, but a practical wisdom that can enhance your daily life.

In the previous section, you discovered some beneficial martial maxims. Other life-improving principles are described below.

➤ *R-E-S-P-E-C-T* Aretha Franklin sang about it. The dictionary says it's synonymous with admiration and esteem. In "martialspeak," *rei* (respect, courtesy or veneration) is an essential element of training. As a student, you'll undoubtedly learn the popular expression, "Martial arts begin and end with respect." Through martial arts study, you'll come to respect your teachers, fellow students, relatives, friends, co-workers and, of course, yourself.

➤ **Steadfast and True** *Cho* refers to the bond of loyalty forged between you and your martial arts teacher and school. As you continue to train for years, you'll probably realize that *cho* is wisely applied to other relationships in your life, such as those with your boss, co-workers, family and friends.

➤ **Do the Right Thing** In Zen phraseology, an unswerving will or spirit is called *fudoshin.* Having *fudoshin* doesn't mean you're stubborn or you refuse to change even when it would benefit you. It means that once you've established the principles and convictions that will guide your life, you won't be swayed by negative influences. This is an especially important concept in light of the effect negative peer pressure can have on children, teenagers and even adults.

Martial Smarts

Honor is like a rugged island without a shore. Once you've left it, you cannot return.

—Nicholas Boileau, Satires

➤ **The Road Less Traveled**   The "way" or "path of the mind," meaning motivation or quest, in martialspeak is *doshin.* There is a popular Zen expression: "The way is already accomplished when one has the right motivation." As you establish goals in martial arts and in life, be mindful of the fact that pursuing them with a pure motivation and single-minded focus can improve your chances of success.

➤ **Ironclad Code of Ethics**   You'll probably learn a code of ethics in your martial arts school. Japanese practitioners call this the *dojo kun.* This code will encourage you to interact fairly with others. Through martial arts, you'll discover the importance of being honorable, ethical, truthful and just. With any luck, this learning will spill over into other areas of your life. The value of this kind of training in a world where morality and ethics seem to be disappearing in schools, offices and even the halls of government shouldn't be underestimated.

➤ **Mission Control**   Self-discipline or self-control in Zen terminology is *kunren.* As a martial artist you'll be taught how to maintain your composure and to persevere through stressful times (from bouts of road rage, to the throes of corporate downsizing, to the loss of a loved one). Lao Tsu summed up this concept as "he who conquers others is strong, he who conquers himself is mighty."

➤ **Good Samaritan**   Martial artists refer to unselfish behavior as *rikoshin no nai.* In times of need, martial artists are often called upon to help other people. The concept of "looking out for number one" doesn't enter into the martial mix. In extreme situations, as a true martial arts practitioner, you are your brother's or sister's keeper.

Martial Smarts

Goodness is the only investment that never fails.

—Henry David Thoreau

Imagine a world where you're applauded for learning from your mistakes. Where you're encouraged to fortify your mind and spirit and achieve clarity of thought.

Where you come to appreciate the little things, strive to withstand negative pressure and improve the lives of others. Where respect, loyalty, a strong code of ethics and concern for your neighbors (those next door and those around the world) are at the top of your agenda. This positive mental and spiritual vibe can come about as a result of your martial arts education.

The Least You Need to Know

➤ Mental strength is an important, nonphysical benefit of martial arts training.

➤ Spiritual training is an essential aspect of many combative artists' education.

➤ The practice of meditation can help you achieve clarity of mind and provide other health benefits.

➤ Many Zen precepts like respect, honor, loyalty and learning from your mistakes can have a positive influence on your life both inside and outside the martial arts classroom.

Knowledge
Respect
Balance
Power

Chapter 8

The Joy of Reaching Your Personal Goals

In This Chapter

➤ How a martial arts goal plan can help you get on track

➤ Tactics for staying motivated

➤ Measuring your progress from White Belt to Black Belt and beyond

➤ Understanding the rank system for color and black belts

➤ Discovering your ultimate aim as a martial artist

Ancient warriors generally had one primary goal: to be alive at the end of the day. Modern "warriors" usually have a more complicated agenda revolving around their physical, mental and spiritual needs and desires.

In this chapter, you'll discover the important role a goal plan can play in helping you achieve your martial arts objectives. You'll learn how to craft and follow that plan, determine what your objectives are, assign timelines to each one and monitor your progress as you move up the rank ladder.

More importantly, this chapter will help you understand what your *supreme* goal should be as a martial artist.

Constructing Your Martial Arts Goal Plan

Before you can develop your personal goal plan for your martial arts education, you'd be well advised to make a personal inventory. You might want to begin by answering the following questions:

➤ Do I have a history of starting, then quitting, things?

➤ Am I frequently late or do I miss appointments?

➤ Do I often misplace or lose things, or forget what task I am trying to complete?

➤ Do I neglect my physical, mental and spiritual health?

➤ As I reflect upon my life, are there few, if any, accomplishments I can celebrate?

No scientific scoring system is necessary to understand that too many "yes" answers mean you might not be the perfect candidate for a martial arts program. But the flip side to this revelation is that if you have a history of starting and quitting things, tardiness, an inability to focus on the task at hand and neglect of your physical, mental and spiritual health, and few moments of achievement come readily to mind, you probably *need* martial arts training! Perhaps that's why you bought this book in the first place. If so, this simple act of deciding whether a martial arts self-improvement program can help you get and stay on track is cause for celebration.

When you begin your martial arts education, you'll be amazed at how organized your life will become, with set class times and target dates for examinations.

Every month or thereabouts, you'll be expected to learn a list of techniques (assuming your school follows an established curriculum, which has been explained to you or detailed in a student handbook). In schools that follow the standard ranking system, if you practice consistently, every few months you'll probably test for a new color belt.

Warrior Words

Whether you call it a *routine*, *habit* or *pattern*, cultivating a learning method that is reinforced through positive repetition is one way of improving your chances of achieving your goals.

If you miss a week or two of classes, a staff member of your martial arts school will likely call you and may even schedule a refresher class to ensure you're able to adhere to your goal plan. He or she may also contact you to remind you about upcoming tests, seminars or other extracurricular activities. All this will help you stay motivated.

The staff at your school will track your improvements and carefully monitor your developmental areas, noting them in your file or on your student membership or report card.

And all you have to do is show up, train and practice at home if necessary. Sounds like a good deal, no? If only your entire life were this well planned!

This Could Be the Start of Something Big

From your very first day as a martial arts student, you'll be encouraged to set and achieve a goal, and then to establish new goals.

When you arrive to take your first class, you'll be asked to complete an application form. Generally speaking, this will include questions about your goals, which may include self-defense, weight loss, toning, fun, fitness, discipline, competition...well, you get the idea. Your martial arts teacher or a program director will review this and other information with you.

This document and subsequent assessments will help you plot your martial arts future.

All in Good Time

Now that you and your martial arts teacher have ascertained your primary goals, you're undoubtedly wondering how much time it will take to achieve them.

That depends on a variety of factors. These include how committed you are to attending classes regularly, how often you'll supplement classroom training with practice at home (or in a gym if necessary) and how well you'll take care of your body, mind and spirit.

Therefore, it is difficult to assign precise timelines to your goals. However, here are a few guidelines to follow for specific objectives:

➤ self-defense – As noted in other chapters in this book, depending upon your chosen martial discipline, it could take you anywhere from a few months to a year to learn basic self-defense techniques.

➤ weight loss, toning, fitness – Again, there are many factors, such as genetics, diet and other physical activity you participate in, that will come into play if these are your primary goals. But, generally, you can expect to look and feel better within a matter of a few weeks or months.

➤ discipline, confidence – As noted, you'll be expected to set goals and begin practicing required techniques from your first day as a martial arts student. Making progress in this area can help you become more disciplined and confident in other aspects of your life. The time it takes before you see a marked change depends largely on your work habits and commitment to improving yourself.

➤ competition – Some schools encourage students to begin participating in tournaments at the novice or beginner level (within 3 to 6 months of starting). Some prefer that you wait until you have more experience (one or more years), while others discourage students from engaging in this kind of activity altogether.

➤ fun – You'll learn interesting skills and make new friends from your very first day as a martial arts student. This experience can bring about a sense of achievement and be extremely enjoyable. Additionally, in a good school, the enthusiasm an instructor feels for his or her martial arts training should be infectious. That is, you should sense his or her passion for training and each class should be informative, challenging and fun.

The Importance of Being Regular

Now that you've determined what you want to accomplish and you've assigned general timelines to each goal, it's time to put your plan into action by developing a regular training schedule. This is easier to do if your school offers classes in the morning, at noon, in the evening and on the weekend, seven days a week. Once you've committed to a weekly schedule, view your classes as appointments with yourself or, more precisely, with the person you're striving to become.

Despite the best-laid plans, unexpected meetings or family commitments will sometimes take precedence over your martial arts schedule. When this happens, get back on track as soon as possible by resuming your training schedule quickly and scheduling refresher classes if needed. If you require makeup classes, be advised that most schools offer a reasonable number of these free of charge, while others require a small fee.

Putting Yourself to the Test

You've determined your goals and figured out how long it may take to achieve each one. You've planned your weekly training schedule to ensure you stay focused and accomplish your objectives. So, what's next? Determining your testing schedule.

Some schools conduct monthly "stripe," or interim, examinations. These are an excellent way of gauging your progress in the short term. Generally, you can expect to receive a stripe or equivalent rank advancement every 8 to 12 classes.

Other martial arts institutions use only periodic color belt evaluations, with students participating every 3 to 6 months on average.

Whatever the case, you should be familiar with the requirements for each rank and know how often you can expect to be evaluated.

Martial Smarts

Many are stubborn in pursuit of the path they have chosen, few in the pursuit of the goal.

—*Friedrich Wilhelm Nietzsche*

Charting Your Progress

We've designed a simple chart to assist you in monitoring your progress in the area of martial arts rank.

Rank Advancement

Belt or Rank	Target Date	Date Received
White Belt or Beginner	_____	_____
_____	_____	_____
_____	_____	_____
_____	_____	_____
_____	_____	_____
_____	_____	_____
_____	_____	_____
_____	_____	_____
_____	_____	_____
Black Belt or Equivalent Rank	_____	_____

This is a general list based on a 10-step rank system that is appropriate for most martial arts disciplines. Consult your instructor in preparing your customized rank advancement chart. Later in this chapter, you'll read more about belts and ranking systems and how they vary from style to style and school to school.

A final word about testing. Like any other activity that requires you to demonstrate your best efforts, martial arts examinations can be a source of anxiety, excitement and, yes, even enjoyment. Learning to master these kinds of physical, mental and spiritual challenges can help you better manage other stressful situations that are part of daily life. Expect to be nervous. Expect to sweat. You'll need the adrenaline boost you're feeling to help you get over the "humps" that occur during tests and to give you a winning edge. And remember this: you've trained for this moment, so rely on what you know. Every teacher, fellow student and spectator in the room has one thing in common with you—they all want you to succeed.

Martial Smarts

Sixty years ago I knew everything. Now, I know nothing. Education is the progressive discovery of our own ignorance.

—*Will Durant*

Getting Practical

In addition to charting rank advancement, you should also develop a simple method of assessing your progress in other martial arts and related areas.

Practical Skills Progress

(1 = needs improvement, 2 = satisfactory, 3 = good, 4 = very good, 5 = excellent)

Area		Rating			
Aerobic Fitness	1	2	3	4	5
Strength	1	2	3	4	5
Endurance	1	2	3	4	5
Flexibility	1	2	3	4	5
Striking Skills	1	2	3	4	5
Kicking Skills	1	2	3	4	5
Breakfalls	1	2	3	4	5
Grappling Skills	1	2	3	4	5
Throws and Takedowns	1	2	3	4	5
Weapons Skills	1	2	3	4	5
Forms or Routines	1	2	3	4	5
Sparring	1	2	3	4	5
Self-Defense	1	2	3	4	5
Terminology	1	2	3	4	5
History, Culture and Philosophy	1	2	3	4	5

This progress chart should be periodically reassessed and revised as needed.

This general checklist will be applicable for most, but not all, martial arts. Consult your instructor in preparing a customized practical skills progress chart.

Rainbow of Belts

The ranking system is one tangible way of measuring your martial arts progress.

If you practice an Okinawan, Japanese or Korean system, you will likely wear a white belt as a beginner and progress through a kaleidoscope of color belts until you reach

Risky Moves

Warning: one way to *decrease* your chances of achieving your martial arts goals is to avoid writing them down. Recording your objectives on paper makes them real, and reading them daily makes it more likely that you'll stick to your plan.

Black Belt. Historically speaking, there were no "color" belts. No one wore orange or purple belts. Practitioners were simply given a white belt whose color darkened with years of wear and tear. But when Kano Jigoro, the founder of Judo, developed a multi-tiered rank system, a spectrum of color belts was introduced. This rank system is still used in the majority of martial arts schools around the world.

The following are the colors of belts in the Okinawan and Japanese system.

1. white
2. yellow
3. orange
4. green
5. blue
6. purple
7. brown
8. black

Some schools include half-steps, for example, a brown belt with a black stripe.

Here are the colors in the Korean belt system.

1. white
2. yellow or gold
3. green
4. blue
5. red
6. black

Some schools add striped belts, such as a yellow belt with a green stripe, or a green belt with a blue stripe.

Master Speaks

If you wear a color or Black Belt and you transfer to another school, even one that teaches the style you've been practicing, you may be required to wear a White Belt. Don't fret. Given your previous martial arts experience, you're likely to progress more quickly than the average student.

While the color belts are generally accepted as the classical belt ranking system, the imagination of North American practitioners is boundless. For example, you might also see camouflage-printed belts that would make even Rambo proud.

As tenure and technical requirements vary from institution to institution, you should be aware that your belts might be recognized only in your school. If, for example, you transfer to another institution, some instructors may permit you to retain your rank and belt, while others may require you to start all over again, as a White Belt or beginner.

Time Travel

You probably know the expression "Good things come to those who wait." In martial arts training, this may or may not be true. Perhaps, good things come to those who work hard, hustle (not the disco dance) and are persistent. If you are patient and you work diligently to achieve your goals, what can you expect as a beginner, novice and intermediate student and how long might you stay at these levels? Read on.

Beginner

It's great to be a beginner. No matter what you do, everyone praises you and you have nowhere to go but up. Enjoy this period of your martial arts education. Think of your training as a long leisurely train ride, rather than a high-speed Concorde flight. Relish (not the condiment!) the journey at least as much as the destination. Build a solid foundation for advancement. Practice proper etiquette, such as bowing. Study how to wear your uniform and tie your belt correctly. Determine the appropriate manner of addressing senior students and instructors. And, of course, learn how to perform basic techniques—safely.

Martial Smarts

Do not despise the bottom rungs in the ascent to greatness.

—*Publilius Syrus*

Novice

The novice level is usually regarded as Green Belt or an equivalent rank, which can take you approximately one year to attain. At this stage, you'll probably possess some good fundamental skills. Perhaps, you're becoming more physically fit and can pump out push-ups with the best of them. You can probably perform most basic techniques with proper form, speed and power. Additionally, at this point in your training, you might be developing areas of preference. Some novice students enjoy practicing forms, whereas others prefer sparring. Some focus on practical self-defense and others enjoy training with heavy bags and pads—usually followed by cleaning up their sweat puddles off the classroom floor.

Intermediate

It could take you 2 to 3 years to reach the Brown Belt or equivalent level. As an intermediate level student, you are skilled at most basic techniques and may even be called upon to demonstrate in front of the class. But don't let your elevated status go to your head. You're being groomed for your Black Belt. As such, you're now a role model and will be held to a higher standard than beginner or novice students. As you climb higher, you'll be expected to demonstrate near-perfect form, coupled with an attitude worthy of a Black Belt.

Risky Moves

Don't be in a hurry to reach your Black Belt or equivalent rank. With advancement comes responsibility or, in the words of Friedrich Wilhelm Nietzsche, "Life always gets harder towards the summit."

Black Belt and Beyond

You've sweated and toiled for 3 to 5 years and now your instructor proudly ties a Black Belt around your waist. This is a momentous occasion. Dust off that vintage bottle of champagne and pause to celebrate everything that went into this achievement, just as you would if you'd earned a university degree, received a promotion at work, purchased your first home or said "I do" (for the first, second or even third time!).

What this moment *doesn't* symbolize is the end of your training. Receiving your Black Belt shouldn't cause you to take a leave of absence (or, for that matter, a leave of your senses). It shouldn't prompt you to slow down your martial arts education.

Staying the Course

At this juncture, you should be less preoccupied with the mere aesthetics of what you're performing. You should also begin researching the deeper meaning and what is often referred to as "the hidden techniques" of the discipline you're practicing. This research may require you to spend less time on individual training and rely on practicing with a variety of partners, assessing how each technique must be adjusted if it is to remain effective against different-sized opponents.

As your study takes on new depth and new meaning, you may become more frustrated than you were as a White Belt just getting the hang of performing the simplest

Master Speaks

When you receive a shiny new Black Belt, the first thing you'll probably want to do is wear it out! A threadbare Black Belt is an emblem of a skilled practitioner. As the fabric becomes worn and loses its color, the belt's white inner core is revealed. This process also symbolizes the cycle of martial arts training: the more you learn, the more you realize how little you know.

techniques. An experienced instructor should work with you to anticipate, understand and surmount these plateaus in your martial arts education.

But how will you continue to stay motivated and feel the excitement of your first day in a martial arts class and the joy of receiving your first stripe, belt or certificate of rank advancement? You'll have to establish new goals and renew your commitment to your martial arts study. An experienced instructor will continue to introduce you to fresh, more complex material with a view to ensuring you evade the perilous pitfall of stagnation and avoid getting sidetracked.

Ten Degrees of Separation

Generally speaking, there are 10 degrees, or levels, of Black Belt. Just as color belts serve as benchmarks of progress for novice and intermediate students, so too do these advanced levels aid students in staying focused on polishing techniques and acquiring more highly evolved martial knowledge.

Typically, the time it will take you to move from level to level (or in some systems, *dan* to *dan*) will correspond to the rank in question. For example, if you're a First Degree Black Belt testing for your Second Degree, you might be expected to train for a minimum of 2 years. Or if you're progressing from Second to Third Degree, it might be 3 years. Moving from Third to Fourth Degree could require a minimum training period of 4 years. Pretty simple?

Yes and no. As you progress even higher, tenure is just one criterion for advancement. Up to the rank of Sixth Degree Black Belt, you'll probably be required to participate in a physical exam. How demanding this test is depends on the discipline or style of martial art you're studying, your school's association with an international organization, and, often, your age and fitness level.

If you're a candidate for Seventh Degree Black Belt and above, it would be unusual for you to engage in a physical examination. Other factors, like contributions you've made to the propagation of martial arts, would be considered before you were approved for advancement. At this level, you'd be expected to encourage the spread of martial arts by teaching, writing books, publishing papers or conducting seminars. You'd likely be queried on how many Black Belt students you've produced and which martial arts you've researched and practiced. Additionally, the length of time you've trained and your age are important criteria. For example, if you were a candidate for the rank of *Hanshi,* or Grand Master level, you would have to have trained for 40 or more years and be a minimum of 65 years of age. It's interesting to note that this is the same age at which North Americans generally retire!

Risky Moves

In your search for a martial arts school, be forewarned. You may encounter numerous Black Belts, some of whom are still in their 20s and who claim to hold the rank of Sixth, Seventh, Eighth, Ninth or even Tenth Degree! While these individuals may have been child prodigies and might possess superlative skills, it's unlikely they've trained for a sufficient period of time to meet minimum tenure requirements for these advanced level grades.

The Ultimate Goal of a Martial Artist

We began this chapter by encouraging you to construct a martial arts goal plan. You've achieved your objectives; getting stronger, fitter and more knowledgeable belt by belt. So far, so good.

Martial Smarts

The angry [people] will defeat [themselves] in battle as well as in life.

—*samurai maxim*

What comes next? We assume that at this stage of your study, you understand that martial arts can make you a better person and, in turn, you as a martial artist can make the world a better place. At this advanced level of training, you probably feel more confident, patient and tolerant than ever before. With these powerful skills, you may come to know a state of *wa* (Japanese) or *wu* (Chinese), meaning "harmony" or "peace." Not the 1960s carry-a-placard version, but rather a serenity that quiets your heart and mind and the collective heart and mind of those who share the martial arts approach to personal discovery. This harmonious feeling can be highly infectious and should be shared with the world around you.

So at the most advanced level of training, what should be your ultimate goal? To focus less on your own personal gains and instead make a positive contribution to the lives of others. While you may pick up some self-defense techniques, or become more physically fit in a matter of months and receive your Black Belt in just a few years, this final objective may take decades or even a lifetime of martial arts study.

The Least You Need to Know

➤ A martial arts goal plan begins with a personality inventory and should include your physical, mental and spiritual objectives.

➤ Assigning timelines, adhering to a training schedule, preparing yourself to test regularly and charting your progress will help you get and stay motivated.

➤ Pre–Black Belt training stages can be summarized as beginner, novice and intermediate.

➤ Generally, there are 10 steps from beginner to Black Belt (or equivalent rank), followed by 10 advanced levels, sometimes called *dan* by Japanese, Okinawan and Korean martial artists.

➤ Most practitioners understand that reaching the Black Belt level marks a new beginning in, rather than an end to, their martial arts training.

➤ The ultimate goal of martial arts practitioners should be to progress from enjoying the positive effects their training has on their own lives, to recognizing the positive influence they can have on the lives of others.

Part 3
How You Can Get Started

Did you read Parts 1 and 2? Have you got a handle on the why and the what of martial arts? What's next? We'll tell you what's next: the how—finding a school and enrolling in a program! This is the good stuff, where we actually move beyond theory to practical application.

In this section, you'll receive expert guidance about which questions to ask and what to look for, and avoid, as you hit the pavement (and perhaps a few inanimate targets!) in your search for a prospective school. You'll get important information that will help you construct a realistic training budget. You'll be armed—so to speak—with knowledge that can help you ease into your first day and month of training. You'll learn how to remain focused on the future and motivated by reassessing your goal plans and setting your sights on what you might learn at a more advanced level.

Chapter 9

Choosing the Right Martial Art

In This Chapter

➤ Rating specific techniques taught by popular martial arts

➤ The importance of availability of schools

➤ How much you'll pay for tuition, uniforms and equipment

➤ Why you and your chosen martial art should be custom fitted

We make this point several times throughout this book, but it's so important it bears repeating: there is no single "best" martial art. When you choose a discipline, the only thing that is essential is finding a suitable teacher and an appropriate institution.

We don't mean to imply that you should ignore the fact that every one of us has different personalities, needs, desires and goals and, as a result, some martial disciplines, and even styles, may offer a better fit.

How, then, will you ascertain which martial art will be the best match for you? That's why we wrote this chapter. If you've read Chapter 3 and others in this book, you have a basic understanding of major combative arts. This chapter will expand on the information you've already learned, with a view to helping you better prepare for your martial arts search. You'll also get some interesting information about tuition fees and the cost of uniforms and equipment, and you'll learn how different disciplines appeal to different personalities.

Details, Details, Details

Chapter 3 contains an overview of popular martial arts that summarizes common disciplines and the benefits you can expect to receive as a practitioner of each one. But it doesn't give you the detailed information you'll find below. For example, which martial arts rate more highly in the area of hand techniques? Which offer more kicking drills or will provide you with the opportunity to learn to defend yourself on the ground? Which place greater emphasis on grappling or self-defense? We've created easy-to-follow indexes designed to answer these questions and make choosing the right martial art even easier. Each listing includes a numerical rating as follows:

➤ 0 = No emphasis

➤ 1 = Slight emphasis

➤ 2 = Some emphasis

➤ 3 = Moderate emphasis

➤ 4 = Substantial emphasis

➤ 5 = High emphasis

As you'll discover when you read Chapters 13 to 23, each system listed encompasses several styles. Each style may place less or greater emphasis on the skill noted in the index.

These are general comparisons and the ratings noted can vary from style to style and instructor to instructor. To keep things simple, we've included only some of the more popular martial arts and have listed them in alphabetical order.

The following is a general rating of martial arts based on the emphasis each places on hand techniques (0 = no emphasis and 5 = high emphasis).

Master Speaks

Avoid having fixed ideas, preconceptions and misconceptions about martial arts. While generally speaking a particular system may be classified as a kicking and striking, or a throwing and grappling discipline, it's becoming increasingly difficult to make these labels stick. Although the lines of combative strategies were clearly drawn at their inception, through cross-pollination that has resulted in blurred boundaries, most of the styles now share common techniques.

The Pull-No-Punches Martial Index

Martial Art	Rating
Aikido	1
Arnis/Escrima	3
Jiu-jitsu	2
Judo	1
Karate	4
Kendo	0
Kobudo	0
Kung-Fu	3
Kyudo	0
Muay Thai/Kickboxing	5
Silat	3
Tae Kwon Do	3
Tai Chi Chuan	2

The following is a general rating of martial arts based on the emphasis each places on kicking techniques (0 = no emphasis and 5 = high emphasis).

The Kick-Start Martial Index

Martial Art	Rating
Aikido	0
Arnis/Escrima	2
Jiu-jitsu	1
Judo	0
Karate	4
Kendo	0
Kobudo	0
Kung-Fu	4
Kyudo	0
Muay Thai/Kickboxing	5
Silat	3
Tae Kwon Do	5
Tai Chi Chuan	2

Master Speaks

Kicking is an excellent mid-range or long–distance defensive tactic. Your legs have greater reach and power than your arms. If your opponent attempts to stifle or "jam" your kicks by crowding you, keep your guard up, move back to regain your distance and then execute your kick.

The following is a general rating of martial arts based on the emphasis each places on techniques that revolve around grappling from a standing position (0 = no emphasis and 5 = high emphasis).

The Root-of-All-"Upheaval" Grappling Martial Index

Martial Art	Rating
Aikido	5
Arnis/Escrima	2
Jiu-jitsu	5
Judo	5
Karate	2
Kendo	0
Kobudo	0
Kung-Fu	3
Kyudo	0
Muay Thai/Kickboxing	2
Silat	4
Tae Kwon Do	1
Tai Chi Chuan	1

The following is a general rating of martial arts based on the emphasis each places on ground-fighting techniques (0 = no emphasis and 5 = high emphasis).

The From-the-Ground-Up Martial Index

Martial Art	Rating
Aikido	2
Arnis/Escrima	1
Jiu-jitsu	5
Judo	5
Karate	2
Kendo	0
Kobudo	0
Kung-Fu	3
Kyudo	0
Muay Thai/Kickboxing	1
Silat	4
Tae Kwon Do	1
Tai Chi Chuan	1

Risky Moves

Many street fights end up on the ground. This is a frightening thought. But more terrifying is the idea that if you fail to construct a personal defensive system that incorporates striking, kicking, throwing and grappling, as well as ground-fighting techniques, you may be "floored."

The following is a general rating of martial arts based on the amount of self-defense skills you may possess after 6 months of study (0 = no emphasis and 5 = high emphasis).

The Personal Protection Martial Index

Martial Art	Rating
Aikido	2
Arnis/Escrima	3
Jiu-jitsu	4
Judo	2
Karate	4
Kendo	0
Kobudo	0
Kung-Fu	3
Kyudo	0
Muay Thai/Kickboxing	2
Silat	3
Tae Kwon Do	3
Tai Chi Chuan	1

As we've already mentioned, it's difficult, and sometimes impossible, to classify every martial art, as you run the risk of pigeonholing each one. In developing a myopic view of each discipline, you may lose sight of the fact that inclusion of other elements can provide each with added dimension. The bottom line is that all martial arts offer

Master Speaks

When it comes to self-defense, all schools, even those that teach the same discipline, take different instructional approaches. For example, generally speaking, as an Aikido practitioner with 6 months experience, your training might have a rating of only "2" ("Some Emphasis") in this category. However, this aspect of martial education carries greater weight among *Yoshinkan* Aikido than among other styles within this discipline.

countless benefits. Some do, as a general rule, place greater focus on different aspects of training and you should seriously consider this factor when assessing their suitability—physically, mentally and spiritually—before deciding if they're right for you.

For example, let's say you're interested in improving your flexibility. Then give Karate, Kung Fu or Tae Kwon Do a try. Want to awaken the warrior within? Then Aikido, Kendo or *Kyudo* may be just the right thing. Interested in testing your strength, endurance and power? Judo, *Muay Thai* or Brazilian Jiu-jitsu might be your answer. Need to work on your balance, posture and breath control? Then give Tai Chi or its sister internal martial arts, Hsing-I and Ba Gua, a spin.

Now that you've got the lowdown on the techniques emphasized by some of the most popular martial arts, let's go shopping.

A Martial Arts Shopping Spree

As you likely noticed in reviewing the overview of popular martial arts in Chapter 3, some disciplines are classified as more "available" than others. This means that as a general rule, if you live in North America, you'll probably find more commercial schools teaching this particular martial art in your hometown. Obviously, if you lived in Manila, the Philippines, the same rating might not hold true.

Martial Smarts

Give me the luxuries of life and I will willingly do without the necessities.

—*Frank Lloyd Wright*

While this overview serves as an ideal jumping-off point (we trust you didn't get hurt when you landed), the following sections expand on the categories noted and provide additional essential details to aid in your martial arts search.

Before we proceed, this is a good time to remind you that your needs and desires—martial and otherwise—will change over time. As a child, you may have relished burgers and milkshakes, but now your preferences veer more toward filet mignon and fine Bordeaux. You've grown up and so have your tastes. In all likelihood, you'll experience this same maturation process in your study of the martial arts. So it's essential, when comparison shopping, that you choose an instructor and school that will grow with you.

How can you be reasonably certain you've found the right place? Begin by looking for a school that teaches one particular martial art. Finding such a school will ensure the instructors have specialized expertise rather than attempting to be Jacks and Jills of all trades. Also inquire about the school's policy with respect to seminars and ancillary activities. Does the institution provide students with an opportunity to expand their martial arts repertoire by attending seminars featuring experts in other disciplines or

Martial Smarts

Start by doing what's necessary, then what's possible and suddenly, you are doing the impossible.

—*St. Francis of Assisi*

styles? In addition to watching a beginner class or two before you enroll in a program, you might consider observing intermediate and advanced classes. Not only will this preview help you better understand the type of training that lies ahead, but you'll also have the opportunity to see whether the enthusiasm present in a beginner class is carried through to other levels.

In this way, you'll ensure there's room to grow—and you'll need it. Although improving your level of physical fitness or acquiring self-defense skills was at the top of your wish list as a beginner, as you evolve as a practitioner, you'll want to gain other benefits from your martial arts study.

We've examined general ratings indicating the types of techniques emphasized by some popular combative systems. As we continue our martial arts shopping spree, the next items on our list are availability of schools, cost of tuition, and equipment requirements and prices.

Coming Soon to a Mini-Mall Near You

In most major markets, there are more listings in the telephone book for martial arts schools than for dry cleaners. It's true! If you don't believe us, take a peek in your directory. It's okay, we'll wait...we're still waiting. *We told you so!*

The information highway is peppered with Web sites for martial arts institutions. In all probability, your local health food store or bookstore has brochures galore for these types of schools. It seems that martial arts schools are sprouting up every day on every corner in every neighborhood in the United States and in Canada.

So what does this mean? Well, it's an indication that you should, as they say in breeding circles, be certain you have the pick of the litter because not all martial arts programs and teachers are created equal. Chapter 10 will help you brush up on your good-consumer skills and aid you in becoming a samurai shopper. The following section will assist you in figuring out how easy it will be to find a school because, while it's clear that there is a dizzying number of training halls, all martial arts are not equally represented. Some disciplines are more difficult to find than others.

Karate and Tae Kwon Do schools are among the most popular. These institutions can be classified under the following general headings:

➤ traditional – The philosophy and history of the martial art are integrated with physical training.

➤ sport – Training is geared to producing future champions.

➤ children's centers – Youngsters are encouraged to learn both martial arts and life skills.

➤ self-defense – The bulk of training is devoted to learning how to prevent or manage physical confrontations.

➤ fitness-based – These schools focus almost exclusively on the physical aspect of training.

Ideally, you'll locate an established school, one with a track record of success, whose curriculum marries these five categories.

Aikido, Judo, Jiu-jitsu, Kickboxing and Kung Fu schools may be plentiful in large urban centers but difficult to track down in smaller communities. Most of these schools are also classified under the headings listed above for Karate and Tae Kwon Do.

Tai Chi Chuan classes, a low-impact martial option that is gaining popularity among the 50-plus set, are widely available through martial arts institutions and continuing education programs taught in high schools, as well as through community centers and fitness clubs.

Silat, Muay Thai and Escrima institutions may be found only in cities where there are Indonesian, Thai and Filipino communities.

Will That Be Cash, Check or Credit Card?

In addition to the basic information provided in Chapter 10 under the heading "The Real Cost of Training," the following sections provide detailed information about the type of investment you should expect to make for your martial arts education.

➤ introductory programs – Trial classes, which generally span a week or month and might include a uniform or school T-shirt, could run anywhere from $20 to $100.

➤ group classes – Most schools are competitively priced. Typically, tuition fees are commensurate with extracurricular educational, fitness and sport activities. Like everything else, you should expect to pay more for classes in New York City, Los Angeles, Toronto, Montreal and other megalopolises than you would in smaller towns. School operators in large urban centers face higher rent, insurance and marketing costs than those in suburban or rural communities. At the beginner level, a year of classes could cost between $400 and $1200.

➤ long-term programs – The increasingly common phrase *Black Belt Club* is not used

Master Speaks

When calculating martial arts tuition fees, the more frequently you attend class, the less your training actually costs you. Why? Because if you're paying between $400 and $1200 per year, your cost per weekly session is $8 to $23. At three times per week, your per-class cost is reduced to $2.60 to $7.60. Training regularly ensures you're getting your money's worth.

107

to suggest that you're guaranteed a Black Belt if you enroll in a long-term program that bears this name. No reputable instructor would make that promise. Rather, this label simply indicates that, at the intermediate level, you're making a commitment to continue your martial arts study with the goal of achieving your Black Belt. Generally, these are 3- to 4-year courses that usually provide more benefits than would a beginner program. A Black Belt Club membership may include a special uniform and crest, access to more advanced classes and invitations to ancillary events, such as workshops and seminars. These long-term programs also afford students and parents the opportunity to tap into substantial savings on tuition fees. For example, although you might pay $1000 for a 1-year beginner program, a 4-year Black Belt Club membership might set you back only $2000 to $3000. Most schools want to reward students for renewing their commitment to their martial arts education and encourage them to continue to achieve their goals.

➤ private classes – If you have special interests or needs, you might opt for one-to-one classes. However, personal training or private tutoring—whether we're talking about martial arts or other activities—does not come cheap. These customized classes could cost you between $40 and $150 per hour.

The above-noted fees are simply guidelines and you'll have to conduct your own school survey in order to formulate a price list that is specific to your neighborhood. Remember, you usually get what you pay for, so don't let tuition be your only, or most important, selection criterion when searching for a martial arts school.

Risky Moves

Initially, some martial arts practitioners may learn more quickly in private classes. This format, however, does not afford interaction with other students and, in the long run, one-to-one training may actually impede your progress. As you graduate through the ranking system, it's essential to test the effectiveness of your skills against partners of varying heights, weights and levels of ability.

Dressing for Success

What you wear can affect the way you feel. Whether it's a business suit, a school uniform or your favorite pair of flannel jammies, you know what we mean.

The same holds true for martial arts uniforms. The very act of stripping off your civvies and putting on your uniform enables you to divorce yourself from the demands of the outside world and puts you in the right frame of mind for training. It can make you feel more confident and more like part of a group working toward the common goal of becoming better human beings.

When you arrive to take your first class, depending on the style taught, you will be outfitted in your school's T-shirt and a comfortable pair of trousers or shorts. Alternatively, you might be given a pajamalike suit called a *gi*, *dogi* or *dobok*. This uniform, which is generally a bit oversized to facilitate ease of movement, can be so roomy that you'll feel like flapping your sleeves in Casper-the-ghost fashion.

The following chart lists what the well-dressed practitioner in each martial art can expect to wear, as well as a price range for these garments.

Uniforms for Martial Artists

Martial Art	Uniform
Aikido	Heavy white uniform ($80–$200). Female students and Black Belts may also be required to wear black *hakama,* or wide trousers ($40–$100).
Arnis/Escrima	Light shoes, loose trousers, T-shirt or vest ($80–$200).
Jiu-jitsu	Heavy canvas white uniform ($50–$150).
Judo	Heavy canvas white uniform ($50–$150).
Karate	Light to heavy white uniform ($40–$200).
Kendo	Heavy blue or white top, and white, black or blue *hakama* ($100–$250).
Kobudo	Light to heavy white uniform ($40–$200). Some schools also require students to wear *hakama* ($40–$100).
Kung Fu	Cotton or satin black or colored uniform ($40–$300).
Kyudo	Black or white top with pinstriped or solid-colored *hakama* ($100–$400).
Muay Thai	Satin shorts and T-shirt ($40–$100).
Silat	Light white or black cotton uniform and colored sarong, or skirt ($40–$100).
Tae Kwon Do	Light white cotton uniform ($40–$100). (International Tae Kwon Do Federation = kimono top; World Tae Kwon Do Federation = V-neck-style top)

Dressed in your fighting finery, you're ready to move on to buying the equipment you'll need to practice your chosen discipline.

Shifting into Gear

Some martial arts require no special equipment, so we've simply provided information about the most commonly used gear and a price range for these items.

Master Speaks

Most martial artists wear a school and organization crest. While this is a good way to express the pride you feel as a result of this affiliation, try to avoid becoming a walking billboard. Consult your instructor about which crests are appropriate and which might be considered garish.

If you're a student of kicking and striking systems, you should, at the very least, splurge for a mouthpiece ($5 to $10) and groin cup ($10 to $30). Some styles of Karate require no safety gear but most use cloth, leather or foam-dipped equipment to protect your hands and feet ($40 to $120) and your head ($30 to $60). Some even go so far as to require students to wear face protectors ($20 to $60). As a Kendo student, you might spend $200 to $400 to purchase armor called *bogu*. If you're a Tae Kwon Do practitioner, you'll typically wear a chest protector ($40 to $100) and headgear ($30 to $60). As a Judo or Jiu-jitsu student, you'll probably purchase kneepads ($10 to $30) and may even don wrestling headgear ($20 to $50) to avoid developing "cauliflower" (of the nonveggie variety) ears. As a practitioner of Muay Thai and Western Kickboxing styles, you'd generally wear ankle supports ($5 to $15), hand wraps ($5 to $10), boxing gloves ($50 to $200) and heavily padded headgear ($50 to $200).

In order to prepare your personal equipment purchase order, one that meets your school's requirements, consult your instructor.

Tools of the Trade

Most schools provide other necessary equipment, so purchasing your own is often a question of preference and finances. Additionally, some training items required for particular martial arts can carry a heftier price tag than others, so your choice of discipline can have an effect on the number of times you'll have to crack open your piggy bank.

For example, if you're a student of Kyudo (Japanese archery), your *yumi* and *ya* (bow and arrows) can cost you close to $1000. If you're studying Kendo, at the novice level you could spend $20 to $40 for a *shinai* (bamboo sword) and, at a more advanced stage in your training, if you're interested in purchasing a "live blade," you might pay $300 to $600 for a modern *katana* (metal-edged sword) or several thousand dollars for an antique version.

As a Kobudo student, you might expect to pay $20 to $60 for a *bo* (wooden staff), $40 to $100 for a pair of *sai* (three-pronged metal truncheons), $30 to $80 for *tonfa* (wood handled baton), $20 to $30 for *nunchaku* (wooden flail), $30 to $80 for *kama* (long-handled sickles) and $60 to $150 for an *eku* (oar).

If you're practicing Arnis/Escrima, you should budget $20 to $100 for ornamental blades and $15 to $50 for a *baston* (rattan or hardwood stick). As an Aikido-*ka* (Aikido student) you may spend $20 to $60 for a *jo* (short wood stick), $20 to $60 to purchase a *bokken* (wood practice sword) and $10 to $30 for *tanto* (wood knives). Kung Fu students may require an arsenal of weapons that can cost from $200 to $300. As a Silat student, you might purchase a *tjabang* (three-pronged metal truncheon) for $40 to $100, *kris* (long knife) for $20 to $100, *toya* (wood staff) for somewhere between $20 and $60 and a *pedang* (machete) for $50 to $150.

Before you whip out your credit or debit card, discuss your school's equipment requirement list with your instructor.

Risky Moves

Purchasing inexpensive safety gear and equipment may prove costly in the long run. Not only will you probably have to replace these items more frequently, but they may not offer the same protection or performance quality as those that are higher priced.

You learned in the preceding sections of this chapter how most popular martial arts stack up when it comes to different techniques. You also know how much it costs for various programs and what you'll have to spend to purchase a uniform and equipment.

What's left? You've still got to select an appropriate martial art.

Custom Fit

Once you've read *The Complete Idiot's Guide to Martial Arts* cover to cover, you should have all the information you need to select an appropriate martial art. If you want to do a little additional research, then pick up a martial arts magazine at your local newsstand or book shop. Rent a few tapes from the video or martial arts supply store located in your neighborhood. Surf the Net or head down to your library. But don't forget, there's no substitute for visiting schools and taking a few trial classes.

An important aspect of your search is to examine each martial art's suitability when it comes to your personality and desires. While we cannot sum up this process in a few paragraphs, what we can provide in this section are a few general thoughts that may help make this match a little easier.

For example, if you're looking for a combative system that is energizing and invigorating, then head down to your Jiu-jitsu, Judo, Karate, Kickboxing or Tae Kwon Do school. If, on the other hand, your aim is to wind down and soothe your jangled nerves, then you might be better off in an Aikido, Kung Fu or Tai Chi class. Is exploring exotic worlds more appealing? Then enroll in an Arnis/Escrima, Kendo, Kobudo, Kyudo or Silat course.

Whatever discipline you choose, with the broad range of systems and styles available and with courses, uniforms and equipment priced to suit everyone's budget, you'll certainly find something that fits the bill.

The Least You Need to Know

➤ Choosing the right martial art will depend on a variety of factors, including which techniques you want to learn, the availability of schools, how much you're looking to spend and your personality, desires and needs.

➤ Most martial arts place greater weight on developing certain skills, but many share common techniques.

➤ Although there appears to be an impressive number of martial arts schools in every community in North America, finding one that teaches the style you're interested in may be difficult and can affect your choice of discipline.

➤ Martial arts tuition fees vary from market to market. You can expect to pay more in large urban centers than you would in suburban or rural communities, but within a given city these prices are generally competitive.

➤ The martial art you choose will have specific uniform and equipment requirements. Be certain you understand what these are and how much you'll have to budget to purchase what you need.

➤ Your personality and needs will influence your search for a martial art that represents a suitable match.

Chapter 10

Finding the School That's Right for You

In This Chapter

➤ What you'll need to know to find the right school

➤ How to decode ads for martial arts schools

➤ What to look for on your first visit

➤ How much will training really cost?

➤ Getting what you want from the program

Now that you've got a basic understanding of the major martial arts, the physical, mental and spiritual benefits of training and some basic do's and don'ts, it's time to search for an appropriate school.

Facts Attack

You probably have a friend who has a friend who's an Eighth Degree Black Belt in martial arts. Or maybe you heard that the new guy in accounting is the current Ultimate Fighting Champion of the world. And you never could get over the fact that your very own seventh-grade teacher was the Olympic gold medalist in Judo in 1960 (even though Judo wasn't introduced to the Olympics until, uh, 1964). While martial arts are more mainstream than ever, getting reliable information on good, well-established schools is about as elusive as finding the Holy Grail. Figuring out what's real and what's not, like finding a good friend, is often difficult—and sometimes impossible. Fear not one whit—that's what this chapter's for.

Martial Smarts

Foolish friends are worse than wise enemies.

—*Dhammadada, Indian philosopher*

First off, take what your colleagues and friends say with a boulder of salt. Folks with perhaps only a few weeks or months of training under their white or yellow belts are generally eager to dispense a flood of advice. Well-intentioned though they might be, some of their counsel may steer you in the wrong direction. For example, their reasons for pursuing a martial arts education might be different from yours. Or maybe they took only a dozen sessions of training before quitting to take up snorkeling.

So how do you know what to look for? You might be considering the classes at your local gym or health club, or at the YMCA (hey, it worked for the Village People). But these classes are usually offered on a limited schedule, are geared primarily to beginners, and their instructors are often novice Black Belts looking to acquire some teaching experience. Similarly, courses offered through community centers, at night school or in adult education programs are generally short term and focus on only one aspect of training, usually self-defense.

In short, what you really want is a school that's devoted to martial arts.

Everything You Wanted to Know but Were Afraid to Ask

Here are the more salient questions you'll want to be asking once you start to scout about for schools. This isn't a comprehensive list, but it'll help you develop your own checklist.

➤ **How Long Has the School Been in Business?**   Look for a martial arts institution that has a history of success going back several years or even decades. Has it received numerous *consumer* awards for providing good service over the years? (Look for these amid all the trophies, medals and plaques.) Are the teachers experienced men and women who will offer competent instruction?

➤ **Is It Safe and Well Equipped?**   Martial arts that emphasize kicking, punching and lots of high-impact activities are probably best performed on a sprung wood floor. Combative systems that focus on grappling and throwing require a well-padded surface. Does the school ensure that students train for a reasonable length of time (on average, 3 months) before engaging in drills with partners like those involving sparring? At more advanced levels, are students required to wear adequate protective equipment? Does the school offer targets and heavy bags or other appropriate equipment that will enhance your training experience? And finally, are dressing rooms, lockers and showers provided?

➤ **Does the School's Schedule Jibe with Your Own?**   Seek out schools that offer daily beginner classes and that have early morning, lunchtime, evening and weekend classes to accommodate even the most harried schedule. Does the school offer separate classes for children and adults?

➤ **Can You Get There Easily?** Is the school's location convenient? Is there ample free parking? Alternatively, if you rely on public transportation, make sure the school is located near bus or train stops. If it takes you hours to get there, you're unlikely to attend classes two or three times per week.

➤ **Can You Try It Out Before You Buy?** Test-driving a program and observing one or several classes is essential before committing to a long-term course. Most reputable schools offer some type of low-cost introductory program. The issue of whether you enroll in a longer program after completing this course is best discussed with the school's program director.

➤ **What's the Instructor-Student Ratio?** A ratio of one instructor or assistant to about eight students will ensure that you'll receive adequate attention. (Senior instructors should be aided by one or more assistants.) Talk to your martial arts teachers to make sure that you've got a clear understanding of the average time required to progress from belt to belt or to acquire specific skills.

Now that you know what to look for, where should you turn? The same place you'd go to find a good plumber or dentist—the Yellow Pages.

Risky Moves

This ain't no spa...Don't expect to find valet parking, organic grooming products or thick terrycloth robes and fluffy towels at your local martial arts school. You're unlikely to enjoy the same type of amenities there as you would at upscale fitness clubs, but that's not why you're enrolling— is it?

Warrior Words

The acronym "TEST IT" might be a good way for you to remember this basic checklist.

T = time in business and reputation

E = equipped and safe

S = schedule that offers a variety of class levels and times

T = transportation and convenient location

I = introductory programs that are affordable

T = teacher–student ratios that will ensure you receive adequate attention

Let Your Fingers Do the Walking

We're focusing on the Yellow Pages because nearly every commercial martial arts school uses them. (If you surf the Net for information, you'll probably find that most local schools don't have a Web site. You might be able to access information about martial arts institutions in New Zealand, but can you imagine the commute?) Some schools also use print and broadcast advertising, direct mail and event marketing to deliver their message, and of course the same guidelines apply.

The phrase "size doesn't matter" is well applied to ads for martial arts schools. Bigger ads aren't necessarily directing you to better schools. Read the copy carefully. Are the instructors more interested in talking about themselves than in addressing the needs and questions of prospective students? Examine the images used in the ad: Do they feature violent scenes that are out of keeping with your goals? Or do they include men, women and children demonstrating the kinds of skills you want to learn?

Here are some ways you can decode the information generally included in Yellow Pages ads.

➤ **Rank and Title** Too many instructors are called "Masters," and even more boast "advanced" Black Belt degrees. But since there's no central governing body for all martial arts styles and systems, these designations don't amount to much. Someone who's trained diligently for 20 or more years and is an excellent martial arts teacher might be only a Second Degree Black Belt, while instructors who have been training for fewer than 10 years and have only 1 to 2 years' teaching experience may be classified as a Third or Fourth Degree Black Belt. Just as there are different martial arts styles and systems, so too are there different requirements for advancement. And keep in mind that there are a variety of school directors who are simply listed in ads for their "marquee value." In short, consider rank and title as only one element in your search for a high-quality instructor.

➤ **International Champions** Unlike other sports, there are almost as many "world champion" titles among martial artists as there are schools and styles. It's important to ask yourself if the world champion in question is qualified to teach you. For example, the 1995 World Brick-Breaking Champion isn't necessarily the one who can best help you become more physically, mentally and spiritually fit—and capable of defending yourself.

Martial Smarts

To treat your facts with imagination is one thing, but to imagine your facts is another!

—*John Burroughs*

➤ **Affiliations with Martial Arts Organizations** Since there are countless associations, the issue of affiliation or whether the school is a "national" headquarters or is "internationally recognized" isn't as important as the quality of instruction you'll receive.

➤ **Hollywood Masters** If the resident

master played Donatello (of *Teenage Mutant Ninja Turtles* fame) or starred in a series of less than memorable films—well, so what? He or she may possess terrific technical ability, but cinematic experience doesn't necessarily translate into good teaching and coaching skills.

➤ **Hall of Fame Members**   In *Black Belt Magazine,* one of the premier martial arts publications of its kind, previous Hall of Fame inductees read like a Who's Who of martial arts: Chuck Norris, Bruce Lee, Olympic gold medalists and so on. But over time we've seen the spawning of numerous other "halls of fame." So just because you see a fancy plaque celebrating the induction of an instructor into one or several halls of fame doesn't necessarily mean he or she will be a good teacher.

➤ **Multidiscipline Schools**   Most business experts agree that you can't be all things to all people. This is especially true when it comes to martial arts schools. While many reputable modern institutions *do* offer a core curriculum that includes elements of other styles and systems, they usually don't take the all-of-the-above approach and advertise themselves as experts in "Tai Chi Chuan, Kickboxing, Karate, Judo, Tae Kwon Do, Kung Fu…" Look for schools that offer a particular expertise, and allow for the fact that more progressive ones will incorporate cross-style, cross-system training where appropriate.

Before you make the final decision to enroll in a martial arts program, nothing will take the place of an on-site visit to one or more schools.

First Impressions Matter

When you arrive at a prospective school for the first time, ask yourself if the commute was convenient and if you'd be able to do it two or three times a week.

What's the physical appearance of the school? Street-level locations with large, clean windows will allow you to assess what's going on inside even before you enter the front door. Peruse the waiting or reception area. Is it clean and comfortable? You're not looking for the Taj Mahal, but there should at least be chairs and a place for your shoes (if you're required to enter the training area barefoot). Are you greeted promptly by courteous staff who look fit and sound professional? Check out the photographs or awards that are displayed. Is the school a shrine to the achievements of the instructor, or a professional educational institution? Do the photographs feature happy faces of students or blood-and-guts scenes for those with cast-iron stomachs? As you're led to an office or training area to fill out the application forms, are you made to feel

Martial Smarts

Of what you see, believe only a little; of what you are told, nothing.

—Spanish proverb

Risky Moves

If you're a woman, an all-female class may appear to be a more comfortable setting in which to learn martial arts, but limiting your practice sessions to working exclusively with other women may not provide you with the opportunity to develop effective self-defense skills. Co-ed classes, on the other hand, can offer more realistic training in the form of male partners.

Warrior Words

Teachers of Kung Fu or other Chinese martial arts are usually called *sifu*. Those who instruct Japanese and Korean combative systems are referred to as *sensei* and *sabom*, respectively—and respectfully! The written characters for these names can be interpreted as "one who has experienced."

comfortable? Does the staff take the time to show you the facility and answer your questions?

If there's a class in progress and your schedule permits, ask to watch for a few minutes. If this simple request is refused because "it's a secret training session" or for some other apparently hollow reason, *leave immediately.* You want a school where you're welcome to watch and ask questions.

Does the class appear to match your needs (that is, is it fitness oriented, skill oriented, safe, properly paced, fun or well taught)? Is there an adequate number of teachers and assistants, and is there sufficient instructor-student interaction? Are techniques clearly explained both physically and verbally? What's the tone of the class? Is it militaristic or unstructured? Does it balance discipline, constructive criticism and fun? Do the relationships between students and teachers appear to be based on mutual respect and camaraderie? Is the general atmosphere one of learning and support?

Look at the students: Is there a wide range of ages and a balance between males and females? (Rarely, if ever, will you find a 50-50 split.) Do participants appear to be energized, challenged physically and mentally, and excited to be in the class?

Most importantly, watch the instructors: Are they proficient at their respective martial art? Can they motivate, inspire and educate you? The role these individuals may play in your martial arts future is extremely important.

Special Notes for Parents

When inquiring about a school for your child, here are a few things to keep in mind.

➤ Although competition can be wonderful for some children, others may find it stressful. Is this aspect of training an option if your child wants to participate in tournaments? Is it a requirement for advancement and, if so, might such training be detrimental to your son's or daughter's attitude about studying martial arts?

➤ Does the schedule offer a broad range of classes divided by age and level of experience? Are they structured to ensure the children are kept moving and motivated for an appropriate period of time (training sessions for preschoolers may run 30 minutes, while older, more experienced children may participate in 45-minute or 1-hour classes).

➤ Do your children share your commitment to their training? Do they have a clear understanding of the school's curriculum and rules? Do instructors encourage them to enjoy the *process* of learning—celebrating even the smallest achievements with some simple form of recognition—while keeping them focused on their goals? Are students evaluated regularly and is their progress carefully monitored and reviewed with them and you? Most progressive schools offer monthly "mini-tests" designed to chart every student's advancement, coupled with regular belt examinations. Furthermore, a reasonable number of one-to-one "refresher" classes should be provided at no charge to ensure students remain on track.

Master Speaks

Does the school give your child a positive message? The better schools encourage students to memorize a student creed or a set of rules designed to improve their behavior, both inside and outside the martial arts classroom.

Sound promising so far? Then let's look at the cost of training.

The Real Cost of Training

Even though a martial arts education can deliver numerous benefits, you'll have to carefully weigh the advantages of training against the tuition. Still, the old saying "If you think education is expensive, remember that ignorance is free" definitely applies.

Here are average rates for the main components of your martial arts education.

➤ **Introductory Programs**   These run from $20 to $100. Look for "test-drive" programs that include a uniform, otherwise you might have to spend another $40 to $100 for one.

➤ **Tuition**   This averages between $40 and $100 per month, and $400 and $1200 per year. Many larger schools offer discounts to the relatives and friends of current students.

➤ **Exam or Testing Fees**   In the larger, more established martial arts institutions, tuition prices include all testing fees. Other schools charge $20 to $40 per belt test and most students can expect to participate in about three exams each year. Black Belt exam fees can run from $75 to $200.

➤ **Equipment**   Requirements vary from school to school and system to system. A Tai Chi Chuan student, for example, might have to buy only a $25 T-shirt. Most reputable martial arts schools require some form of safety gear at the intermediate level, at an average cost of $100 for both hand and foot pads. If you enroll in a Kendo program, you might expect to pay $400 for *bogu* gear. So make sure to ask

119

about any special equipment requirements before enrolling in a school. (See Chapter 9 for more details about equipment costs.)

➤ **Association Dues** Many schools that maintain international links may require students to pay an additional membership fee, which could run from $10 to $30 per year.

➤ **Tournament Fees** Some martial arts facilities conduct tournaments and special events throughout the year. Some of these activities are optional, while others may be a requirement for rank advancement—and could command an additional fee upwards of $20.

Now that you know how to shop around for an appropriate school and you have a fairly good idea of what your training will cost, here are some last words on what you should expect from your classes.

Master Speaks

If you're eager to progress and you enjoy supplementing in-class training with at-home study, you can purchase videotapes, books and CD–ROMs through your school. Prices will vary greatly.

Martial Smarts

To rise in the world, one should veil ambition with humility.

—Chinese proverb

Friends, Comrades and Assorted Others You Never Knew Existed

People from all walks of life enjoy martial arts study. As you begin your training, you'll undoubtedly encounter some very interesting fellow classmates: lawyers and entertainers, doctors and construction workers, university professors and models, students and full-time parents. While the material you're practicing should be challenging, getting to know your fellow students shouldn't be! Instead, the atmosphere of your chosen school should exude teamwork and cooperation. You should feel comfortable and look forward to returning regularly to train.

The teacher-student relationship should blend professionalism and friendship. Martial arts teachers are often called upon to wear many hats: instructor, parent, coach and comrade. So it's essential that your *sensei, sifu* or *sabom* put his or her ego on the back burner, and work tirelessly to ensure that you get all you can from your martial arts education.

The relationship between a martial arts student and teacher is a unique one. On the surface, it appears as though it's the student who works hard to nurture this exchange. But in reality, it's the teacher who serves the student.

The Least You Need to Know

➤ Ask around for advice in locating a good martial arts school, but keep in mind that others' interests, goals and experiences might be drastically different from your own.

➤ Compile a checklist to help you screen prospective schools. Consider how long the school has been operating, the qualifications of its instructors, its class schedules, its approach to safety and whether it offers an introductory program.

➤ Understand martial marketing lingo before you tour the Yellow Pages. Fancy titles don't necessarily mean competent instruction.

➤ Inspect the facility before you enroll. Watch a class or two and observe the behavior of staff, students and instructors.

➤ Program length and tuition options vary from school to school. Ask about any additional expenses like exam fees, association membership dues or equipment costs.

Chapter 11

What to Expect in the First Month and Beyond

In This Chapter

➤ Anticipating and conquering fears about your first day

➤ Learning to bond with your instructors

➤ Cultivating relationships with fellow students

➤ Overcoming first-test stress

➤ Establishing new goals

Did you know that one-third of all martial arts students, even those with the highest of hopes, quit training after just a few months? Why? Probably because these individuals failed to do their homework before deciding which martial art to study and where to enroll.

If you read *The Complete Idiot's Guide to Martial Arts* from cover to cover, you'll be armed with knowledge these students probably didn't possess. You'll know how martial arts came about and have a general familiarity with the major types. You'll have a rudimentary understanding of their physical, mental and spiritual benefits, and their rank or advancement systems. You'll also know what to look for, and avoid, as you search for a teacher and school.

Once you've done your research and you're heading off to your first martial arts class, you'll likely be excited and, to tell the truth, at least a little nervous. Will it be all you've expected? Will the transition from newest kid on the block to a member of a team be smooth as "butta" or an experience you'd wish on only your worst enemies?

123

Only time and determination will tell, but this chapter may help you make the journey a little more smoothly.

The Learning Curve

As discussed in Chapter 10, one of the best ways to get acquainted with a martial arts program is to enroll in a low-cost introductory or orientation course.

The purpose of this type of program is twofold. First, it will help you and the instructor establish your martial arts goals from day one. Having made and confirmed your first introductory class appointment, you should be greeted at the door or in the office when you arrive. You'll probably be asked to complete a simple questionnaire that will include a few questions about why you want to study martial arts. This form will assist you and your instructor in assessing where you are and where you want to go as you begin to construct your martial arts goal plan.

Second, this kind of program will give you a more realistic feel for the type of training you'll receive at a particular school. Some students arrive at a martial arts institution with visions of Power Rangers or Chuck Norris dancing in their heads. Others imagine themselves as a future WWF world champion or the next Jean-Claude Van Damme. An introductory program can put a more realistic spin on what you can actually hope to gain from martial arts practice.

You won't have to hock the family silver or cash in your mutual funds to pay for these mini-courses. Generally, these introductory programs will cost anywhere from $20 to $100. They will include a few private classes, where you'll learn some basic martial arts techniques and even a few self-defense drills. Many packages include a martial arts T-shirt or complete uniform. The instructor or program director will also give you information about the martial arts school (such as class schedules, tuition fees, regulations and curriculum details). These types of preparatory classes give you a chance to test-drive a program before committing to a long-term course.

More importantly, introductory programs will provide you with the opportunity to

Master Speaks

If you've read Chapter 10, you know which questions you should ask, and which will be asked of you, during your first visit to a martial arts school. Don't forget to observe a few group classes and inspect the facility. Is it clean and professionally run? Do students appear to be stimulated, motivated and enjoying themselves? Will you be comfortable in the months and years to come?

soften the learning curve. Instead of starting off in a group class, where students seem to already know what they're doing, you'll ease into your training. As a result, you'll be less likely to abandon your martial arts education.

Home Sweet Home

After you've completed your school's introductory or trial course, what comes next? Your first day in a regular group class.

Remember your first morning at nursery or grade school? Recall your first day on campus or at the office? This is the stuff of which antiperspirant commercials are made! And perhaps nothing is as intimidating as entering a martial arts group class for the first time. The sights, sound and smells are probably not like anything you've experienced. Students whirl in frenzied activity in response to strange commands. Loud shouts punctuate every movement. While this experience may mark the realization of a long-held dream, it's possible that, at this frightening moment, the only thing you want to do is go home to your Mommy.

This nervousness is a common reaction. But we assure you that, like many other things in life, crossing that threshold and entering the classroom will become easier in time. If you read *The Complete Idiot's Guide to Martial Arts,* take an introductory course, observe a group class or two and carefully select your teacher and school, then not only will you become more comfortable as you train for a few days, weeks, months and years, but you'll probably come to *love* the place!

Occasionally, as you push your body, mind and spirit to new limits, you might wonder why you're not at home, vegging out in front of the television. Or you might sometimes think you've lost your mind and believe you'd be better off in some martial arts "chat room" on the Net, rather than in a martial arts classroom in your neighborhood. Don't worry. Time and patience will help you get through the first few challenging months of training. So will a few other things, as explained in the following sections.

Bonding

Locating a good teacher is probably the single most important factor in your martial arts success. This individual should be competent in his or her field of expertise. He or she should be a compassionate person, a good communicator and motivator, and a great role model. Chapter 4 provides some instructor "profiles" that will assist you in assessing the appropriateness of different types of instructors.

Risky Moves

Just because a fellow student possesses enviable technical skills doesn't necessarily mean he or she deserves your respect as a martial artist. The ability to kick high, to punch with optimum power or to throw an elephant across the room isn't indicative of someone's level of maturity, wisdom, compassion and genuine concern for others.

Connecting with your martial arts teacher will be based, to a large extent, on mutual respect. We've already explained some of the qualities and skills a teacher should possess in order to earn your respect. Just remember that it's a two-way street. If *you* want to be respected as a martial artist, you'll find the following beginner do's and don'ts useful.

Beginner Do's and Don'ts

Do	Don't
Arrive promptly to warm up and practice	Be late for class
Maintain good hygiene	Wear a dirty uniform
Bring necessary equipment to each class	Forget your equipment
Raise questions in a respectful manner	Talk out of turn in class
Attend classes regularly	Miss classes
Strive to follow school regulations	Neglect school rules
Respect the value of your training	Abuse what you learn

As we've already mentioned, in all likelihood your school has its own list of rules. Following these guidelines can help make your first month, year and decade of training more enjoyable and productive. The suggestions we've offered above can also help you establish your credibility as a serious practitioner and help you to bond more easily with your teacher.

Master Speaks

Even *if* you possess no natural ability and have difficulty remembering which is your left foot and which is your right, give every training session 100 percent effort and you'll probably be rewarded. Instructors seek out students who try their best, often responding by giving these individuals additional attention and more one-to-one instruction.

With a Little Help from Your Friends

In your first month of training, you'll probably know no one in your school. If you attend classes regularly, however, you'll become familiar with your instructors and fellow students, and they'll have the opportunity to get acquainted with you. This will enable you to establish and reinforce relationships with people who may be very similar to—or very different from—you. You'll meet doctors and lawyers, architects and accountants, teachers and construction workers, psychiatrists and models, full-time parents and students, and actors and politicians. But you and your fellow students will have one thing in common: an interest in martial arts that may, in time, grow into a burning passion.

Men and women and boys and girls who were once strangers will become your training partners, perhaps even your friends. If you and they adhere to martial arts goal plans, you may advance through the ranks together. In time, you may share a beer or a coffee as you exchange ideas on everything from martial arts to the latest movie. Or you may attend tournaments, seminars and other extracurricular events together. Treat these relationships as the precious commodities they are, but don't lose sight of your purpose at the martial arts school: you're there to learn skills that can help you become a better person, not a better date or social director! When kept in perspective, becoming part of your school's "pack" and making new friends can enhance your training experience.

After your first month of training and the months that follow, your martial arts instructors and fellow students will probably begin to play a bigger role in your life. We've already provided you with some suggestions as to how you can win the respect of your martial arts teachers. What follows are a few recommendations that can help you gain the respect of your fellow students.

Tips for Getting Along

Do	Don't
Keep your mouth closed and body moving	Whine or complain
Give each technique your best shot	Give up
Demonstrate control even as a beginner	Be overly aggressive
Strive to remain humble	Show off
Respect your body and uniform	Neglect good hygiene

Again, most of this stuff is common sense. Training purposefully and demonstrating optimum control of your techniques and power, while remaining humble and "springtime fresh," will help you become the kind of partner everyone seeks.

Risky Moves

Unless you're a doctor on call or a birthing coach, it's a bad idea to bring your activated cellular telephone to martial arts classes. Be courteous. Turn it off or, better yet, leave it at home.

One Small Step for Martial Artists, One Giant Leap for You

After a few months of training, your instructor may advise you that it's time for your first belt exam. You'll probably experience a mix of emotions: joy, apprehension, excitement, dread. If the prospect of exhibiting your skills before a panel of Black Belts brings images of the Spanish Inquisition to mind and makes you want to run for cover, then follow these simple guidelines and the advice of your teacher to make the experience a little less traumatic.

Getting Down to the Wire

If you've followed your martial arts goal plan, attended classes regularly and practiced at home when necessary, you probably know the material that will be covered on your first test. Depending on your discipline and school, exam criteria might include basic techniques, "forms" (routines resembling dance) and one-step self-defense drills. In most schools, you'll also be evaluated and scored on your level of strength, flexibility and endurance. Some institutions may require you to complete an oral or written examination at every rank level.

Typically, students who are testing are notified one or more weeks in advance of the exam. Many schools post an exam schedule, which notes the name of each candidate. This schedule will determine your final preparation period before the big day.

Master Speaks

When approved to take exams or gradings, most students insist they're not ready. Trust the judgment of your instructors and do everything in your power to ensure you're prepared. There's a popular bit of advice that goes, "Bite off more than you can chew, then chew it...plan more than you can do, then do it!" You may be surprised at how well you rise to the occasion.

Conquering Performance Anxiety

Fear and self-doubt can be brought on with the anticipation of being evaluated for your first (or any) martial rank and can be extremely debilitating. There will be nights when you awaken from your happy little slumber in a cold sweat, wondering why you or anyone else has to test at all.

The real lesson to be learned from the experience of completing a martial arts exam is not how to model a fancy new belt or where to display rank certificates. This nerve-racking ordeal can yield big payoffs in the form of unbridled joy and increased self-confidence, which will fill your heart and mind. If you learn to master the fear that comes from having to perform every martial technique you know in front of your teachers, fellow students and spectators, you may gain a sense of empowerment that can carry over into your home life, relationships, academic studies or career.

Before you head down to your local pharmacy to pick up a prescription for valium, or drink gallons of soothing herbal tea, we'd like to share some tried and true relaxation techniques that can help you conquer martial stage fright.

➤ **The Week Before** If your school practices some form of relaxation drills or meditation, the week prior to testing might be the appropriate time to begin this type of training. You'll learn to sit quietly, breathe naturally and focus on filling your consciousness with positive thoughts. (See Chapter 7 for more information about meditation.)

➤ Next, solicit the advice of senior students. Not only can they help you put the finishing touches on many techniques, critique your form and give you sage advice about 11th-hour improvements, but they can also lend you a sympathetic ear (or supportive shoulder).

➤ Ensure that you're well rested, you maintain sound nutritional habits and you *practice.* If you were a boy or girl scout as a child, you know the value of being prepared!

➤ **The Day Before** This is also a great time to apply visualization techniques. Meditation may also come in handy. Simply find a quiet place and eliminate any mental distractions. Imagine yourself performing each movement flawlessly. Analyze each technique as you engage in "mental video playback." Your heart may begin to race and beads of sweat might form on your brow as you "feel" yourself executing forms, self-defense and basic drills.

➤ In the last 24 hours before the big event, it's advisable to ease up on your training routine. Light stretching, a leisurely stroll, laundering your uniform and preparing any necessary equipment (just to give your body and brain something simple to do) are terrific, low-stress pretest activities. Eat a balanced carbohydrate-rich diet (see Chapter 4 for tips on nutrition). Allowing your body to rest and refuel will give you the energy you'll need during the test.

Master Speaks

One way to minimize test terrors is to observe one or more examinations before you're actually a candidate. It's a great way to preview what's to come and, perhaps, shrink your fears down to a more manageable size.

Warrior Words

Shinsa (Japanese) or *simsa* (Korean) refers to rank tests conducted in your school. When Black Belts are participating in exams for First to Sixth Degree, their tests may be held in a gym or auditorium. Candidates for Seventh Degree and above may have to travel to Asia and perform before the director of their style.

Master Speaks

If you're counting calories, you may want to consume an additional 500 to 1000 the day before your big test. This will help ensure you have adequate reserves.

➤ **The Final Hours** You've probably visited the washroom a dozen or more times, so let's see…what else is there to do? Once again, if meditation is your thing, then get going by unwinding. But we don't mean that you should be overly relaxed. The adrenaline boost you're probably feeling is a guaranteed "hump clearer." It will come in handy when you think you don't have another ounce of energy to spare. What we are suggesting is clearing your mind of any negative thoughts, monitoring your breathing pattern and re-minding yourself that you and your teachers have worked diligently to prepare for this moment. You've earned the privilege of demonstrating your skills, and your fellow students, as well as relatives and friends in attendance, are there to support you and celebrate this wonderful occasion. And remember those washroom breaks? To avoid coming up dry, you'll have to drink adequate amounts of water or a low-sugar isotonic drink to remain hydrated.

➤ **The Moment of Truth** You arrive promptly and take your place among the other exam candidates. Perspiration pours. Your heart pounds. Much of what goes on is a blur, like some high-speed, out-of-focus movie. As you wait your turn, watching other students perform, maintain a clear, calm, focused mind. Take comfort in the fact that as you push yourself to new limits—perhaps a level of physical, mental and spiritual exhaustion you thought impossible—at the end of the day, you'll emerge a more skilled practitioner and, perhaps, a slightly better human being.

Martial Smarts

My mother drew a distinction between achievement and success. She said that achievement is the knowledge that you have studied and worked hard and done the best that is in you. Success is being praised by others, and that's nice too, but not as important or satisfying. Aim for achievement and forget about success.

—*Helen Keller*

Pats and Congrats

Kudos! Way to Go! You did it! You've achieved your first martial arts rank. Looking back on the exam, you may be surprised at how easy it actually was—most things seem that way with the benefit of hindsight. And it may become apparent that these tests are not as much an assessment of your skills as they are an appraisal of your ability to exhibit grace under fire.

Remaining calm and focused on the task at hand is an essential skill whether you're facing a physical confrontation, a job interview, or having to defend a doctoral dissertation.

And while martial arts examinations can be the ultimate stress tests, the resultant sense of personal pride that you'll likely experience will make them all worthwhile.

Reassessing Your Goals

Now that you've spent a few days admiring your newly belted image in the mirror, it's back to the grindstone—or, at least, back to the classroom.

Martial Smarts

When a thing is done, it's done. Don't look back. Look forward to your next objective.

—*General George C. Marshall*

Before the last champagne bubbles fizzle and fade, it's time to begin learning new material. And guess what? In a few short months, you and the Exam Demon will be staring one another in the face once again. But perhaps next time, you'll feel more relaxed and ready to do battle—in a manner of speaking.

Having taken a few minutes to conduct your own cross-examination, you've assessed your performance and made mental notes on which areas need improvement. You may also have stopped to realize that your once-lofty goal of advancing in martial arts rank is accessible if you don't underestimate your potential and are willing to work hard.

Armed with newfound confidence, should you dare to now think of reaching your Black Belt? *You bet you should!* Time is of the essence, so revise your goal plan and get back to your training schedule pronto. In the time it takes to achieve your Black Belt, your coach potato buddies could have packed on 50 pounds and raised their cholesterol levels to an all-time high.

The most frustrating and amazing thing about martial arts training is that there's always more. More to learn. More to share. And more to achieve. So raise that bar and get busy. Let the inscription on the Hopkins Memorial (located at Steps, Williams College) be your training motto: "Climb High/ Climb Far/ Your goal the sky/ Your aim the star."

The Least You Need to Know

➤ Participating in a martial arts introductory course can help you overcome initial fears, provide a more realistic view of training, assist you and your teacher in establishing your goals and improve your odds of achieving them.

➤ Your first month or two at a martial arts school can be filled with a mix of emotions. Following a few guidelines can help make this crucial period less difficult.

➤ Developing a bond with your teachers and fellow students can enhance your training experience.

➤ Fear and self-doubt aside, your first belt exam can be a source of pride and serve as a catalyst for continued martial arts progress.

➤ Having achieved one goal—your first belt—it's essential to establish new objectives if your aim is to be a Black Belt one day.

Chapter 12

The Higher Level of Martial Arts Learning

In This Chapter

➤ Reading would–be attackers' verbal and nonverbal cues

➤ How to defend yourself against more than one assailant

➤ Strategies for armed confrontations

➤ Looking at martial arts tournaments

➤ Breaking objects can test your power and boost your confidence

➤ Discovering what it takes to teach

There are two types of martial arts students. The first are the individuals who happily coast in the realm of the familiar. Having achieved limited ability in performing required techniques, these students, restricted by fear and doubt, refuse to exceed self-imposed boundaries. Then there are the envelope-pushers: students who strive each day to better themselves, both inside and outside the martial arts classroom. Nurturing an indomitable spirit, they seek new and innovative challenges that will help them exceed physical, mental and spiritual expectations—both their own and those of other people.

How would you classify your own attitude about martial arts? About life in general? This chapter can help you answer these and other questions about higher levels of martial arts training.

Martial Smarts

A man cannot be too careful in the choice of his enemies.

—*Oscar Wilde*

All for One and One for All?

Neanderthals to the left of you. Cro-Magnons to the right of you. And you're armed...with your briefcase or lunch box?!

You've been studying martial arts for a year or more. And although the bookies in Las Vegas might not give you great odds in a match with the current world boxing champ, you're reasonably certain that you can block a punch, slip a kick or release any number of holds. But what if fists are flying in your direction, from every direction? Imagine countless kicks connecting as you cower for cover in a corner (we couldn't resist a little alliteration).

Take a deep breath and read on. The next section will provide you with several strategies for dealing with multiple opponents. These might be difficult for you to grasp if you are a beginner. But after you've got some experience under your "belt," you should be ready to learn these more advanced techniques.

Danger Signs

Multiple attacks, like one-on-one confrontations, rarely happen without advanced warning. If you learn to read the signs, you can improve your ability to sense, and ideally avoid, an attack.

No two defensive situations are identical. Some occur spontaneously and are fueled by unbridled passion (for example, group violence at a soccer match or gang clashes in inner cities). Others are premeditated crimes.

Indications that a spontaneous attack by multiple assailants may occur include—

> ➤ A change in tone or volume of people's voices or repetition of heated, angry words. Stress or anxiety may cause vocal cords to constrict, altering the way individuals would normally speak. They might also say things that generally wouldn't enter their vocabulary.

> ➤ Excessive sweating. While some experienced assailants might appear cool, other more nervous attackers may, as their anxiety builds and their blood pressure rises, begin to perspire.

> ➤ Body Language. Before any individuals in the group initiate an attack, they may tighten their jaw or clench their fists.

These are but a few of the telltale signs that warn of a possible attack. In response you can—

1. diffuse the situation by gently talking and walking away

2. keep "mum," say nothing and sympathetically listen as your would-be attackers spew

3. do unto others before they have an opportunity to do unto you (this means a pre-emptive whacking) or

4. do options 1 and 2 while passing your assailants a can of deodorant and a bottle of muscle relaxants, skillfully avoiding—at all costs—option 3.

Other assaults are less spur of the moment, entailing more advance planning. They may be materialistic in nature. That is, your attackers' motive may be stripping you of your property. Alternatively, they may be premeditated physical crimes, such as sexual assault or murder. Indicators of these types of crimes include the following.

➤ People showing unusual interest in your property. They may make comments about the value of your goods, such as "That must be an expensive watch" or "Can I take a look at your Walkman?" Such interest might be a sign that an individual is assessing the value of your possessions.

➤ Crowding of your personal space. One or more individuals touch or bump into you.

➤ Being followed or stalked. An individual, group or vehicle appears to be following you and, despite numerous changes in direction, continues in pursuit.

Listen to how people speak and the words they are using. Read nonverbal cues like facial contortions and clenching fists. Remain sensitive to any other unusual behavior, such as heightened interest in you or your property or the fact that a caravan seems to be forming behind you, and you may be able to recognize that a physical confrontation is imminent, and, more importantly, be better able to avoid it.

Martial Smarts

Good judgment comes from experience, which comes from poor judgment.

—*Anonymous*

Practical Training

Now that you understand how to interpret the signs pointing to physical confrontations, how can you better prepare yourself physically through martial arts training to address these situations?

The "science" of combating multiple opponents is practiced in most martial arts schools at the intermediate or advanced level by means of numerous drills, including those described below.

➤ Blocking multiple attacks – With two or more students surrounding you, block, deflect or sidestep a barrage of unrehearsed attacks. After dealing with one assailant, quickly reposition yourself, preparing for the next opponent. Throughout the exercise, keep your eyes on the other students and carefully read their physical signals. This drill is often performed in a circle but may be less structured. Begin slowly and gradually increase the speed of both the attacks and defensive techniques.

➤ Striking multiple pads – Position a number of focus pads at different angles and attempt to strike each one with speed, accuracy and power. Decrease your response time gradually until you're able to launch each counterattack rapid-fire, like the most experienced *Top Gun* pilot.

➤ Striking multiple heavy bags – If your school has several heavy bags positioned in rows, move from one to the other while executing strikes and kicks. This drill can greatly improve your footwork and reaction time as you skillfully move to avoid swinging targets.

➤ Holding and striking multiple attackers – While one student grabs you, another attempts to hit you. You'll have to learn to release the hold and respond to the strike by slipping, blocking, moving out of the way and launching a countering technique.

Master Speaks

Protection versus vigilantism. If you find yourself faced with a physical confrontation and are unsuccessful in talking your way out of the situation, be certain before you respond physically that you're familiar with the legal ramifications of your actions. Consult your instructor on what, precisely, constitutes "reasonable force." Otherwise, you, rather than your assailant, might be left standing before a judge.

➤ Fighting from the ground – In preparing for self-defense scenarios with one or more attackers, in addition to learning to protect yourself from a standing position, you'll also have to become adept at fighting from the floor. Kneel, sit or lie down. Several students will launch attacks as you defend yourself and attempt to move to an upright position.

➤ Sparring with padded opponents – This drill will require use of heavy-duty padded protective gear (face masks, body shields, leg and arm guards) worn by two or more partners. To protect yourself from spontaneous attacks, you'll defend and counter in full-contact fashion. This exercise, like many of the others listed, will not only test your power but also measure the efficacy of your techniques.

➤ Deflecting objects – Encircled by numerous opponents, you'll attempt to deflect or side-step focus pads thrown in your direction.

The objective of this exercise is to protect yourself against these objects, while trying to exit the circle.

In addition to honing the physical skills to better manage an attack by multiple

Risky Moves

Some students experience fight–or–flight anxiety when practicing multiple opponent drills. It can be unnerving to have several people using you for target practice. But *not* learning to protect yourself in this situation can be even more unpleasant should you suddenly be confronted by several attackers. In the words of Edgar Watson Howe, "A good scare is worth more to a person than bad advice."

assailants, the above-noted exercises can assist you in preparing psychologically for these situations.

Strategies for Multiple Attacks

If you've studied the preceding sections, you know some of the nonverbal and verbal indicators that may signal an attack by several individuals. You are also familiar with numerous drills that can be practiced in your martial arts school to help you become better prepared, physically and psychologically, should an attack be unavoidable.

What remains is learning several strategies that can help you address these frightening situations. Before we delve into these, we thought it essential to remind you that Plan A should always be to *talk your way out of a bad situation and walk—or run—away.* Don't let your ego get in the way of your survival. A fender-bender in your new RV, stinging insults aimed at you, your family or your football team, or some mugger's overwhelming desire to own your Rolex aren't reasons to put your physical well-being or your life on the line. (See also Chapter 1, which covers other aspects of personal defense inside and outside your home.)

Okay, so you've tried to gab or gallop out of harm's way, and cheerfully indicated a willingness to part with your baubles but, for a variety of reasons only a forensic psychologist could fathom, these strategies haven't worked. You're now faced with the prospect of defending yourself against several opponents. What to do? Go to Plan B:

1. Stay calm. This is the most difficult advice to follow. Seize the first opportunity to flee and call for help.

2. Maintain a defensive posture by keeping your hands up.

3. Keep all attackers within your line of vision.

4. Maintain a safe distance and make it difficult for attackers to reach you.

5. If there's a wall, position yourself in front of it to protect your rear.

6. When struck by one assailant, block and quickly move to avoid others.

7. If you must counterattack, use short strikes and kick in several directions.

8. Attempt to line up your attackers, positioning them one behind the other.

9. Don't wrestle one attacker to the ground if others are still around you.

10. Use your entire body, including your hands, feet, head, teeth and nails, as weapons.

Martial Smarts

War is an unmitigated evil. But it certainly does one good thing. It drives away fears and brings bravery to the surface.

—Mahatma Gandhi

Attacks by multiple assailants can be chaotic and terrifying. You should do everything in your power to avoid these situations, as well as confrontations with one individual, at all costs. If, however, you have no other alternative and you've prepared yourself physically, mentally and spiritually, your martial arts training will greatly increase the odds of your emerging in one piece.

Armed and Dangerous

This section deals with another intimidating subject: confrontations with armed assailants.

As in the above section, we caution you that no two attackers or confrontations are exactly the same and it's always better to avoid a fight than to stick around and play Joe or Jane Avenger.

Imagine, though, that you've taken every precaution but are now at the mercy of an armed thug. If you've read the previous section, you've attempted the diplomatic approach and even tried the 40-yard dash. If these attempts did not work, you're now face to face with the most threatening self-defense situation. What are your options? Well, your responses will depend on the weapon used.

Let's examine some common weapons you may encounter on the street, or even in your home, school, or office, and some self-defense strategies that you can employ against them.

The Cutting Edge

In this category, you'll find several weapons, including single- and double-edged knives. Most people are, quite rightly, afraid of being cut. With some extra caution, you can use many of the same empty-hand defensive techniques you've practiced in the classroom to control and disarm a knife-wielding opponent.

Two essential skills you'll need to develop in preparing for this type of attack are—

1. Maintaining a defensive distance – If you're too far away from the knife, your attacker will keep coming at you. If you're too close, you may be cut.

2. Controlling the weapon – Resist what may be your natural reaction to push away the hand holding the weapon. Instead, strive to control that hand.

One way to overcome your fear of bladed weapons is to initially practice using wooden or rubber varieties. Allow your partner to slash and slice, striking you from a variety of angles. Another drill involves use of uncapped washable markers wielded by your fellow students. This exercise can be messy but at least you'll get a pretty good idea of how your techniques would work in a street situation. (Just don't wear your favorite uniform on the day you practice this drill.)

Risky Moves

To control an opponent holding a knife, firmly grab his or her hand or wrist. If, by some unfortunate chance, you grab the blade instead and your assailant pulls the weapon back, it's essential you avoid resisting. Maintain your grip and go with the flow while striking your attacker's vital, highly vulnerable points.

As your skills improve and you become more confident, you may progress to a blunt knife and, at a more experienced level, to sharper weapons. Obviously, these techniques should be part of a gradual learning process as you move from basic to intermediate drills, and should be practiced only under the supervision of your instructors.

Babe Ruth Would Have Been Proud

Many of you probably grew up watching baseball players send a little, round white object soaring out of the ballpark. Both the athletes and the spectators understood the value that a bat, in the hands of a skillful player, could have at home plate.

In the movie *The Untouchables*, Robert DeNiro's Al Capone demonstrates that this same object can do some serious damage off the playing field. Even if you didn't see this film, think about your cave-dwelling, club-carrying ancestors and let your imagine run wild!

As weapons go, bats, clubs and even nine irons and tire irons are infinitely easier to deal with than guns and knives. Two basic strategies for defending against bat attacks are described below.

1. Move inside the range of the strike while keeping your guard up to protect your head, stomach and groin. At the same time, shift your legs to avoid lower body strikes (such as those aimed at the shins and knees). Even if you are hit, you've minimized the impact of the blow by shortening the distance between you and the weapon and reduced the number of vital areas that might be struck. Use your striking or grappling skills to disarm your attacker.

139

2. Move outside the range of the strike by shifting back and allow the swing to pass. Keep your guard up and rush in, "jamming" your attacker's shoulder and thereby preventing a return pass. Use your striking or grappling skills to disarm your attacker.

Risky Moves

Remember that the "Lambada" is an ever-annoying dance. "Lumbago" is your ever-aching back. And a *lobatomy* can be the ever-painful result of misjudging the timing of a bat attack. It can also follow foolish attempts to recreate scenes from action films where the protagonist ducks under a swinging club, only to have his or her head connect with what is affectionately referred to as the "business end" of this object.

Bat defensive strategies require in-class practice in which you face one and, as you become more skillful and confident, several opponents under the supervision of your instructor. You might begin with foam or rubber objects and progress to props of a more durable nature. Learn to apply striking and grappling skills to control your attacker's wrist and hand rather than concentrating on the weapon.

Chain Reaction

Any Las Vegas lounge lizard worth his or her salt knows the appeal of a glitzy assortment of gold chains. Chains can be fashionable accessories, decorative ornaments or flexible and extremely frightening weapons. In the hands of an angry individual, swinging bicycle or tire chains are dangerous because you never know where they will make contact. The same basic strategies you would use to defend yourself against knife and club attacks are applicable if you're faced with an enraged chain-swinger. Your options include moving inside or allowing the weapon to swing past and then rushing in on your opponent. You would then rely on striking and grappling techniques to control the assailant's wrist and hand rather than the weapon itself.

You're Not Faster Than a Speeding Bullet

Unless you are outfitted in blue tights, wear a red cape and have an aversion to kryptonite, it's highly unlikely you'll be able to outrun a bullet. So what are your options if faced with a firearm? The old joke is to be 100 miles away—but what if this isn't possible? Once again, attempt to talk your way out of the situation. Assess what the attacker wants. Your wallet? Car? Jewelry? We don't have to remind you (we hope!) that material possessions aren't worth risking a physical confrontation.

What if the stakes are higher, however, and your life is on the line? One strategy is to attempt to deflect the barrel of the gun by grasping your attacker's hand or wrist and aiming the weapon away from you. Using striking and grappling techniques, you might then move to disarm the assailant.

Begin by training with wood, plastic and rubber guns. When your skill level has improved, use metal cap or starter pistols, which will teach you to respond to a weapon that is more realistic—in terms of its appearance, its weight and, perhaps most frighteningly of all, its sound. Practice disarming drills in your martial arts school under the supervision of an instructor who has experience dealing with firearms. This kind of expertise is even more crucial with guns than with other weapons.

Martial Smarts

When you pet a stray dog with your left hand, make sure you're holding a rock in your right hand.

—*Chinese proverb*

A final word about these types of assaults. The good news about armed confrontations is that many times the assailant doesn't intend to use the weapon—it's simply a negotiating tool. The bad news is that sometimes it's not merely a prop. As your wise old grandmother might have advised you, always keep your wits about you. Avoiding rather than managing these, and all, assaults is always preferable. However, you should recognize that facing and surviving an armed attack is serious business and train for these terrifying encounters physically and psychologically. Discuss and rehearse practical defensive strategies with an experienced martial arts instructor and don't neglect the protective value of ordinary objects like briefcases, books, chairs or even a steaming cup of java. These simple things can be used to distract or distance an attacker and to block his or her strikes.

Are Tournaments for You?

Once you've reached the intermediate phase, perhaps after 1 to 2 years of training, you may experience an overwhelming desire to test your skills. You can either 1) drive the family station wagon down to the local biker bar, fearlessly announce, "You're all a bunch of sissies" and wait for the sparks to fly; or 2) register for the next local martial arts tournament. The second option can be a lot more fun and result in a lot less wear and tear on your bod.

As visions of hardware—in the form of trophies, medals and plaques—begin dancing in your head, let's examine what's involved in participating in the competitive arena.

A Sporting Chance?

Most popular martial arts like Jiu-jitsu, Judo, Karate and Tae Kwon Do include a sport component. Local, national and international tournaments are popular and plentiful and offer dozens of categories broken down by martial arts styles, age, gender, weight and rank as well as by division, such as forms, weapons, sparring, self-defense and breaking (objects).

Calendars of events, which can be found in most martial arts publications and flyers

141

Warrior Words

While a broad range of techniques are practiced and have equal value in the martial arts classroom, only a handful hold any tournament value. Some techniques that are more useful when attempting to score points include the *seionage* (shoulder throw) in Judo events, *gyaku-zuki* (reverse punch) in Karate contests and the *dollyo-chagi* (roundhouse kick) in Tae Kwon Do competitions.

mailed to your school, publicize a plethora of upcoming contests. These include open tournaments, which feature a modern or eclectic structure, and traditional events, as well as sanctioned and nonsanctioned competitions. Some martial arts tournaments are designed to appeal to students and fans of Muay Thai, American Kickboxing, French Foot Boxing (Savate) and other forms of full-contact combative systems, and feature amateur and professional bouts. Contests aimed at Jiu-jitsu practitioners and students of other free-form grappling systems are gaining popularity. Escrima events, where contestants wear padded protective gear and spar with rattan batons, are targeted to aficionados of this form of Filipino stick combat. Even the more serene martial arts like Tai Chi and Aikido have climbed aboard the tournament train. Tai Chi students can be seen at competitive events, demonstrating "pushing hands" (drills resembling sparring) and showcasing their forms skills. Students of Tomiki (a type of Aikido) participate in contests where they are judged by their ability to defend themselves against a variety of unarmed and armed attacks.

Tournaments for Children and Teenagers

Children and teenagers can quickly become excited about numerous activities—including martial arts—and just as quickly lose interest in them. Tournaments, when kept in their proper perspective, can add another dimension to martial education and, as such, might enable boys and girls to stay interested in, and focused on, this worthwhile activity for years.

Most martial arts competitions are very safety conscious. Protective gear is mandatory at the majority of events and competitors are divided by age, size and rank. Teenage divisions frequently include separate male and female sparring categories.

Through competition, children and teens (and adults, for that matter) can learn to take pride in their accomplishments and comprehend the value of good sports behavior. Understanding how to win and lose gracefully is a lesson that can positively affect the lives of all participants.

The Adult Competitor

Are you looking for something shiny that can stand beside last year's bowling or golf league trophy? Or maybe you're seeking an opportunity to see how your martial skills compare with those of other men and women of the same age and rank level.

If you have the right attitude, tournaments can shed some interesting light on your strengths and the areas you need to develop. For instance, if you lose a sparring match to a Karate student, you might want to reexamine your competitive arsenal and add more lightning-fast hand strikes or kicks. Or perhaps you didn't fare as well as you thought you might going one-on-one with a Jiu-jitsu practitioner. If so, you may need to polish your grappling skills. Maybe your empty-hand or weapons forms didn't place you among the top three competitors, leaving you to head back to the drawing board. You can use this opportunity to advance your martial arts study by analyzing what went right—and wrong—and discussing your performance with your instructor.

Furthermore, competing in martial arts tournaments can offer the same broad range of benefits to adults that this experience can provide youngsters. You'll learn how to be a good winner and loser, cultivate an appreciation for other martial arts styles and disciplines, and perhaps make a few new friends—or even bump into Mr. or Ms. Right along the way. You'll also have the opportunity to take pride in the progress you've made while recognizing you've still got a long way to go.

And on Sunday, God Rested

While the "supreme being" might take Sunday or Saturday off, these are the days when martial arts tournaments are generally conducted, usually in high school or college gymnasiums. Typically, these events will begin in the morning and run through the evening hours. Registration costs vary depending on the number of divisions you enter, but on average will run from $20 to $60. Noncompetitors usually pay a nominal spectator's fee of $5 to $15. Some promoters permit spectators and coaches to videotape or photograph divisional activities. Others strictly prohibit the use of any recording or photographic devices.

Divisional winners generally receive trophies, which can be as tall as 6 feet, or nearly 2 meters. Medals and plaques may also be presented. Some events give attendees a certificate acknowledging their participation. Others also award points that are recognized by a federation, association or league. Many competitors travel to events throughout the year, accumulating points that will make them eligible for national ranking.

In conjunction with these tournaments, ancillary events, such as trade shows, banquets, photo sessions with celebrities, charity fundraisers and seminars, may be conducted. You can purchase videotapes or T-shirts, dine or take pictures with local, national and international celebs, make a donation to a food or clothing bank or some other worthy cause, or participate in a seminar or workshop featuring top-ranked competitors. While some event directors offer all-in-one price packages (generally in the range of $60 to $100), other promoters opt to sell tickets for each activity.

Rules are fairly uniform but they can vary slightly from competition to competition. Be certain you're familiar with all tournament requirements in advance. Train and compete with these guidelines in mind. You can obtain event schedules and detailed regulations from promoters.

143

Risky Moves

Martial arts teach children respect, humility and self-control. Tournaments can reinforce (or weaken) these positive values. Unfortunately, many parents and spectators who attend these competitions have not acquired the same values. All too often, well-intentioned family and friends seated along the sidelines display negative behavior toward event officials, competitors and other spectators when things don't go their way.

If you're interested in obtaining information about tournaments that is specific to different martial arts styles and systems, refer to Chapters 13 to 23 and Appendix F in this guide, consult your instructor or local school, or contact the associations listed in Appendix E.

Smashing Success

Once you've begun practicing martial arts, well-intentioned friends may begin asking you if you can break a brick or chop your coffee table in half. Fortunately, with millions of men, women and children practicing martial arts around the world and increased awareness about the real value of these combative systems, ridiculous requests like these are fast becoming a thing of the past.

What has not diminished, however, is the interest of students in testing their speed, focus and power—whether they're aiming their techniques at a heavy bag, brick or slab of ice. What, then, can be gained from breaking inanimate objects?

The primary reason for board, brick and ice breaking is to instill confidence in a martial artist, by giving him or her tangible proof of the power of each technique.

Before squaring off against a defenseless solid object, your instructor should teach you how to prepare yourself by performing strikes against pads, heavy bags and other apparatus, like *makiwara* (striking posts). You may then proceed to hitting plastic breakaway boards, before progressing to single and later multiple wood boards or other solid targets.

It is essential that you execute each strike with appropriate form, breath control and focus, and that

Martial Smarts

Bruce Lee said "Boards don't fight back." He meant this as a warning that the power with which you hit a stationary target is no measure of your true fighting skill.

the holder knows how to position the board correctly; that is, they must brace their elbows against their body and keep their fingers out of the line of the strike. Concentrate on passing through the target, aiming at the holder's chest (not fingers), rather than simply hitting the surface of the object.

As with other combative exercises, splintering wood, shattering bricks and cracking ice with your bare hands and feet can help you face and overcome your fears. With each successful "breakthrough," you'll come to realize your infinite potential, which extends beyond the martial arts classroom to every corner of your life.

Let's now discover another important aspect of higher levels of martial arts training: teaching.

Teacher, Teacher

There's no doubt about it. Teaching is a noble pursuit, provided your intentions are—as gun-toting folks in the backwoods say—honorable.

Before you update your résumé, scan the want ads or inundate your instructor with requests to join your school's teaching roster, stop and ask yourself one question: *Is my aim to improve the quality of training at our school and to make students' learning experience more productive and enjoyable, or am I simply seeking a showcase to demonstrate my own abilities?* An honest response to this one query will speak reams about your reasons for wanting to teach martial arts.

Put rank, experience, academic credentials and physical talents aside. While these things may be factored into the teaching mix, they are by no means a true measure of your qualifications. What counts is whether or not you have a burning desire to help others gain optimum benefit from their martial arts education.

If you've been training for a few years and your aim is to share your knowledge with other students and make their martial arts journey a more wonderful experience, then discuss this goal with your instructor. He or she might construct a plan detailing how you can begin to get some practical experience and hone your teaching skills. You may start by assisting with beginner classes or by leading students through warm-ups and basic drills. You may be asked to teach introductory programs. Your instructor might assign you to teach off-site courses, such as those in local schools or community centers. Furthermore, from time to time, you may be asked to fill in as a substitute teacher. Your instructor may begin to educate you about how to write and implement your own class plans, using your school's student manual or curriculum guide. In this manner,

Martial Smarts

The true teacher defends his [or her] pupils against their own personal influences...and guides the eyes from the teacher to the spirit that quickens them.

—*Amos Bronson Alcott*

145

your instructor and other teachers will have ample opportunity to assess your ability to teach, direct a class and interact with other staff, students, parents and the public. This gradual, hands-on approach will also give you the chance to learn by doing, providing you with necessary practical experience. If all goes well, after a reasonable apprenticeship period, you could become a staff instructor.

In sum, as your martial arts training progresses, you may begin practicing for multiple and armed attacks, participating in tournaments, testing your power by breaking objects, and expanding your knowledge through teaching.

The Least You Need to Know

➤ At the intermediate stage of training, you may seek out innovative ways to push your martial arts limits.

➤ Learning to read a would-be assailant's verbal and nonverbal cues can help you pre-empt an attack.

➤ At an intermediate level, you may begin practicing self-defense drills that can help you protect yourself against more than one attacker or against armed individuals.

➤ Tournament competition can provide you with an opportunity to test your skills, learn interesting techniques and make new friends.

➤ Breaking solid objects can assist you in assessing the power and accuracy of your techniques and help you conquer your fears.

➤ If you're interested in teaching martial arts, an apprenticeship program can help you gain the necessary practical experience.

Part 4
Major Martial Arts in Detail

In earlier chapters you became familiar with the most popular martial arts being practiced in North America today. Now you're ready to put these combative systems under the microscope. If you're imagining martial masters squirming around in a petri dish, well forget it! That's not what we mean.

This entire section is devoted to educating you about the origins and development of major combative systems—and even a few eclectic ones. You'll get the historical and cultural lowdown on these unarmed and armed martial disciplines. And here's an exciting aspect of Part 4: you'll actually have the opportunity to "participate" in classes because these 10 chapters include lots of technical information and instructional photographs. These will give you a good idea of what you will learn as a student, and how a typical training session would be structured.

Chapter 13

Enter the Dragon with Chinese Kung Fu

In This Chapter

➤ Examining Kung Fu's development

➤ How religion influenced Chinese martial arts

➤ Comparing different systems

➤ Looking at Kung Fu training techniques

Although you can trace the roots of Kung Fu back to 2000 B.C., it is martial arts supernova Bruce Lee who is, more often than not, credited with launching the Kung Fu craze of the 1970s. Remember the disco hit "Everybody Was Kung Fu Fighting"? In the early days of his career, Bruce Lee graced the small screen as "Green Hornet" sidekick Kato. His brief but memorable celluloid credits include martial arts megahits such as *Enter the Dragon, Fists of Fury* and *The Big Boss*.

While the legendary Lee died in 1973 and the Kung Fu craze has dwindled somewhat, this martial art remains popular. This chapter will help you understand different types of Kung Fu, their evolution and the benefits they can offer you.

Martial Smarts

"You have offended my family and the Shaolin Temple." This is one of the most memorable, revenge-justifying phrases uttered in any action film. It was said by Bruce Lee in the *Citizen Kane* of martial arts movies, *Enter the Dragon*. This single sentence gave him carte blanche to destroy anything in his path!

Martial Smarts

At the time of the warring states (around 300 B.C.), the population of China was estimated to be between 50 and 60 million! With so many mouths to feed, the reigning lords of various states appropriated—that *is*, borrowed with no intention of returning—their neighbor's land. This "borrowing" was generally by force so, obviously, superlative martial skills were highly valued.

Animal Attraction in the Middle Kingdom

China was called Zhong Guo, which means "The Middle Kingdom." For several thousand years, China's ruling elite regarded their country as the center of the universe. Its influence on the rest of Asia touched all areas: cultural, artistic, spiritual, religious and scholastic.

If you lived in China during the Hsia dynasty (2200 B.C.), you probably would have struggled alongside your compatriots: tribe against tribe, nation against nation. As China's government gained power, its military forces overtook neighboring countries with Pac Man-like frenzy!

Military leaders quickly came to appreciate the value of soldiers adept at both armed and unarmed combat. Numerous schools, defensive systems and training regimens emerged, with the aim of improving the fighting skills of military personnel. Many of these systems mimicked the protective movements of animals (such as the tiger, panther, snake and monkey), birds (crane, eagle, hawk), insects (praying mantis) and even mythical beings—no, not Sailor Moon or Conan the Barbarian, but rather the dragon and phoenix.

In addition to imitating defensive techniques, if you practiced these systems, you would have tried to develop the characteristics often associated with these creatures, for example, the heroism of the tiger, the speed of the panther and the cunning of the snake. You could have used these techniques as ancient personal growth programs!

Ssshh! Secret Training

Since these martial systems were closely guarded, few written accounts, public performances or exchanges between schools were permitted. During this time, if you were applying for admission to most martial arts schools, in addition to fulfilling technical requirements, you would have had to demonstrate patience, appropriateness of character and an allegiance to your teacher. It would not have been unusual for you to devote 10 or more years to martial arts study before you would begin learning "secret" material. This material was divided into four principal areas: conditioning and physical exercises, hand striking and kicking, seizing and controlling techniques, and the application of Chinese medicine in treating the injured (bone setting, acupuncture and the use of herbs and tonics).

Damo the Mysterious Monk

While martial arts practitioners may argue about some things, most agree that even without Jules Verne's time machine, or an elaborate Day-Timer, the origin of Chinese martial arts can be traced back to approximately 5000 B.C.

In A.D. 527 the emperor Wu Di (a religious groupie) invited a mysterious Indian monk, Bodhidharma (Damo, in Chinese), to China. Bodhidharma is credited with establishing a curriculum and authoring several instructional books that helped spread Chinese martial arts. He is also famous for developing the Chan sect of Buddhism (Zen, in Japanese). You probably wonder what might have happened if this monk had had access to the Internet!

Warrior Words

A little Zen goes a long, long way! Zen, translated as "meditation," is a sect of Buddhism that focuses on the here and now, as opposed to the hereafter, or rebirth. A popular Zen exercise is the *kung-an* (or *koan*, in Japanese), which relies on the use of riddles that sharpen your intellect. For example: What is the sound of one hand clapping?

Bodhidharma wasn't your average yes-man. In what we might call a career-limiting move, the monk often gave the emperor vague responses to religious questions. It is no wonder, then, that shortly after Bodhidharma's much anticipated arrival, the emperor gave the monk his walking papers (or in "Zenspeak," Bodhidharma heard the sound of one hand slamming the door behind him).

After journeying throughout China, Bodhidharma came upon the Shaolin-si (Young Forest) Temple in Henan province, where he found the monks to be weak and sickly. If you were a monk at this time, you would have meditated a lot and exercised very little, if at all. Without a national health care program in place, Bodhidharma took matters into his own hands. He shifted into high gear by *sitting down*—for 9 years—in a meditative position called *biguan,* as he pondered this serious issue. When he awoke, Bodhidharma wrote two books that resembled ancient health guides. One *(Yi Jin Jing)* featured exercises to help you develop external strength. The other *(Xi Sui Jing)* was about meditation, breathing and circulation.

Shortly after, Bodhidharma authored a third book, titled *The Eighteen Hands of Lohan (Shi Bao Luo Han Shou),* which was based on his experiences in India as a member of the Kshatriya cast (warriors and rulers). This text included choreographed defensive routines called *kune* (Chinese Kung Fu), *hyung* (Korean Tae Kwon Do) or *kata* (Japanese Karate) and is widely regarded as the first how-to manual of offensive and defensive martial movements.

There are few written records about Bodhidharma's life and death. Additionally, information regarding the impact he had on the evolution of Chinese martial arts is mostly speculation. Furthermore, burning questions—like how you can sit for nearly a decade without a bathroom break—remain a mystery.

Warrior Words

What's in a name? The name *Bodhidharma* can be translated as "truth" or "wisdom of Buddha" *(Bodhi)* and "law" *(dharma).*

Risky Moves

Long ago, children as young as five entered the Shaolin Temple and, even at this tender age, were expected to practice martial arts for many hours a day, seven days a week. Modern parents should take care to ensure that their youngster's martial arts training is balanced with other extracurricular activities.

The Shaolin Temple

While the part played by Bodhidharma in the development of Chinese martial arts is based largely on educated guesses and interpretation, the role of the Shaolin Temple, or more precisely *Temples,* is rooted in fact.

There were several Shaolin Temples across China. (Think of these as the earliest martial arts franchises.) Two of these temples stand out as institutions of martial arts learning: Henan Temple, in the north, and Fukien, in the south. The former was built in A.D. 495 by order of Wei emperor Xiao Wen. There is no recorded date for the construction of the latter. Initially, these were centers for religious learning. However, with the Manchurian invasion of China in A.D. 1127, their focus shifted to more political issues.

The mission of the first abbot, Batuo, of the Shaolin Temple in Henan province was to construct a state-of-the-art religious institution. He never imagined that his beloved temple would become a center of political unrest and intrigue.

If you were a monk living in the Henan Temple in China in A.D. 621, you and a dozen of your monastic brothers would probably have been drafted by the emperor Li Shi-ming. Skilled in the martial arts, you could have played a crucial part in overthrowing the government of the Sui dynasty. With your support and that of 12 of your close and personal friends, Li would have been established as the first emperor of the Tang dynasty. In return, the big guy would have given you and your buddies 600 acres of land, which you would have used to expand your temple (talk about an impressive return on investment!). The emperor also encouraged temple officials to house and train their own soldiers, who served as an elite police force to protect surrounding villages against hordes of marauding bandits.

If you were a monk living in China during the Sung dynasty, from A.D. 960 to 1279, you would likely have traveled across the country to exchange combative ideas. Once you had become very proficient at martial arts and were called a "master," you would have visited temples to train and demonstrate your skills, in what today might be described as trade-convention style!

Monks for Hire

If you were a Shaolin monk during the Manchurian rule of China, from A.D. 1644 to 1911, you would probably have been called upon to test your combative skills in the name of patriotism. Calls to "Overthrow the Qing and Restore the Ming" would have echoed throughout your temple's hallowed halls. This slogan summarized the feelings of the indigenous people, the Han, toward the oppressive Northern Qing dynasty, which was viewed as barbaric and cruel (displaying what in psycholingo could be classified as "anger issues"). The seed of rebellion blossomed, giving rise to secret societies, whose purpose was to encourage Chinese nationalism and prevent efforts toward tyrannical control by outsiders.

At the Shaolin Temple, you and other skilled warriors would have been busy training a disillusioned population. For this reason, you would have been viewed as a threat to the ruling dynasty. Therefore, the emperor Yong Sheng (1722–1735), your basic take-no-prisoners guy, would have ordered the burning of the temple and the mass execution of you and your fellow monks. If you survived, you and your comrades would have continued to teach martial arts as you fled across the country.

State of the Art

Use of the term *Kung Fu,* which can mean "human struggle" or "special skill," became popular in North America in the late 1800s. In China, it was called Chuan Fa (use of the fists) or Wushu (formerly martial art, now martial sport). Given the wide acceptance for the term *Kung Fu,* however, even the Chinese have adopted this westernized name for their martial art.

Master Speaks

Nothing comes easy. There are no low-maintenance (simple) systems or styles. All require effort and commitment, and natural ability counts for little, if anything. As the old Chinese proverb says, "If the power to do hard work is not talent, it is its best possible substitute."

Martial Smarts

It's not line dancing—it's *lion* dancing. Chinese New Year's celebrations often include folk dancing featuring two or more performers outfitted in a lion's costume. This is more than a colorful tradition, as the lion is the mascot of most Kung Fu schools. Great pride is taken in the choreography and execution of the performance, which represents either Northern or Southern styles of Kung Fu. In addition to mimicking the lion's mannerisms, the performers, who are usually martial artists, demonstrate a variety of combative techniques, including low stances, kicks and evasive tactics like rolling and tumbling. Look out Disney World!

Modern Kung Fu is divided into three systems: Koshu (arts of self-defense), Wushu (martial sport) and Chi Kung (exercise for health and longevity).

Kung Fu x 4

There are four types of Kung Fu:

1. Northern styles

2. Southern styles

3. External styles

4. Internal styles

These styles are outlined in the following section.

Warrior Words

There are two types of Chi Kung. One focuses on cultivating general good health (improved circulation, increased range of motion) and an overall sense of well-being. The other, called "Iron Body" Kung Fu, is devoted to the development of martial skill. If you become very good at Chi Kung, you could, at least theoretically, absorb and redirect power from an assailant. Any volunteers?

North versus South

The Yangtze River (Long River) crosses China from east to west.

North of the river, you would find fertile fields, dry steppes and desert, while in the south, where it rains frequently, there are lots of rivers and waterways. This difference in climate and terrain is illustrated in the popular Chinese expression: "Southern boats, northern horses." This saying refers to means of travel used in these two regions. While this might hold true for the wealthy, if you're poor, a more appropriate expression would be "Northern walk, southern sit."

Whether body shape is a function of nature (genetics) or nurture (environment), if you were northern Chinese, you would likely be tall, have long legs and be more slender than your southern neighbors. If, on the other hand, you hailed from the south, you might be shorter and have a stockier build and a stronger upper body. Among Kung Fu practitioners, this difference in body type is summarized as "Fists in the south, kicks in the north."

If you were practicing Southern boxing styles, you would use deep, rooted (firm) stances. One common position is the "horse stance," a variation on the ever-popular squat, where your weight is equally distributed on both legs with the knees bent at a 90-degree angle. You would also assume a "front stance," which is similar to a lunge and requires a weight distribution of 80 percent (on the front leg) and 20 percent (on the rear leg).

As a student of Southern styles, you would use hand techniques like punching, chopping and grabbing. Your blocks would be direct and circular, and most of the time you would deflect rather than intercept attacks. You would use kicks sparingly, generally aiming them at low targets, like the knees and shins.

As a Southern stylist, you would favor close or mid-range defensive tactics that require little or no movement to reach your target. You might use a series of in-close techniques that could finish with an unbalancing, grappling or locking attack.

As a Northern stylist, you would rely on a variety of explosive (quick, dynamic) movements including acrobatic blows with your feet (where you would attempt to execute

Warrior Words

Remember, in martial arts, a "system" incorporates a variety of styles.

Master Speaks

Don't get caught with your pants down! As a Kung Fu student, you would wear a thick sash, approximately 6 to 9 feet (2 to 3 meters) long, to protect your abdomen and lower back. In contrast to the Japanese and Korean belt system, as a beginner you would be outfitted with a black sash. Once you became an expert, you would wear white or gold, symbolizing enlightenment.

two, or even three, kicks while airborne). You would also use high stances coupled with low leg sweeps (off-balancing tactics), and postures balanced on one leg. Your kicks would be performed from kneeling, standing and jumping positions. You would strike with both a closed fist and the palm of your hand. For the most part, you would shift out of the way of an attack, rather than relying on blocking or deflecting movements. You would place very little emphasis on grappling or locking tactics.

As a Northern stylist, you would utilize long-range attacks requiring you to take one or several large steps to reach your target.

Warrior Words

Wushu is an intensely physical sport based on traditional Kung Fu forms (choreographed routines). It is both a martial art and an acrobatic form of entertainment. As a Wushu stylist, you would use death-defying kicks and lightning-fast strikes, dramatic head turns and expressive facial movements (think Peking Opera) coupled with superhuman power, speed and agility.

Risky Moves

Don't jump the gun! Regardless of the style or method you practice, it will take time to develop the ability to defend yourself. For example, it might take 3 to 6 months before you are comfortable with some self-defense techniques.

From the Inside Out

External styles of Kung Fu are derived from "Shaolin Fist" (martial arts that were developed at the Shaolin Temple). They rely on physical conditioning—translation: the stronger you are, the more power you can unleash. If you practice External styles, you could develop large, rippling, Schwarzenegger-esque muscles and thickly callused knuckles, as a result of repeatedly striking heavy bags and padded posts.

Your well-positioned strikes would cause surface, or visible, damage to your target, and while they might bruise, it's unlikely they would be life threatening.

Conversely, if you're an Internal stylist your physique might be closer to Mr. Rogers's than Mr. Schwarzenegger's! You would be concerned with developing your *chi,* or internal energy. You could achieve this by practicing exercises like *nui gung.* This involves focusing your energy "into the depths" of your opponent's body. When practicing *nui gung,* you would perform a series of repetitive movements, breathing techniques that originate in the *tan dien* (a point located 3 inches, or 8 centimeters, below your navel) and balance drills. These could improve your ability to concentrate and help you develop internal power.

As a student of Internal systems, you would generally be required to make a greater time commitment than your External counterparts. Having mastered the nuances of Internal martial arts, you could inflict severe damage on your opponent. As a result, you would use your skills only in life-threatening circumstances.

Warrior Words

You should never be "off-*ki.*" In addition to physical strength, Kung Fu practitioners strive to develop their internal life force, called *chi* or *qi* in Chinese, *ki* in Japanese. This entails using postures that can realign your meridians (invisible energy lines) and transport you to a higher spiritual plane.

Class Action

When you enter a Kung Fu class, regardless of style, you address the individual at the helm as *sifu*, which means "master" or "teacher."

In a typical Kung Fu class, you and your fellow *si-di* (students) would participate in—

➤ warm up, stretching and conditioning exercises

➤ stances and movement drills

➤ hand and elbow strikes

➤ footwork and kicking

➤ blocking and evasion techniques

As a more advanced student, you would also practice:

➤ forms with and without weapons

➤ pressure-point training

➤ takedowns and sweeps

➤ ground fighting

➤ healing techniques using medicines and massage

You would use special Kung Fu training equipment, including the following:

➤ heavy bag (large cloth bag) filled with sand that you can hit or kick to produce powerful hand and foot techniques

➤ square bag filled with rice, beans or pebbles that you can strike to condition your hands and arms

Master Speaks

If you were practicing Iron Body Kung Fu, a type of Chi Kung, you would perform a series of isometric and deep breathing exercises, which are done slowly, with dynamic, deliberate tension in each muscle group. These are designed to strengthen different parts of your body, including your throat, forehead, chest, rib cage, groin and legs.

Risky Moves

It's not safe to strike hard targets early in your training. If you want to condition your fingers, fists, palms and feet, begin by striking soft surfaces and gradually progress to those that offer more resistance.

➤ wooden dummy (*mook jong*) with movable "arms" and "legs" that you can use to improve your blocking, catching, striking and kicking skills, as well as your timing and coordination abilities

These are three of the most popular training apparatus.

The Least You Need to Know

➤ Kung Fu, the westernized name for Chuan Fa or Wushu, is a popular Chinese martial art that was developed and spread by Buddhist monks.

➤ Many Kung Fu styles are based on animal movements.

➤ Kung Fu has three distinct systems: Koshu (self-defense arts), Wushu (martial sport) and Chi Kung (health and longevity exercises).

➤ There are four styles of Kung Fu: Northern, Southern, Internal and External.

➤ Under the supervision of a teacher or master, who is called *sifu,* as a Kung Fu student, you can use a variety of apparatus to enhance your training.

➤ Some of the reasons for you to study Kung Fu include learning self-defense skills, improving your health and, perhaps, entering martial arts competitions.

Getting Technical

The photographs on the following pages illustrate typical Kung Fu techniques that you would perform as a student of this martial art.

Figure 13–1 (a, b, and c)

Figure 13–2 (a, b, and c)

Chapter 14

The Samurai Martial Art of Jiu-jitsu

In This Chapter

➤ Investigating samurai martial arts

➤ Understanding the evolution of major types of Jiu-jitsu

➤ Learning about the ranking system

➤ Some benefits of Jiu-jitsu practice

➤ Training techniques

Even if you know nothing about Japanese samurai or the martial art of Jiu-jitsu, you probably have seen or at least heard of great films like *The Seven Samurai* (or its American knockoff, *The Magnificent Seven*). You might also have read Miyamoto Musashi's *Book of Five Rings* or comic books romanticizing the samurai lifestyle.

These movies and books continue to create knowledge and awareness about the samurai subculture. They stand in tribute to brave individuals who represent the Eastern counterpart to the Western hero.

This chapter will help you understand the martial art of these mysterious warriors—Jiu-jitsu.

The Cult of the Samurai

By the third century, although Japan appeared to be a unified country governed by a single ruler, the reality was that numerous clan leaders, or *daimyo*, ruled the country.

Martial Smarts

Like Miss Manners, the well-behaved samurai had rules to follow in order to maintain proper etiquette. These rules are still greatly valued in modern Jiu-jitsu schools today.

These powerful individuals were lawmakers who had large, private armies. Within the ranks of their military forces, the elite samurai did the bulk of the fighting.

Law and Order

If you were a *daimyo* living at this time, you would have helped create the Eight Principles of a Warrior. These were rules based on Confucian laws of human behavior and included guidelines to govern fair play, even when you and other *daimyo* were pillaging and plundering.

The Eight Principles of a Warrior are—

➤ 1. *Jin* – Develop a sympathetic understanding of all people.

➤ 2. *Gi* – Preserve correct ethics.

➤ 3. *Cho* – Demonstrate loyalty to your master.

➤ 4. *Ko* – Respect and care for your parents.

➤ 5. *Rei* – Show respect for others.

➤ 6. *Chi* – Enhance wisdom by broadening your knowledge.

➤ 7. *Shin* – Remain truthful at all times.

➤ 8. *Tei* – Care for the aged and those of humble station.

From time to time, as a *daimyo,* you might have wondered if this code of behavior proved a source of comfort for overtaxed peasants, merchants and neighboring lords. Could they, having recently had their land destroyed and their property appropriated, rest more easily knowing that the hired mob that had just attacked them operated with a higher purpose in mind?

Operating as a sort of Robin Hood in reverse, you and other regional lords would have taken from the poor and, once your coffers grew, given to the rich in the form of lavish gifts. With vast financial resources at your and other clan leaders' disposal, like good CEOs or even families on a budget, you would have constructed leaner, meaner organizations that would provide significantly more bang for your investment buck. So, you would have replaced foot soldiers, barely dressed, armed with only the crudest of weapons and the simplest of combative skills, with a new breed of superwarrior—the samurai.

Warrior Words

The word *samurai* means "one who serves."

Über-*Soldiers*

Imagine yourself as a samurai serving your lord during this period. You would have been an *"über*-soldier," mounted on horseback, clad in lightweight body armor and equipped with state-of-the-art weapons. Like modern executives in boardrooms today, you would have been a professional warrior, handsomely compensated for your services. With paycheck and purpose in mind, you would have braced for a "hostile takeover" and faced the battlefield with new commitment.

In order to understand the philosophy behind the warrior mask, you might want to trek off to your local video store and rent classic samurai films. Celluloid celebs such as Toshiro Mifune (Japan's answer to John Wayne or Clint Eastwood) will undoubtedly impress you as you watch the star neatly dispatch dozens of attackers in a nanosecond. Faster than you can say "Cuisinart," the samurai's glittering sword will "slice 'n' dice" until he, alone, remains.

No Macramé, Please!

In years gone by, as a highly skilled samurai, you would've had to practice, practice, practice! When you were not invading neighboring territories, you would devote every waking hour to perfecting each combative element, with your training revolving around the Twenty-Three Arts of the Samurai.

While macramé, home economics and early child care are *not* among required areas of study, the Twenty-Three Arts of the Samurai do consist of the following:

➤ 1. *Kyu-jitsu* – bow and arrow techniques

➤ 2. *Ba-jitsu* – horse-riding skills

➤ 3. *Ken-jitsu* – sword-fighting skills

➤ 4. *So-jitsu* – small-point spear techniques

➤ 5. *Naginata-jitsu* – long-blade spear techniques

➤ 6. *Sumo* – unclad grappling

➤ 7. *Kumi-uchi* – armor grappling

➤ 8. *Genkotsu* – assaulting vital points

➤ 9. *Jiu-jitsu* – hand-to-hand combat (some weapons use)

➤ 10. *Uchi-ne* – hand-throwing arrows

➤ 11. *Iai-jitsu* – art of sword "quick draws"

➤ 12. *Shuriken-jitsu* – throwing bladed weapons

➤ 13. *Fuki-bari* – blowing needles from your mouth

➤ 14. *Gekigan-jitsu* – using a ball and chain

➤ 15. *Chigiriki-jitsu* – employing a pole and heavy chain

➤ 16. *Jutte-jitsu* – using a metal truncheon

➤ 17. *Tessen-jitsu* – application of an iron hand fan

➤ 18. *Tetsubo-jitsu* – handling a long iron rod

➤ 19. *Bo-jitsu* – staff art

➤ 20. *Jo-jitsu* – stick art

➤ 21. *Kusariga-jitsu* – use of a sickle and chain

➤ 22. *Sodegarami-jitsu* – employing a barbed pole

➤ 23. *Sasumata-jitsu* – entrapping with a forked staff

Like Sun-tzu's *The Art of War* or Musashi's *Book of Five Rings,* this training guide would have prepared you and other samurai for even the toughest battle. Could it—with some obvious editing—aid today's rising executives as they prepare for the heat of corporate conflict? Or, on the family front, might it help parents and children resolve their differences? We caution you to refrain from "blowing needles from your mouths" or "entrapping (someone) with a forked staff." Furthermore, "employing a barbed pole" or "unclad grappling" (ouch) might be viewed as career-limiting, and relationship-damaging, moves!

As a samurai, you would also have been skilled in the areas of camouflage, swimming and fighting in water while wearing armor, and the use of fire as a weapon or for signaling. You would even have been schooled in the fine art of *retreating* from a losing battle.

Martial Smarts

Only the samurai, who were considered to be upper-middle class, were permitted to carry two swords. These weapons were both a status symbol and an indication of their owner's martial prowess. The *katana,* or long sword, and *waki-zashi,* or short sword, were worn in the belt *(obi)* during the Momoyama (1573–1603) and Edo (1603–1868) periods.

Birth of the "Gentle Method"

Jiu-jitsu is a composite martial art incorporating striking, kicking, throwing and seizing. It existed in Japan for centuries and closely resembles its Chinese predecessor, Shaolin Kung Fu. It has had various regional names throughout history. The list of names includes *Tai-jitsu,* which means "way of unbalancing," *Kempo* (fist law), *Gyakute* (reversing hand), *Koshi no Mawari* (hip throwing) and *Sumai* (wrestling to the ground).

Martial artists agree that Jiu-jitsu originated from three probable sources. The first was visiting Buddhist teachers from China who were skilled in the "ways of the Shaolin Fist." The second was samurai warriors seeking ways to unbalance or restrain their opponent while wearing armor. The last was commoners with a need to develop personal protection skills to cope with the challenges of daily life. In all likelihood, Jiu-jitsu stemmed from all three sources.

Warrior Words

It was not until the seventeenth century that the more popular name, Jiu-jitsu, meaning "gentle method" or "lighting method," came into use.

Study, Study, Study

Though perhaps not the first *ryu* (school) of Jiu-jitsu, the first recorded learning center for this art was Take-ryu, founded by Takenouchi Hisamori in the seventeenth century.

If you were a Jiu-jitsu student training in this center at this time, you would have followed a curriculum that included—

➤ kicking

➤ striking

➤ kneeing

➤ throwing

➤ choking

➤ joint-locking

➤ using weapons

➤ restraining an enemy

Master Speaks

A little restraint goes a long, long way! If you want to gently control an opponent without risk of severe injury, you can use a number of restraint techniques, commonly referred to as "come-alongs." These might come in handy when escorting an aggressor who has had one too many bottles of *sake!*

The Golden Age of Jiu-jitsu

From the late seventeenth to the mid-nineteenth century, Jiu-jitsu's "Golden Age," hundreds of schools appeared, all teaching their version of this martial art.

Throughout the prefectures (provinces), schools sprang up, usually near Buddhist or Shinto temples. Training outdoors in the temples' courtyards and gardens ensured practitioners would have ample space. In an effort to cover their bases, these training centers, more often than not, bore both a spiritual name and the name of the founder.

This provided a type of omnipotent insurance coverage for the growth of these schools. (Hey, when it comes to the fighting arts, it doesn't hurt to have the deities on your side.)

Predictably, as gun-powdered weapons made their appearance, the need for hand-to-hand combat skills among the military began to disintegrate, and the preservation of these techniques was entrusted to the civilian population.

And, as in China, the infusion of religio-philosophical beliefs resulted in the dilution of combative skills, and many Jiu-jitsu schools slipped into oblivion.

Today, dedicated practitioners, the majority of whom are Westerners, continue to work tirelessly to revitalize and propagate Jiu-jitsu. They are motivated by the belief that this martial art, when taught in its true form, can offer you one of the best methods of self-defense, and perhaps more importantly, serve as a unique vehicle for self-improvement.

From the Battlefield to the "Cage"

If you were practicing Jiu-jitsu during the feudal period (1185–1868), your combative traditions were handed down on a one-to-one basis. As a recipient of this information, you would have to be a member of a select group of highly devoted practitioners. As such, it's unlikely you would have abandoned your passion for the martial arts in favor of, say, golf or tennis.

With the dawn of the twentieth century, interest in the martial arts shifted and hobbyists contributed to the splintering of complete systems of combat. Niche styles like *Tai-jitsu* (a method of throwing an opponent to the ground) and *Nihon Kempo* (specialized methods of striking an adversary) emerged.

As a practitioner with limited access to more diversified systems, you, like other students during this period, would have migrated from teacher to teacher, rather than bonding with a single instructor. This migration, or more precisely cross-pollination, would give rise to a multitude of hybrid systems. Over time, methods of grappling and striking would be fused together and renamed *Nihon* (Japanese) Jiu-jitsu. This replaced classical Jiu-jitsu.

Modern Jiu-jitsu "101"

During this time, in a typical class, you would step onto the *tatami* (Japanese mats made of rice straw) and begin practicing numerous Jiu-jitsu techniques.

These techniques include—

➤ *jitsu taiso* – coordination exercises to improve your reaction time

➤ *ukemi waza* – breakfalls (methods of landing safely)

➤ *tai sabaki* – body shifting and avoidance

➤ *uchi* and *keri waza* – striking and kicking

➤ *atemi waza* – pressure-point control (striking and manipulating vital areas)

➤ *shime waza* – neck restraints

➤ *torite waza* – joint restraints

➤ *nage waza* – throwing

➤ *suwari waza* – defending yourself from standing, sitting and kneeling positions

Martial Smarts

Innue Shian, founder of Hontai Yoshin-ryu Jiu-jitsu, in comparing the attitude of beginners and advanced practitioners, said, "Novice Jiu-jitsu students worry about making big gains; experts pay attention to the smallest detail."

"X-Treme" Jiu-jitsu

Classical Jiu-jitsu stems from samurai arts that were based on battlefield strategies. Modern Jiu-jitsu was born of a need for people to defend themselves against violence of a more personal nature. The next generation of this martial art, which could be dubbed "X-Treme" Jiu-jitsu, a.k.a. "reality bouts" (no-holds-barred, anything-goes contests involving striking, kicking and grappling), is the hot ticket on pay television.

If you were a student or instructor eager to capitalize on this trend toward blood-sport contests, you would likely forget about the history, culture and philosophy of the martial arts. Your opponent's submission would be your ambition. Mastering techniques where you would compel—in the strongest sense of the word—your opponents to "tap-out" (tap the mat to

Risky Moves

Learn to go with the flow. When practicing Jiu-jitsu, it's important to redirect, not oppose, your partner's force. If you weigh 120 pounds (54 kilograms), it could be dangerous to meet the attack of a 250-pound (113 kilograms) person head-on! Instead, redirect your partner's weight by shifting your body and employing a technique called "blending." As the great Jiu-jitsu master Okuyama Yoshiji put it, "when pushed, pull... when pulled, push."

indicate they no longer can continue the bout) is the only thing that would matter to you and other advocates of this ultraviolent type of martial arts.

The First Family of fighting of the octagonal variety (so named because bouts are generally conducted in octagonally shaped cages—yes, *cages*) are the Brazilian brawlers, "The Fabulous Fighting Gracies."

As a teenager growing up in South America, Carlos Gracie trained with the great Japanese teacher Maedakama Hitsui. The young Gracie was a skilled street fighter who combined Maedakama's grappling techniques with Western-style boxing. This amalgam, a lethal style that was refined on the streets of Rio de Janeiro, enabled Carlos to confront and defeat all challengers.

Carlos's younger brother, Helio, has been called one of the most gifted Jiu-jitsu practitioners in the world. Helio, a natural athlete, moved with pantherlike agility. He is famous for issuing challenges to martial artists throughout South America and later, North America, inviting them to demonstrate their skills in no-holds-barred bouts. The match wouldn't end until someone was knocked unconscious or tapped out.

Helio brought Brazilian Jiu-jitsu, and his sizable family, to the United States. His sons, Rorion, Royce and Rickson, continue to be virtually unbeatable.

Your Rewards

Jiu-jitsu is first and foremost a system of self-defense that can give you a feeling of confidence and peace of mind.

Beyond the obvious physical benefits, as a Jiu-jitsu student, you can develop a strong spirit and a "can do" attitude that can positively impact other areas of your life. Quite frequently, this development is inextricably linked to advancement and achievement of rank.

Warrior Ranking System

Historically, Jiu-jitsu has had a dual ranking system. The traditional rank method is based on the warrior classes of yesteryear and awards *menkyo* (certificates of proficiency). A more modern version is the belt and *dan* (degree) system similar to that used by other martial arts. Schools that adhere to the traditional system generally award merit certificates at the novice, intermediate and advanced levels. Some schools also present the award of *menkyo* to teachers, and *menkyo kaiden* to instructors who are more proficient. In *dojo* (schools) that follow the modern ranking structure, however, individuals are classified by their level of ability and the length of time they have studied martial arts.

Warrior Words

Many Japanese words are spelled and pronounced the same way in both the plural and singular forms. For example, the Japanese word for one or several martial arts schools is *dojo*.

Modern Ranking System

The modern version mirrors the one established by the legendary founder of Judo, Kano Jigoro. Kano Sensei was the son of a successful *sake* mill owner. As a member of the merchant or lower class, rather than the elite samurai class, he was undoubtedly all too familiar with the limitations of a rigid social system. Therefore, his goal was to develop a martial arts ranking system that would be devoid of class distinction. His system rewards the ability and commitment of the student, and is structured as follows.

The beginner levels are—

➤ *Jukyu* – Tenth Level

➤ *Kukyu* – Ninth Level

➤ *Hachikyu* – Eighth Level

➤ *Shichikyu* – Seventh Level

➤ *Rokukyu* – Sixth Level

➤ *Gokyu* – Fifth Level

➤ *Yonkyu* – Fourth Level

➤ *Sankyu* – Third Level

➤ *Nikyu* – Second Level

➤ *Ikkyu* – First Level

After the above-noted color belt tiers are several degrees *(dan)* of Black Belt, which qualify as the intermediate levels:

169

➤ *Shodan* – First Degree

➤ *Nidan* – Second Degree

➤ *Sandan* – Third Degree

➤ *Yondan* – Fourth Degree

The expert levels are—

➤ *Godan* – Fifth Degree

➤ *Rokudan* – Sixth Degree

➤ *Shichidan* – Seventh Degree

➤ *Hachidan* – Eighth Degree

And finally, the master levels are—

➤ *Kyudan* – Ninth Degree

➤ *Judan* – Tenth Degree

Your Jiu-jitsu Class

When you enter a Jiu-jitsu *dojo* (which means "place of learning the way" or "school") for the first time, you'll notice that the floor is covered with a thick, padded material. This will help protect you and other students as you learn to fall and roll.

The teacher, or *sensei,* will guide your class through numerous drills, including—

➤ conditioning exercises (such as those to strengthen the neck)

➤ breakfalls (methods of landing safely)

➤ maneuver drills performed from the ground

➤ methods of forcing your opponent to the mat (padded floor)

➤ restraint and immobilization techniques

The average class might last 1 or 2 hours, and most students attend two to three practice sessions per week. Jiu-jitsu can be a highly demanding, physical art that can provide you with a well-rounded fitness program: cardiovascular endurance, stretching and strengthening exercises, combined with effective self-defense skills.

You might devote a lifetime to your study, or train for a shorter period of time. You could prepare for competition or simply regard Jiu-jitsu from a recreational standpoint. Whatever your motivation, clearly, Jiu-jitsu can provide you with invaluable skills, as well as a broad range of physical, mental and spiritual benefits.

The Least You Need to Know

➤ The samurai, or warrior class of feudal Japan, often served as mercenaries (paid soldiers) and obeyed a strict code of behavior, which was based on Confucian philosophy.

➤ Ancient Japanese combat systems that incorporated striking, kicking, throwing and seizing evolved into Jiu-jitsu.

➤ Ultramodern versions of this martial art include "X-Treme" Jiu-jitsu, in the form of pay-per-view caged bouts.

➤ Some Jiu-jitsu students practice their chosen art for competition; others have a more recreational interest. Some will train for years or even decades; others may be interested for a shorter span of time.

➤ While Jiu-jitsu continues to be practiced as a means of self-defense, it is, more importantly, viewed as a method for perfecting your character.

Getting Technical

The photographs on the following pages show the types of techniques you would learn as a Jiu-jitsu student.

Risky Moves

The majority of Jiu-jitsu's self-defense strategies focus on throwing and grappling. To ensure you practice safely, these techniques should be performed on a cushioned surface under the supervision of more experienced students or your *sensei.*

Master Speaks

Make a fashion statement. Be sure to wear a Jiu-jitsu uniform *(gi)* made of heavily woven canvas, designed to withstand the rigors of training (grabbing and pulling). Depending upon the quality of this uniform, it can cost anywhere from $50 (basic model) to $150 for a top-name brand. (Jean Paul Gaultier does not design a *gi*—if he did, this price structure would, obviously, be dramatically different!)

Figure 14–1 (a, b, and c)

Figure 14–2 (a, b, and c)

Chapter 15

Navigating Karate's Sea of Styles

In This Chapter

➤ Understanding how a tiny island nation developed Karate

➤ Discovering the differences between Okinawan and Japanese Karate

➤ How Karate made its way to mainland Japan

➤ Four people who changed the course of martial arts history

➤ Most popular styles of Japanese Karate

If there is one martial arts term that has become a household word, it's *Karate,* which means "empty hand." This combative system enjoys worldwide popularity. Regardless of where you live, you know that a pajama-clad expert can smash a pile of bricks faster than you can say "Van Damme!"

But if your Karate knowledge is limited to what you've learned at your neighborhood multiplex movie theater, then read on!

Tropical Punch

The island of Okinawa, located on the Ryukyu archipelago in the East China Sea, is a tropical paradise with pristine beaches, exotic birds and abundant vegetation. Glorious flora and fauna are contrasted, almost schizophrenically, against the familiar golden arches of McDonald's and red roofs of Pizza Hut. The island's lush landscape is punctuated with convenience stores and gas stations.

This paradoxical patchwork extends to Okinawa's culture, which is a mélange of native, Chinese, Japanese and, relatively recently, American influences. It has also had an impact on Okinawan combative styles and disciplines, which in turn, have contributed in no small way to the global popularity of the martial arts.

Although Okinawa has played an essential role in spreading martial arts around the world, little is known about the origins of its indigenous system of self-defense, called *Ti* or *Te*. What *is* known about the evolution of Okinawan martial arts is detailed in the next section.

Warrior Words

The first written record of the name *Ryukyu,* or *Loo Chew* in Chinese, appeared in A.D 608. The name of these islands was changed to Okinawa in 1879.

The Sum of Its Parts

When you're examining the evolution of Okinawan martial arts, you'll come across lots of myths and legends. There are, however, three known contributing factors that are at the center of the development of these systems.

➤ **Mainland Warrior Arts** Frequently, after wars in mainland Japan, soldiers would wander the countryside to rest and regroup. Okinawan *anji*, or chieftain rulers, welcomed these highly skilled martial castaways, who possessed formidable fighting skills, coupled with all-important experience.

➤ **The Chinese Connection** As far back as the Tang dynasty (A.D. 618–907), historical records show contact between Okinawa and China. During the fourteenth century, a Ming dynasty official advised Okinawans that their country

Martial Smarts

It's a family affair. In 1393, a Chinese mission was established in the thriving commercial center of Okinawa, Naha city, where 36 Chinese families had settled in Kume village. Among other things, these settlers brought with them a wealth of knowledge about Chinese fighting traditions. In addition to these families' taking up permanent residence in Okinawa, frequent trade missions would be conducted for the next five centuries. Goods and raw materials from Okinawa flowed into China. In exchange, *sapposhi,* special envoys appointed by the Chinese government, would aid Okinawa's development in a variety of categories. These individuals were artists, technicians, teachers and martial arts experts who shared their skills with local residents.

would become a tributary colony of China. Exchange with China also included sharing martial arts.

➤ **Ryukyu Kingdom Weapons Ban**
For centuries, the *anji* struggled to achieve domination and personal wealth. Although the leadership of the Sho clan enjoyed growing stability, the threat of regional lords loomed large. In an effort to control these regional nobles, King Sho Shin, who ruled from A.D. 1477 to 1527, instituted a law forbidding anyone other than members of the ruling class from possessing weapons.

With an unarmed population surrounded by skilled soldiers with steel-bladed weapons, the comfort zone of the ruling elite increased several fold. Unbeknownst to the nobility, the weapons ban simply led to the growth of empty-hand systems. In addition to hand-to-hand fighting skills, these systems incorporated ordinary items like the wood staff *(bo)*, oars *(eku)* and sickles *(kama)*, which quickly took on a new role as implements for personal defense.

Master Speaks

Empty-handed versus empty-headed! The romantic image of peasants fending off attacks with nothing more than their hands and feet is a fallacy. Most teachers in Okinawa believed in balancing unarmed and armed combat practice. The latter can help you develop strength and coordination.

Martial Smarts

The "father of modern Karate," Funakoshi Gichin, believed in the life-affirming properties of the martial arts, evident by the fact that he said, "The ultimate aim of Karate-do does not lie in victory or defeat, but in perfection of the character of its practitioners."

What You Should Know about the Debut of *Kara-te*

Since the tenth century, Okinawa's native *Ti* was combined with Chinese and Japanese martial arts to form one, unified system. In the seventeenth and eighteenth centuries, this system was labeled *Kara-te* or "China hand," and was quickly adopted by Okinawa's warrior and merchant classes as a means of personal protection. If you lived in a rural farming and fishing village during this time, you and your neighbors would probably have practiced a simplified form of Karate for self-defense purposes.

As a Karate-*ka* (Karate student), your arsenal stretches from your fingertips to your toes. At the turn of the twentieth century (and even in some schools today), you would have relied on extreme training measures to fortify each weapon. You would have struck *makiwara* (padded posts) and trees, or hit heavy sand-filled bags. Additionally, you would have lifted heavy rocks and jars as a means of developing strength. These seemingly masochistic training methods certainly lend credence to the old saying "That which does not kill you will make you stronger."

Ti Time for Three Okinawan Karate Systems

Martial historians estimate that, until the seventeenth century, there was one form of empty-hand combat in Okinawa. It was called *Ti* or *Te,* which means "hand." Over time, three regional Karate systems emerged. Each displayed unique characteristics and bore the name of the area in which it was developed: *Shuri-te,* named for the capital of the Ryukyu Kingdom; *Naha-te,* which originated in the commercial center; and *Tomari-te,* which came from the port of the same name. Let's look at these three primary systems.

Shuri-te

Shuri, the area surrounding Shuri-jo, the city's castle, was the seat of the Sho ruling class. It was populated by Ryukyu nobles called *anji.* If you were a member of this elite social group, you would have been born with a silver chopstick in your mouth, and your household would have included bodyguards and other security personnel who were assigned to protect your family. In addition, teachers, who were scholars and martial arts experts, would have tutored your children. You and your family would likely have become skilled in a martial style characterized by fast linear movements and agile footwork, performed from a tall, natural stance. The most popular modern Karate style that emerged from the *Shuri-te* system is *Shorin-ryu,* which means "young forest style."

Naha-te

This system was practiced in Naha, which was then the commercial hub of the Ryukyu Kingdom. If you studied the unique elements of this style, you would have learned circular hand movements (due to the influence of Chinese martial arts), deep breathing and low, rooted stances, combined with body conditioning drills. If you were an Okinawan trader, you would have conducted business in this area with representatives from abroad. Trade would have included the exchange of manufactured goods and agricultural products. *Sake* (rice wine) and *awamori* (a strong, clear alcoholic drink), which were really valuable, were also exchanged. If you were hiring individuals to safeguard these lucrative items, you would have looked for people who possessed top-of-the-line martial skills. The most popular modern Karate style that evolved from the *Naha-te* system is *Goju-ryu,* which means "hard and soft style."

Tomari-te

As the Ryukyu Kingdom's port and fishing center, Tomari was home to several popular drinking-and-dining establishments (most of which would not have been listed in the *Michelin Guide* of the period). If you were a *sake*-soaked seafarer, you and your drinking buddies would probably have been skilled in Chinese martial arts, which employed open-hand strikes, low kicks and sweeping techniques. While no single style emerged from the *Tomari-te* system, many of its techniques are still easily recognizable in the moves of modern practitioners.

Master Speaks

You can clean up by "sweeping." This does not refer to tidying your home with the aid of a broom, but rather, to leg and hand off-balancing tactics that force your opponent to fall. In addition to striking and hitting, sweeping is an important defensive skill.

It's a Question of Style

A "style" of Karate is, quite simply, the teaching methods and personal beliefs of its founder. While individual ideology may differ slightly and training methods may be at opposite ends of the teaching spectrum, there is no single style that is "best."

There are two primary Karate systems: Okinawan and Japanese. At the turn of the twentieth century, Okinawan martial arts arrived in mainland Japan. Both systems have changed dramatically since their debut.

The following are general characteristics that apply to most Okinawan styles, including *Shorin-ryu, Goju-ryu, Uechi-ryu, Matsubayashi-ryu, Isshin-ryu* and Okinawan *Kempo*. They are contrasted with general characteristics of Japanese styles like *Shotokan, Shito-ryu, Goju-kai, Kyokushin-kai* and *Wado-ryu*.

If you were an Okinawan Karate stylist, you would use soft, circular blocks to thwart an attack. You would then grab an opponent's arms or legs to exert control. On the other hand, if you were a Japanese practitioner, you would use direct powerful blocks to deflect an attack and generally not follow up with a grab.

As an Okinawan Karate student, you would view the entire body—from fingertips to toes—as a natural weapon. As a Japanese stylist, you would rely on a closed fist and the ball of the foot as your primary weapons.

Your stances as an Okinawan practitioner would be fairly high (upright), resulting in more natural movement when fighting. As a Japanese martial artist, you would use lower stances allowing greater range of hip movement (rotation) and enabling you to generate more power when striking.

As an Okinawan practitioner, you might terminate a bout with a restraining or controlling technique. If, however, you are practicing Japanese Karate, you might depend on a powerful finishing blow, coupled with a piercing yell *(kiai)* to bring an attack to an end.

Risky Moves

For adults only: the *makiwara* (striking post) should not be used by children, as the bones of their hands are still developing. Generally, around the age of 16, teenagers can begin this type of training under the supervision of an experienced instructor.

Martial Smarts

Your place or mine? Karate legend, Funakoshi Gichin, when discussing the benefits of martial arts training both inside and outside the traditional classroom, said: "Some youthful enthusiasts of Karate believe that it can be learned only from instructors in a dojo, but such individuals are mere technicians, not true 'karate-ka.' There is an old saying...any place can be a dojo and...anyone who wants to follow the way of Karate must never forget 'Karate-do' is not only the acquisition of certain defensive skills, but also, the mastery of the art of being a good and honest member of society."

Your Okinawan Karate training would emphasize *kihon* (basic drills), *kata* (choreographed routines designed to improve your blocking, striking and shifting skills), *yoku soku kumite* (sparring sequences) and conditioning drills utilizing a variety of implements like the *makiwara* (striking post). As a Japanese Karate student, you, too, would practice *kihon* and *kata,* with free sparring (unrehearsed attacks and counterattacks) and heavy bag work rounding off your training.

Karate's Fantastic Foursome

While countless individuals played an instrumental role in the development of martial systems, four teachers—who today would be labeled a "Karate Dream Team"—are credited with making an impressive impact on the advancement of the combative arts.

➤ **Martial Arts' Goodwill Ambassador** Higaonna Kanryo was born in 1853 to a poor family in Naha city. His martial arts teachers, or *sensei,* were Arakaki Seisho and the famous Chinese master Ru Ru Ko (also called Wan Shien Ling). He died in 1916, but was famous for creating and organizing a variety of Okinawan and Chinese martial techniques, which would become *Goju-ryu*. Like many masters who develop their own style, he named a successor to carry on his martial arts teachings after his death. This individual was Miyagi Chojun, a very famous *Goju-ryu* expert.

➤ **The "Hard and Soft" Teacher** Miyagi Chojun lived from 1888 to 1953. As noted, he inherited and modernized the teachings of Higaonna Kanryo. Like his teacher and many other martial arts experts, he traveled to Fuchou, China, where he studied *Kempo* (Chinese Kung Fu). Miyagi Sensei was one of the most famous Okinawan masters who traveled to mainland Japan to teach his brand of martial arts, *Goju-ryu,* which became a very popular style.

➤ **The Safety Conscious Sensei** Itosu Anko was born in 1830 and studied with several famous martial arts teachers, including Matsumura Sokon. Itosu Sensei was proud of his strong striking ability, which resulted from a strengthening method that involved hitting stalks of bamboo with his bare hands. After a somewhat wild youth, a more subdued Itosu sought to develop a safer brand of Karate. This required the retooling of several *kata*, eliminating many lethal techniques. This was not entirely acceptable to his martial arts peers, and was met with considerable criticism. His teaching emphasized physical and mental conditioning rather than self-defense exclusively. It was introduced into the Okinawan school system in the early twentieth century. Like many modern teachers, he also promoted the other benefits of a martial arts education: developing self-discipline, self-esteem and self-confidence in practitioners of all ages. Itosu Sensei passed away in 1915. While many of his students continued his martial tradition, the most famous of these was Funakoshi Gichin.

➤ **The Father of Modern Karate**
Funakoshi Gichin, born in 1869, is called "the father of modern Karate." He was also a prolific writer who founded a popular style of Karate that would later be called *Shotokan*. As noted, he was a student of Itosu Anko. Funakoshi Sensei also trained with some of the most notable teachers of the period, including Azato Anko and Matsumura Sensei. On numerous occasions in the early 1900s, Funakoshi Sensei was invited to demonstrate Okinawan Karate on the mainland. There, he was befriended by the famous founder of Judo, Kano Jigoro, who persuaded Funakoshi to remain in Tokyo. In 1936, after teaching in several universities, Funakoshi established his own *dojo*, which would bear his pen name, *Shotokan*, meaning "house of the whispering pines." After his death in 1957, this became the name of the popular style that is currently practiced by more than six million people worldwide. Like Itosu, Funakoshi Sensei believed martial arts training would enlighten practitioners while offering the additional benefits of improved health and increased longevity.

Master Speaks

Japanese people list their last name first and their first name last (example: Smith Anne). Your title would be presented after your family name. If you were a Karate teacher, you would be Smith Sensei.

Warrior Words

The word *ryu* means "school" or "style." Traditionally, martial arts experts who launched their own *ryu* generally passed their knowledge, and the title for that style, on to their children or favorite students.

Risky Moves

Don't get stuck in a time warp. Some martial arts schools employ only the training methods that were taught to the teachers by their predecessors. More progressive schools may maintain a traditional, or classical, foundation infused with modern training methods. Were he alive today, forward-thinking Master Funakoshi might have used water-filled heavy bags!

Martial Smarts

One of the first events that brought Okinawa's fighting prowess to the attention of the mainland was a well-publicized boxing contest held in Kyoto in 1921. A European boxing champion invited anyone with combative ability of any kind to engage in a pugilistic contest. As no one else accepted this challenge, an Okinawan Karate teacher, Motobu Choki, entered the ring and faced this most formidable of opponents. Dwarfed by the European, the diminutive Motobu released an impressive *kiai* (Karate yell of spirit) and felled the boxer with a single blow. As his youthful opponent lay motionless for some time, the 51-year-old Karate master bowed and exited the ring.

To the Mainland or Bust

Once transplanted to the mainland, Okinawan Karate began to enjoy widespread acceptance.

In sharp contrast to classical Japanese styles of combat like Jiu-jitsu and *Ken-jitsu,* which were steeped in etiquette and formality, Okinawan Karate took a more meat-and-potatoes approach to self-defense.

Additionally, unlike these other martial arts, Karate could be taught to large groups of students by one teacher at the same time. In the early 1920s and 1930s, it was not uncommon to see 100 or more students, under the direction of one Karate teacher, practicing in university gyms. Conversely, *bugei* (classical martial arts) relied on a low student-instructor ratio, generally one or, at most, a few students to each teacher.

Supported by the Japanese Ministry of Education, which viewed Karate as a valuable tool in molding the bodies and minds of the country's future leaders, this martial art continued to flourish. Furthermore, the Japanese government had a less noble agenda in encouraging the spread of combative arts. It aimed to develop a strong army while cultivating a sense of national pride in the country's youth.

Japanese "Super Styles"

While there may be dozens of recognized styles of Japanese Karate, five dominate the field. Let's discover something about each of these "super styles."

➤ *Shotokan*   This is a very popular martial art practiced by more than six million men, women and children around the world. It was founded by Funakoshi Gichin and further popularized by his students Nakayama Masatoshi and Nishiyama Hidetaka. As a Shotokan student, you would practice a style characterized by low stances, broad open movements, pronounced hip rotation resulting in increased power, and thrusting kicks.

➤ *Goju-ryu*   The name of this style means "hard and soft." Goju-ryu is a popular style that was developed by Miyagi Chojun and popularized by the martial arts legend Yamaguchi Gogen (nicknamed "The Cat" because of his felinelike speed and prowess). As a Goju practitioner, you would use small, narrow steps (designed to protect your groin), open hand strikes and elbow and knee techniques, all of which are appropriate self-defense tactics for in-close combat.

➤ *Shito-ryu*   Mabuni Kenwa, who lived from 1889 to 1952, combined the circular movements of Goju with the straight-line techniques of Shorin-ryu to create this style. If you were studying Shito-ryu, you would use soft blocks and fast counterstrikes and place little emphasis on grappling with your opponent. Instead, you would probably prefer to kick and strike quickly to defend yourself. Your Shito-ryu syllabus would include more than 50 self-defense routines, called *kata*.

➤ *Wado-ryu*   Wado-ryu, or "way of harmony," was developed by Otsuka Hidenori, who was born in 1892. He trained with Funakoshi Sensei and a variety of Jiu-jitsu teachers. If you were practicing Wado-ryu, you would rely on a combination of the direct, linear techniques of Shotokan, together with Jiujitsu's softer, grappling movements. This combination, according to Otsuka Sensei, is "a softer, more natural means of self-protection." The name also illustrates its founder's ultimate goal, which was the use of Karate to stop conflicts in a nonviolent way, and to create *wa*, which means a "harmonious existence" or "ultimate peace."

Warrior Words

What's in a name? The difference between *Karate* or *Karate-jitsu* and *Karate-do* can be summarized as follows: In Okinawa, *Karate-jitsu*, with the suffix meaning "technique" or "true technique," was used solely as a fighting art. *Do*, on the other hand, means "way" or "path" and was adopted to demonstrate the new purpose of this martial art—as a vehicle for self-perfection.

Master Speaks

Remember: many martial arts styles or techniques mimic the movements of animals. In the immortal wisdom of Muhammad Ali, "Float like a butterfly, sting like a bee."

Martial Smarts

Oyama Masatatsu was renowned for performing incredible feats of strength. He routinely chopped stacks of bricks and roof tiles, smashed rocks and "cut" bottles, all with his bare hands. He is best remembered for sparring with—and defeating—bulls, until international animal rights groups brought this unusual activity to a halt. Animal-rights issues and opportunities for psychoanalysis aside, Oyama was one strong guy.

➤ *Kyokushin-kai*   This style of Japanese Karate was founded by one of the martial art's most colorful exponents, Oyama Masatatsu. As a practitioner of Kyokushin-kai, you would use deep breathing exercises, striking drills and bare-knuckle sparring bouts to perfect this more modern Japanese martial art. After winning the All Japan Karate Championship in 1947, Oyama shaved off his hair and eyebrows and embarked on a journey of self-discovery. He traveled into the mountains, where he would smash rocks, kick trees and lift heavy boulders (look out, Outward Bound). Clearly, this new and improved version of Oyama was, to say the least, intimidating to his martial peers. The name of the style he created, Kyokushin-kai, is translated as "the ultimate truth."

In the next chapter, More Karate: Going to the Next Level, you will explore the technical side of this martial art.

The Least You Need to Know

➤ *Ti,* or *Te,* is an ancient Okinawan martial art that was blended with Chinese and Japanese combative techniques to form Karate (empty hand).

➤ The primary contributing factors to the development of Karate were mainland Japanese warriors, Chinese who traveled to Okinawa and Okinawans visiting China, and weapons bans.

➤ Okinawan Karate developed in three areas, Shuri, Naha and Tomari, and later was exported to mainland Japan.

➤ Karate is generally classified into two types: Okinawan and Japanese.

➤ The five major styles of Japanese Karate are *Shotokan, Goju-ryu, Shito-ryu, Wado-ryu* and *Kyokushin-kai.*

➤ The primary areas of Karate training include *kihon* (basic techniques), *kumite* (sparring) and *kata* (choreographed forms).

Chapter 16

Taking Karate to the Next Level

In This Chapter

➤ Developing your body, mind and spirit with Karate

➤ Why *kata* is called the "vital exercise"

➤ Understanding Karate tournaments

➤ What are the belts, ranks and titles?

➤ A typical class

So, now that you have a basic understanding of the "why" of Karate, let's learn more about the "how to" of this empty-hand art of defense.

This chapter will show you how Karate can help you expand your mind, soothe your spirit and buff your body, while you kick, punch and have some fun!

Ancient Lessons for a Modern World

The name *Karate* evokes images of fists and feet moving with blinding speed as they shatter bricks, splinter wood, chop concrete blocks, smash solid ice or dispatch opponents with a single blow.

While these images are certainly accurate portrayals of the lethal power you as a Karate-*ka* (practitioner) might wield, they do not tell the entire story. In reality, the true purpose of Karate is not to master new and innovative ways to crush inanimate

Warrior Words

Tamashiwara, the practice of breaking solid objects, means "test of strength." The purpose of this training is not to make kindling for your fireplace or brick chips for your garden, but to help you overcome fear and self-doubt. When you safely learn to break one or more boards or bricks, the resultant sense of empowerment will be transferred into other areas of your life.

(or animate) targets. On the contrary, this martial art can—like a new-age self-help program—enable you to recognize and defeat your own shortcomings!

As a student of Karate, you'll strive to develop yourself on three levels:

➤ 1. physical – ability to defend yourself and promote good health

➤ 2. mental – improved concentration and the fortitude to withstand hardship

➤ 3. spiritual – internal harmony

Martial Smarts

In clarifying the rigors and rewards of martial arts training, Grand Master Nagamine Shoshin said: "The Dojo is the place where courage is fostered and superior human nature is bred through the ecstasy of sweating in hard work. It is a sacred place where the human spirit is polished."

Based on the teachings of ancient martial arts masters, who developed Karate as a means of both self-protection and self-perfection, the above-noted three-pronged approach to martial arts training is called *sanchin,* or "three struggles." Karate practitioners believe that a balance between these key areas is necessary in order to achieve self-actualization.

Is *Kata* a Dance or Vital Exercise?

Over time, the primary focus of Okinawan Karate study shifted away from exercises, like sparring, that were designed to prepare martial artists for combat readiness, and toward *kata*. At the most basic level, *kata* is a series of choreographed defensive and offensive techniques that include hand and foot strikes, as well as footwork and shifting movements. *Kata* can help you develop body awareness through balance and breathing training.

At a more advanced level, *kata* serve as a personal textbook detailing the teaching philosophies and methods of various martial arts legends. These individuals crafted routines based on actual combative experiences. This lent an air of authenticity to *kata* practice that would better prepare Karate-*ka* in the event of physical confrontation. Additionally, these forms would bear the distinctive markings of each expert, in the sense that they would include the favorite techniques of each teacher. Depending on their individual style or area of expertise, these martial artists would incorporate the following techniques into each form:

Master Speaks

While there are many similarities between Okinawan folk dance and Karate *kata*, and numerous martial artists contend that there is a relationship between these two disciplines, most modern teachers do not share this belief.

➤ blocking, body shifting and trapping

➤ strikes to vital points

➤ unbalancing and throwing

➤ methods of control

As you practice *kata* for an extended period, the meaning of each form will likely change with every passing year. With time and maturity, the exercise ceases to be merely physical and becomes a form of moving meditation. This results in numerous benefits, some of which are improved circulation and stress reduction, making *kata* an essential exercise for the body, mind and spirit.

As noted in the previous chapter, the three primary styles, which developed in Okinawa, are *Shuri-te*, *Naha-te* and *Tomari-te*. A list of the most popular Karate *kata* practiced by each of these styles, as well as a translation for their names, follows in the next section.

Shuri-te Kata

Some of the more popular *Shuri-te kata* and the meaning of their names are—

➤ *Pinan* – peaceful mind

➤ *Naihanchi* – holding your ground

➤ *Passai* – penetrating a fortress

➤ *Seisan* – thirteen

➤ *Chinto* – Chinese martial expert

➤ *Kushanku* – Chinese martial expert

➤ *Gojushiho* – fifty-four steps

➤ *Chinte* – mysterious hand

➤ *Jion* – temple sound

➤ *Jitte* – ten hands

Naha-te Kata

Some of the most popular *Naha-te kata* and common translations for their names are—

➤ *Sanchin* – three battles

➤ *Saifa* – breaking and tearing

➤ *Seipai* – eighteen

➤ *Seiunchin* – walk far to conquer

➤ *Seisan* – thirteen

➤ *Shisochin* – fighting in four directions

➤ *Sanseiru* – thirty-six

➤ *Tensho* – changing hands

➤ *Kururunfa* – to stop breaking

➤ *Suparenpi* – one hundred and eight

➤ *Unsu* – hand in a cloud

➤ *Sochin* – to preserve peace

➤ *Niseishi* – twenty-four

Tomari-te Kata

The following are some of the most well-known *Tomari-te kata,* along with an acceptable translation for their names:

➤ *Wansu* – Chinese military envoy

➤ *Rohai* – vision of a crane

➤ *Ananku* – peace from the south

➤ *Wankan* – king's crown

Warrior Words

The names of *kata* indicate the number of movements, explain a deeper philosophical meaning connected to the form or pay tribute to their creator or place of origin.

A Sporting Advantage

Not all Karate students train to compete in tournaments. If you do, you may participate at the international level, or, like other weekend warriors, you may limit your involvement to local competitions.

Theoretically, the purpose of Karate tournaments is to provide you with a forum for fostering new friendships, exchange martial concepts and further develop the art of Karate-*do*. The reality of competition is, quite often, a different story.

With divisions drawn along stylistic and national lines, the modern tournament scene is all too often plagued with bias and political intrigue that would rival Washington, D.C., on its best day.

This sad fact aside, tournament competition can serve as a valid barometer for assessing your martial arts skills in a relatively injury-free environment. Furthermore, you and other students who successfully compete in tournaments might face other stressful situations in life in a more resolute and positive fashion. You may also come to recognize your abilities and welcome the opportunity to showcase them.

The Tournament Scene

There are three popular types of Karate competition:

1. In Japanese-based events, sometimes called WUKO (World Union Karate Organization) tournaments, contestants compete in four divisions: individual

kata, kumite (sparring), team *kata* (three persons) and team fighting (five persons).

2. Okinawan-based events are conducted in accordance with rules developed by leading Karate masters and the Okinawan prefectural government. Contestants compete individually in *kata, kumite* and *kobudo* (weapons) categories.

3. North American–based events feature a broader range of competitors, not simply those who practice traditional Karate, but others who train in a variety of martial arts styles and disciplines, both classical and modern. Divisions are usually broken down as follows: forms (open and traditional), weapons and sparring. Additionally, self-defense and board-breaking divisions are sometimes added.

Master Speaks

Be prepared! While, generally speaking, training two to three times per week is adequate for most students, if you are a competitor, you should plan to devote more time and energy to your regimen. You may also need to incorporate cross-training activities into your program, and be prepared to practice diligently. The bulk of your preparation time should be devoted to your chosen area of expertise (forms, sparring, self-defense and weapons use).

Rules of the Game

While rules may vary slightly from tournament to tournament, generally, they are as follows:

➤ **Kata.**   After performing a form that is suitable to the division, you (or your team) will receive scores from several judges and, quite simply, the highest score wins. In the event of a tie, you may be required to perform another *kata* or your score might be recalculated, with judges adding any marks that might have been eliminated (for example, highest and lowest scores).

➤ **Weapons**   Like unarmed forms divisions, after performing, you and other competitors (or teams) receive scores from several judges and the highest sum wins.

➤ **Sparring**   As a participant, you would score by "tagging" your opponent first with a kick or punch that touches specific targets (for instance, the chest). Generally, there is a center referee, who controls the match, and judges positioned in several corners. Judges award a point to you by gesturing in your direction. Alternatively, your points may be indicated when judges raise a flag: a white flag represents a point scored by that player, while a red flag indicates the point was awarded to the other competitor.

Some matches are timed (2 or 3 minutes). Safety equipment is mandatory at many tournaments. Excessive contact to the face or head can result in a warning,

Master Speaks

Let's go to the videotape...As a *kata* competitor, you would be well advised to choose an appropriate form (one you can perform at an optimum level). Having selected a particular *kata*, you should strive to refine the form by rehearsing it with competition in mind and solicit the input of an instructor, coach or experienced competitor. A videocamera can also aid you in this area.

Risky Moves

Be aware that some traditional tournaments will not permit you to wear protective gear of any type. Extreme caution should be exercised if you are going to participate in sparring and other exchange activities without safety equipment.

loss of points or forfeiting of the match to your opponent. As in other divisions, if you are the competitor with the greatest number of points, you win. Some events also feature team sparring divisions.

➤ **Self-defense**   Judges will score the efficacy of one or more of your self-defense routines performed against one or several opponents.

➤ **Breaking**   You and other competitors will receive scores for demolishing one or more objects (such as blocks of ice, boards or bricks).

You can obtain specific rules governing martial arts competitions from tournament promoters, associations or martial arts publications.

Ranks and Titles

There are three ways that your status as a Karate practitioner is recognized: rank, title and position of authority.

Rank refers to your belts and certificates, which are generally awarded based on your overall skill, your performance of *kata,* sparring and self-defense abilities, and your understanding of Karate history and traditions. The white belt is the symbol of a beginner, while a black belt is bestowed upon skilled practitioners.

While it can take you approximately 3 to 5 years to achieve Black Belt *(Shodan,* or First Level), titles, measured in *dan* (degrees, or levels of Black Belt), can take you upwards of 20 years of devoted practice, as described below:

➤ *Renshi* (Polished Practitioner) – When you are a Fifth or Sixth *Dan* and have practiced for more than 20 years, you may receive this title.

➤ *Kyoshi* (Polished Teacher) – This title might be bestowed upon you when you are a Seventh or Eighth *Dan,* are an accomplished teacher and have practiced for at least 25 years.

➤ *Hanshi* (Polished Master) – At Ninth or Tenth *Dan,* after you have produced numerous *Renshi* and *Kyoshi* and you have trained for a minimum of 40 years, you may receive this title.

➤ *Shihan* (Master) – If you are a practitioner above the rank of Fifth *Dan,* you might also be referred to as *Shihan.* Unlike for the other titles noted, there is no prescribed minimum training period.

In addition to the above-noted titles, you may achieve a level of authority by holding a post within your school or within organizations. You could be referred to as—

➤ *Dojo Cho* if you head a *dojo,*

➤ *Kai Cho* if you are the local or international branch director of an association,

➤ *Kan Cho* if you are a director of a large international organization, or

➤ *Soke* if you are the founder of a style.

Martial Smarts

Belt it out! While most schools continue to teach that "Black Belt is a symbol of achievement," a line from the PG-rated film *The Karate Kid* provides a different perspective on the issue of rank. The beloved Karate teacher, Mr. Miyagi, said, "I don't need a 'black belt.' I have a leather belt and it holds my pants up."

Risky Moves

Don't be dazzled by diplomas. It's often difficult to know exactly what title and rank a teacher holds because most certificates are printed in Japanese!

Taking a Class

In most schools, at the beginning of every class, you and your fellow students will line up in neat rows by rank, before performing *makuso* (brief period of seated meditation). This enables you to clear your mind in preparation for your training session (mentally erasing that morning's fender-bender or the most recent water-cooler gripe session).

This may be followed by a warm-up, basic drills, punching-bag and focus-pad training (using small or large hand-held targets) and, depending upon the type of Karate or school, *makiwara* (post striking) practice. Use of these implements can improve your reaction time and power.

Next on your class plan may be *kata* training (basic to advanced forms, which correspond to the school's curriculum and ranking system). You might then practice self-defense and sparring. As a beginner, you will likely perform *ippon kumite* (one-step drills, where you are taught to block and counterattack). Around the sixth month of training, you may begin participating in a more impromptu version of these exercises called *jiyu kumite,* or free sparring.

Finally, your class may culminate in a short cooldown, which can include a brief meditation period, *hansei* (during which you can reflect on material covered in the class), and a motivational message from your *sensei,* at which point you and your students bow and leave the *dojo.*

Risky Moves

To ensure both you and your training partner are adequately protected during exchange activities, purchase and wear protective gear. Minimally, this should include a groin cup and mouthguard. Higher up the food chain of safety equipment is canvas, leather or foam–dipped gear designed to protect hands and feet, head, chest and ribs.

The Least You Need to Know

> ➤ Karate is a unique self-defense and self-perfection program. It can help you improve yourself physically, mentally and spiritually.

> ➤ An essential component of Karate training is *kata* (choreographed series of blocks, punches and kicks). This important exercise is viewed as "moving meditation."

➤ Another key training technique is *tamashiwara,* which involves breaking boards, concrete blocks and bricks. In addition to helping you develop speed, focus and power, *tamashiwara* can also assist you in overcoming your fears and provide a sense of empowerment that can be transferred to other areas of life.

➤ Though not for every practitioner, participation in Karate tournaments can provide you with a unique forum for exchanging ideas and sharing your martial arts knowledge.

➤ Tournaments generally adhere to one of three formats: Japanese, Okinawan or North American. Divisions can include *kata* (forms), *kumite* (sparring), *kobudo* (weapons) and, at some events, self-defense and breaking (of objects).

➤ The efforts of Karate-*ka* are recognized by rank, title or appointment to positions of authority.

Getting Technical

The photographs on the following pages illustrate some common Karate techniques you would perform in a typical class.

Figure 16–1 (a, b, and c)

Figure 16–2 (a, b, and c)

Chapter 17

Going for the Gold with Judo

In This Chapter

➤ Discovering Judo's "gentle, soft way"

➤ How Judo made its way to the West

➤ Learning how some Judo techniques are performed

➤ Discovering the rules of international Judo competition

Judo is both martial sport and martial art. If you watch Judo-*ka* (Judo students) roll, tumble and fly, you will undoubtedly be impressed with the efficient, explosive power they possess.

In this chapter, you'll learn how some popular Judo techniques are performed, as well as how Judo began and developed. You'll also see how Judo traveled from the Far East to the West, how it was transported from the hallowed halls of the Kodokan (Judo's headquarters) to the silver screen and how it evolved from martial art to Olympic sport.

Inch by Inch and Throw by Throw

With little effort, a skilled Judo-*ka* tosses you. As you fly through the air with the greatest of ease, with only seconds before you land on your proverbial "keester," there is perhaps no better time to ponder the curious meaning of Judo's name—"the gentle, soft way."

This comically painful moment illustrates the paradox that is Judo: Olympic sport and martial discipline, art and combative methodology, as diverse and complex as its founder, Kano Jigoro.

Born in 1860, Kano Sensei eventually earned a doctorate in Physical Education. It was his belief that classical Jiu-jitsu placed too much emphasis on disabling an opponent. He researched and refined various forms of Jiu-jitsu and the end product was the modern martial sport of Judo. It featured techniques that would not permanently injure the Judo-*ka* and provided practitioners with the opportunity to test their combative skills in a setting that posed minimal risk.

In addition to being credited with Judo's development, Kano Sensei worked tirelessly, traveling the globe for more than 50 years, propagating his unique martial art. It was on a return trip from Cairo, where he had attended an International Olympic Committee meeting, that Kano Sensei died aboard ship. After his death in 1938, an army of skilled teachers continued his mission to spread Judo throughout the world.

Building Blocks of Judo's Development

As a young practitioner, Kano Jigoro made an interesting observation: pain was the primary motivator in performing techniques correctly. Placing stress on a partner's wrist, elbow or shoulder in a manner designed to ensure optimum discomfort was often the most effective means of diffusing an attack. The word *leverage* is as important to the vocabulary of a Jiu-jitsu practitioner as it is to that of a savvy business tycoon. It refers to unbalancing an opponent. But in Kano Sensei's opinion, with respect to Jiu-jitsu students, this unbalancing often came about only through application of brute strength. Having conducted exhaustive research utilizing an infinite number of techniques, Kano crafted a method for throwing an opponent, relying on mental (rather than physical) muscle and employing skill rather than sheer strength.

As a Judo-*ka,* your skills will rely on your ability to interpret or "read" your partner's body movements and launch an appropriate physical response. Although your opponent may be larger, you can easily subdue a stronger attacker by combining your strength with his or hers and by pushing when he or she pulls, or vice versa. It is upon this fundamental precept that the foundation of Judo is constructed.

Judo's Kodokan Headquarters

The Kodokan, Judo's first learning center, was established in 1882 on the grounds of the Eisho-ji Temple in Tokyo. The name means "an enlightened place where one studies the 'way.' "

If you were a student practicing at the turn of the twentieth century at this fledgling institution, you would have been joined by only eight other pupils. In an area 16 by 16 feet (5 by 5 meters), all nine of you would have studied Judo. Your mission was neatly printed on the reverse side of your diploma: "Only through mutual help and mutual concessions can an organization, made up of a large or small number of individuals, reach complete harmony and bring about serious progress."

Climbing the Rungs of Judo's Rank Ladder

At the turn of the twentieth century, if you were a senior Judo student, you probably would have worked with Kano Sensei to formulate what would become the popular martial arts ranking system. The varying levels of ability of students—from beginners to advanced—were indicated by color or *kyu* belts.

Martial Smarts

At the time of Kano Jigoro's death in 1938, it is estimated that there were in excess of 100,000 Black Belts practicing Judo across the globe.

Risky Moves

Learn to fall head over heels! Before you can throw, you have to learn to fall safely by practicing breakfalls, called *ukemi.*

Martial Smarts

Kano Jigoro was a martial arts pop star. The 1943 movie *The Judo Saga,* which marked the cinematic debut of Oscar-winning director Akira Kurosawa, was loosely based on Kano Sensei's life story. This was a clear tribute to Kano Sensei's growing celebrity.

Additionally, this system included 10 levels of Black Belt, called *Dan.* From First to Fifth *Dan,* you'd wear a plain black belt. After you had studied Judo for many, many years

Warrior Words

A *sakura* (cherry blossom and symbol of rebirth among the Japanese) superimposed over the country's flag was chosen by Kano as the symbol for the Kodokan.

Master Speaks

When practicing Judo, you will wear a heavy canvas uniform called a Judo-*gi*. As with many other martial arts, your uniform will include a belt indicating your rank or level of expertise, from white for beginners, to black for more experienced Judo–*ka*.

and were at the level of Sixth, Seventh or Eighth *Dan,* you would wear a belt that is made of alternating red and white squares of fabric. A red belt in Judo would signify that you are at the Master Level and would generally be worn when you are a Ninth and Tenth Degree Black Belt.

By 1920, the Kodokan created the following Judo syllabus:

➤ *kuzushi* – pushing someone off balance

➤ *tsukuri to kake* – preparing and executing an attack

➤ *ukemi* – breakfalls

➤ *nage no kata* – methods of throwing your opponent

➤ *katame no kata* – grappling or holding

➤ *goshin-jutsu* – self-defense routines

➤ *kime no kata* – submission techniques

If you were a Judo practitioner in the 1940s and 1950s, you would have observed that the focus of the Kodokan during these decades shifted from training instructors to producing world-class teachers of this martial art. It was during this period that numerous Japanese nationals and foreigners were trained and certified by the Kodokan.

Martial Smarts

Bring your own compass! From its humble beginnings, Judo's headquarters has grown. The Kodokan is now a city block wide and seven storeys tall. It houses several *dojo* (training areas), administrative offices, shops, a museum and an arena for competition. You just may need a compass or map to find your way around!

James Bond and Judo in the West

In the 1964 classic Bond film *Goldfinger,* the amorous advances of the perennially tuxedoed hero are brought to an abrupt halt when a beautiful blonde pilot tosses him into a haystack. A flabbergasted "007" utters the now famous line "Pussy, who taught you Judo?"

Sexism and camp aside, clearly, Judo was coming of age in the West, a mere 75 years after Kano staged the first Judo demonstration outside Japan. In Marseilles, France, in 1889, at what would become Judo's first Western home, Jean-Joseph Renaud and Guy de Montgrillard became the world's first non-Japanese teachers of this martial art.

In 1918, on the other side of the channel, the first British *dojo,* the Budokwai (Martial Arts Group) was established under the direction of E.J. Harrison. (In all probability, Judo was being practiced informally in the U.K. prior to the opening of this school.)

Meanwhile, across the pond, among their other prized possessions, Japanese immigrants brought their Judo skills to North America with them. Even the heat of the Second World War could not cool interest in this popular martial sport.

One of the first Americans to study at the Kodokan in Japan was Walter E. Todd, who received his *Godan* (Fifth Degree Black Belt) in 1949. Todd Sensei currently heads the prestigious Shudokan Martial Arts Association (*shu* – to learn by rote with spontaneity, *do* – the path or way, *kan* – house).

Master Speaks

As a Judo-*ka,* you will practice *randori*. These are essential impromptu sparring sessions in which you as the *uke* (the partner who submits or gives way to the attack) are tossed to the mat and pinned by the *tori* (someone else who does the throwing).

Martial Smarts

From 1964 to 1968, the most winning pair of Judo-*ka* were two heavyweight Dutchmen, Anton Geesink and William Ruska. Their victorious record was significant, as it marked an end to Japan's domination of the sport and paved the way for numerous non-Japanese champions, who would follow in their footsteps.

In 1964 (which, coincidentally, is the same year that *Goldfinger* hit theaters around the world), the phenomenal popularity of Judo led to its acceptance by the International Olympic Committee. (It also didn't hurt that the Games were held in Tokyo that year.) Curiously, it was this metamorphosis from combative art to medal sport that, in the view of many martial arts historians, proved to be the silver bullet for Judo. The superhuman properties heretofore associated with Judo as depicted on the big screen were minimized—in every sense of the word—to fit the small screen. In television's flickering glare, Judo lost some of its magic and mystery and became a sport like any other.

Break(fall)ing into a Typical Class

As your feet step onto the *tatami* (mat made of rice straw, whose modern equivalent is the foam variety) for the first time, you will undoubtedly notice a large framed portrait of Kano Sensei hung conspicuously above the training area.

In a sense, in addition to being under the watchful eye of your *sensei* and fellow students, your training is being "observed" by Judo's founder. As in other martial arts schools, you and your fellow students would bow to these photographs, acknowledging the contribution made by individuals who preceded you (your teacher's instructor and the founder of your style).

Following a warm-up, your breakfall practice will begin. These techniques will teach you how to land safely and defend yourself on the ground. As in other martial arts drills, you, as a beginner, will learn basic falls and gradually progress to more advanced techniques.

Throwing drills including *harai goshi* (hip throws), *kata murana* (shoulder throws), *tai-toshi* (off-balancing an opponent by pulling him or her over your leg) and *deashi buri* (foot sweeps) will be repeated until they become reflexive.

Arm and neck restraints, which can enable you to limit an aggressor's attacks, generally follow. You will practice these defensive tactics from a variety of positions—standing and lying on the ground. Your next level of practice will likely be groundwork, wherein you will develop the ability to pin, or hold down, your opponent.

Like other martial arts, training in Judo can be fun and safe and provide many benefits when you practice with a qualified *sensei*.

Risky Moves

"Tap" into safety. When pinning or restraining your partner, it is important for you to listen for the tapping sound your partner will make by striking the floor or mat. This sound indicates your partner has reached his or her maximum pain threshold (a.k.a. Uncle!) and it's time for you to release your hold.

Rules of the Game

Are you interested in tournaments? Then read on, because this section summarizes the rules of competition as dictated by the International Judo Federation.

Competition Area and Officials

You'll participate in a *tatami* or foam-covered area 14 by 14 meters (46 by 46 feet) or 16 by 16 meters (52 by 52 feet). You can score points only in a designated area, called a "safety zone." One referee, who moves with the players in order to closely monitor exchanges, is positioned in the center of the ring. He or she is assisted by two judges positioned in opposite corners, as well as two timekeepers and a scorekeeper.

Master Speaks

It's a "numbers" game. Rather than performing an entire technique a few times, you will learn more efficiently if you dissect a complete sequence, analyzing each of its components, and practice every section dozens of times. The two primary elements are the entry (initiating the throw) and breaking (ascertaining your partner's center of gravity for the purpose of off-balancing him or her). This rapid practice of small components is called *uchi komi*.

Uniforms

As a competitor, you'll have to wear a standard Judo uniform. This means a white or off-white heavyweight canvas or cotton Judo-*gi*. This uniform must be clean and in good repair. Your top must reach your mid-thigh, and your sleeves have to cover your forearms, but not hang beyond your wrists. Your uniform pants must cover at least half your calf, but not extend beyond your ankles. You're also required to wear a belt corresponding to your rank and either a white or red sash differentiating you from your opponent. Additionally, if you're a female participant, you'll wear a plain white or off-white short-sleeved T-shirt under your top.

Your personal hygiene must meet the satisfaction of event officials (that means, clip your toe- and fingernails and tie back your hair).

Match

The duration of a match can vary from 3 to 20 minutes. The end of a match is indicated with an audible signal by the timekeeper. Clocks and scoreboards or manual systems are used at international events.

After ensuring that all officials are ready, the center referee will "bow in" the players, who have been paired by weight and gender. Once the match begins, judges will indicate points awarded to competitors by raising a white or red flag. Scorekeepers record these points. A competitor must beat an opponent by one full point or two half-points to win a match.

Point System

➤ *ippon* (full point) – A full point is awarded when a player throws an opponent (generally on his or her back) with force and speed, holds an opponent for no less than 30 seconds, or forces his or her opponent to "tap out" (or when the referee determines a player cannot make these gestures).

➤ *wazari* (half-point) – There are two ways a player can score a half-point: a competitor uses a technique that is lacking in maximum extension or power, or a contestant holds his or her opponent for 25 seconds.

➤ *yuko/koka* (additional techniques) – In the event of a tie or if time runs out without either player scoring, the center referee will decide which competitor is the winner based on attempted techniques and display of better "fighting spirit."

➤ fouls – Contestants who commit minor infractions are cautioned with a *shido*. More severe offenses receive a *hansoku*. In the event of a tie, these can keep you from winning a match.

You can obtain more detailed information about international competition rules by contacting your local Judo school or association.

The Least You Need to Know

➤ Judo, "the gentle, soft way," was founded by Kano Jigoro, who adapted Jiu-jitsu techniques to develop a unique martial art and sport.

➤ Judo features a variety of throws, off-balancing maneuvers and restraints to subdue an opponent using mental, rather than physical, muscle.

➤ Judo's ranking system, which was developed by Kano Sensei, is employed by most martial arts disciplines today.

➤ Movies like *Goldfinger,* status as an Olympic sport and the establishment of schools outside Japan helped solidify Judo's popularity worldwide.

➤ Judo is practiced in many countries around the world, and its headquarters, the Kodokan, is an impressive complex located in Tokyo.

➤ Under the supervision of a qualified *sensei,* you can practice Judo safely, have fun and enjoy the numerous benefits this martial art provides.

Getting Technical

The photographs on the following pages illustrate the kinds of techniques you would perform as a Judo-*ka.*

Figure 17–1 (a, b, and c)

Figure 17–2 (a, b, and c)

Chapter 18

Getting Defensive with Aikido

In This Chapter

➤ How an educated warrior developed Aikido

➤ Aikido's throwing and controlling methods

➤ Getting physically, mentally and spiritually fit with Aikido

➤ Generating internal energy

➤ Examining typical training techniques

Remember Steven Seagal in the movie *Above the Law?* He managed to toss barroom bad guys around like ragdolls without messing up his ponytail. Impressive scenes like these illustrate the self-defense value of Aikido, which relies on redirecting an opponent's aggressive energy. But this brand of movie magic doesn't tell the whole story.

The philosophy of this Japanese martial art, whose name means "harmony energy way," has, at its core, the belief that you should strive to develop yourself not just physically, but mentally and spiritually as well. This chapter will help you figure out how that's done.

Martial Smarts

At age 84, after 66 years of practice, Ueshiba Morihei, the founder of Aikido, said, "I have only taken a first step...I am still a baby in the martial arts."

The Warrior Scholar

Ueshiba Morihei was born to a samurai family in the Motomachi district of the city of Tanabe, Wakayama prefecture, Japan, on December 14, 1883. When Ueshiba was a child, his parents encouraged him to study Buddhism of the Shingon (true word) sect, which subscribes to the idea of reaping rewards in the here and now, as opposed to the hereafter. Members of this sect believe you can become a "living Buddha" during your existence. This passionate interest in theology and a belief in a divine spirit ("Divine Buddha," called *Vairokana*) and five deities (called *Myo-o*) would play a large role in Ueshiba's life and, consequently, the evolution of Aikido.

At 18 years of age, Ueshiba embarked on a lifelong study of *budo* (a personal improvement program based on practice of the martial arts), enrolling in the Kito-ryu School of Jiu-jitsu and the Shinkage School of Ken-jitsu (where he learned sword-fighting skills). Two years later, he enlisted in the military. There are two conflicting opinions regarding his career in the armed forces. Some martial historians contend that Ueshiba displayed unparalleled combative prowess and courage under fire, thereby earning the unofficial title of Gunshi no Kami, or "God of Soldiers." Others assert that, due to his diminutive size, it is unlikely he performed active duty and instead he was posted to the reserve in Osaka.

In 1908, Ueshiba was discharged from the armed forces. He received a teaching certificate from the head master of the Shinkage-ryu and opened a *dojo* in Tanabe. Seven years later, the life of Ueshiba Morihei would be altered forever when the martial arts master Takeda Sokaku accepted him as a disciple.

Rooted in generations of battlefield experience, Takeda's martial teachings were, by most reports, realistic and extremely effective.

Warrior Words

Loosely translated, a "disciple" is a student who dedicates him- or herself to an intensive study of the martial arts.

Martial Smarts

Takeda Sokaku explained his inclination toward the martial arts with the following quote: "As a child, I used to play on the battlefields with discarded weapons as toys."

Body and Mind

In true warrior-scholar fashion, Ueshiba's training was divided between the corporal and the cerebral. Takeda addressed the physical portion of Ueshiba's emerging martial form, which would serve as the foundation for Aikido. Deguchi Onisaburo, a self-proclaimed prophet, trained Ueshiba's mind and provided spiritual guidance. Deguchi was the leader of the Omoto-kyo religious movement, whose purpose was to establish a "mystical nation state." In an effort to create a home base, Deguchi and his followers, including Ueshiba, traveled throughout rural Japan, Manchuria and China, eventually settling in the town of Ayabe, near Kyoto.

The heyday of the Omoto-kyo cult came to an abrupt end in Waco-esque fashion in the late 1930s, when its compound was razed by a bevy of police and an army of bulldozers.

Creating the Aikido "Buzz"

Removing himself from public life to further develop his martial art, Ueshiba transferred the duties of propagating Aikido to his son Kishomaru. This enabled the elder Ueshiba to focus his energies on refining this combative system. Public interest in Aikido was fueled by numerous demonstrations and resultant media exposure, which helped to create a buzz about this martial art. In 1949, the Ministry of Education assisted Ueshiba Sensei in establishing a *dojo* in central Tokyo. This school would serve as a training academy for up-and-coming teachers. Nearly two decades later, in 1967, an ultramodern school was opened that would house the Aikido Hombu (central headquarters) Dojo. He had hardly begun to enjoy the fruits of his labor when, in 1969, Ueshiba Sensei passed away.

Warrior Words

Although martial historians debate the exact date Ueshiba created Aikido, the generally accepted time frame is between 1925 and 1926. It was during these years that the name *Aikido*, which can be translated as union or harmony *(ai)*, vital breath or energy *(ki)* and path or way *(do)*, made its debut. Most martial arts experts agree that Aikido, like other combative systems, remains a work in progress.

ABCs of A-I-K-I-D-O

As a student of Aikido, you would be called an Aikido-*ka* (not "okeydokey"). Your training uniform is a thickly woven, white pajama-style outfit called a *dogi*. When you achieve the rank of Black Belt, you also wear a wide, black, skirtlike garment, called a *hakama*. Some Aikido schools subscribe to the color belt ranking system used by other martial arts *dojo:* white for novice students, color belts at the intermediate level and black belts for more experienced practitioners.

Master Speaks

Here's a fashion tip! It's important to recognize that a *hakama* is not really a "skirt" at all. It's a pair of very wide trousers (think palazzo pants or long culottes). Originally worn by the samurai, *hakama* came into vogue in the Nara period (A.D. 710–794).

If you were an Aikido-*ka,* your curriculum would include 720 techniques or combinations. These would be divided between two main areas: *nage waza* (throwing techniques) and *katame waza* (controlling techniques). The ABCs, or essentials, of your Aikido training will revolve around freeing yourself from a hold, throwing your partner to the ground and immobilizing opponents by exerting pressure on their joints.

Unique Techniques

Aikido does not fit neatly under the heading of exercise, sport or martial system. It is none of the above *and* all of the above, as well as a discipline whose aim is to transport you to a higher, more spiritual plane. This approach represents a dramatic departure from its initial purpose, which was decidedly more "martial" than "art." Over the years, Aikido's hard edges have softened. Whether this transformation is attributable to the aging of its founder or is simply a shift in emphasis to the use of *ki* (internal energy) rather than external strength is unclear. Today, a great deal of etiquette and morality is attached to its combative principles. For example, although some striking techniques exist in Aikido, they are used primarily to distract your opponent, allowing you to employ alternative methods for *gently* controlling your attacker.

As an Aikido-*ka,* you would practice five basic defensive techniques:

1. *atemi* – You strike vulnerable parts of the body using your fingertips, knuckles and sides of your hand.

2. *tai sabaki* – You shift out of the way of an attack or use your body weight to amplify a defensive technique.

3. *irimi* – You practice forceful, committed ways of entering the space of your attacker.

4. *rofuse* – You throw an opponent to the ground using pressure on his or her joints.

5. *kansetsu* – You immobilize a partner using joint restraints.

Let Your *Ki* Fly

People just like you are attracted to the study of Aikido for a variety of reasons: learning personal defense skills, cultivating a spiritual balance or harmony, and minimizing stress. With its emphasis on etiquette, Aikido offers you a unique method for understanding Japan's intriguing culture. Additionally, by practicing a discipline that is steeped in Zen philosophy, you can also develop an appreciation for the simplicity of other aspects of Asian culture and even life itself.

Risky Moves

Practice your primal scream. The *kiai* (meaning "meeting of energy" or "cry that gives strength") is a yell used in Aikido and other Japanese martial arts to purify your mind, focus your energy and help you deliver maximum power into techniques. While performing the *kiai* may feel strange at first, you'll get used to it. You may even start to enjoy it. (But avoid developing laryngitis.)

➤ **Let's Begin at the Beginning** To begin practicing, you are paired with other students to perform techniques appropriate to your skill level. You and your partners will alternate your roles as *uke* (assailant) and *nage* (defender). Once thrown, the *uke* will use soft, rolling or diving breakfalls *(ukemi)* to absorb the impact of the counterattack and minimize risk of injury.

At the intermediate level, you may study ancient weapons like the *bokken* (wooden sword), *jo* (short wood staff) and *tanto* (wooden knife). These represent arms carried by samurai.

Martial Smarts

Less is more. The Japanese martial training hall *(dojo)* is generally modeled after the traditional teahouse. The driving concepts behind the simple construction of both structures are *wabi* (not *wasabi*—that's Japanese horseradish that you eat with sushi), which can be translated as "quiet elegance," and *sabi* (no, not *sake*), or the "quietness of nature." The unadorned decor of both the teahouse and the *dojo* is a celebration of minimalism: from natural wood floors and paneling illuminated by soft, recessed lighting, to modest calligraphy scrolls and unobtrusive flower arrangements. The room is spartan except for a bell or sword, which may be added to provide a focal point.

➤ **Taking It to the Mat**   Japanese feudal forms of combat, whether unarmed or armed with a sword or dagger, were often performed from a kneeling position. This type of training, called *suwari waza*, is still used in Aikido to test the angles of various techniques and better assess their combative possibilities. Nearly all Aikido techniques can be, and often are, executed from this position against attackers who are standing or kneeling. Practicing trapping, locks and throws while on your knees can help you develop excellent balance and allow you to pay special attention to even the most minute details.

➤ **Group Fun**   To further develop your Aikido skills at an advanced level, you'll need to tussle with multiple opponents. Attacks may be either "static," meaning your opponents restrain you, or "dynamic," meaning they converge upon you in a free-for-all. Learning to defend yourself against two or more opponents can help you improve your timing and distance skills, but more importantly it can help you learn to remain levelheaded and in control when facing even the most challenging situations.

Martial Smarts

Tohei Koichi, a Tenth Degree Black Belt in Aikido, explained the importance of mental training when he said "It is the mind that leads the body."

Risky Moves

Don't underestimate the power of words. *Kotodama* (meaning "true word") originated in China. It refers to the practice of aiming the vibration of your voice to heal or destroy your opponent. So, shout with extreme caution!

Mind over Matter

Once you have graduated from the physical level of training, as an advanced Aikido-*ka*, developing your mind and cultivating *ki* will become more important to you.

➤ **Martial ESP**   Aikido practitioners believe that, through countless hours of *zazen* (seated meditation) and physical practice, you can achieve an intuitive state—which means you should be able to anticipate and pre-empt an attack. This requires you to have a light, unpreoccupied yet highly focused mind housed in a finely tuned body.

➤ **Air "Force"**   An essential step in developing *ki* (internal energy) is learning the technique of deep abdominal breathing, called *kokyu*. This involves deep inhalation and exhalation combined with mental imaging. To begin, you would sit cross-legged or in a kneeling position and then inhale a thin stream of air through your nostrils, feeling your breath travel from your chest to your abdomen. Then, you exhale through your mouth while an "aah" sound resonates in your throat. The number of breaths you take per minute will be reduced as you become more experienced. For example, an average adult takes 14 to 20 breaths per minute, but a seasoned practitioner will require only 6 to 10. At the same time, using mental video "playback," visualize yourself performing Aikido techniques perfectly. This fusion of body, mind and spirit—the marriage of the physical, mental and spiritual—is the ultimate aim of all serious Aikido-*ka*.

The final stage of your Aikido training is the study and understanding of *ki*. As the founder of Aikido, Ueshiba Morihei, put it, "No '*ki*,' no Aikido!"

➤ **The *Ki* to Unlocking Your Power** Through consistent, disciplined practice, you can generate *ki* (internal energy) in your *hara* (stomach) and transmit it to all points of your body. Think of it as central heating or air conditioning feeding energy to your entire being, creating a Star Trek–like force field that can protect you against armed and unarmed attacks. Too good to be true? If you witness the swift and seemingly effortless way Aikido masters are able to fend off opponents, you will, no doubt, be left wondering how you too can find the *ki* to unlock your power!

The Least You Need to Know

➤ Aikido was developed by Ueshiba Morihei.

➤ At the color belt levels, you and other Aikido students wear a *dogi* (uniform) and at Black Belt level, you will also wear *hakama* (wide trousers).

➤ The ABCs of Aikido include throwing and controlling techniques. At the intermediate level, you may also begin practicing with ancient weapons.

➤ At the most advanced level of your Aikido training, you will strive to cultivate *ki* (internal energy that can function as a type of "force field").

➤ Initially, Aikido was primarily a combative art but, since its inception, its focus has softened and now its primary aim is self-improvement.

➤ As an Aikido-*ka,* you can enjoy not only physical or self-defense benefits, but also the opportunity to be transported to a higher spiritual level.

Getting Technical

The photographs on the following pages illustrate techniques you would perform in a typical Aikido class.

Figure 18–1 (a, b, and c)

Figure 18–2 (a, b, and c)

Chapter 19

Trading Blows in the Pacific Rim

In This Chapter

➤ Cross-cultural influences on martial arts in Southeast Asia

➤ How Muay Thai made its way from stadiums to gyms

➤ Discovering how 200 Silat styles began with one peasant woman

➤ Understanding Filipino stick fighting

➤ Getting a glimpse of typical techniques

The Pacific Rim is a hodgepodge of cultures including Thai, Indonesian and Malaysian, and Filipino. While each embraces the fighting traditions of its neighbor, all are proud of their individual combative heritage. Additionally, these three ethnic groups have exported their respective field-tested martial arts throughout the world.

Martial artists from this region run the gamut from lean and limber Muay Thai kickboxers and stick-wielding Escrima practitioners, to sarong-wearing Silat stylists. This chapter will help you understand the exotic, and lethal, martial arts of Southeast Asia.

Read This Before You "Thai" One On!

As an enthusiastic spectator enjoying the weekly Thai Boxing match at the Lumpini Stadium in Bangkok, Thailand, you might be unaware of this sport's long fighting tradition, which dates back to the Kingdom of Siam. As a devoted fight fan, busily munching peanuts and washing them down with a cold Pepsi, you're probably

Martial Smarts

The Lumpini and Rajadamnern Stadiums are the main venues for Muay Thai (Thai Boxing) events, which play to standing-room-only crowds. These extravaganzas feature musical accompaniment in the form of drums, flutes and cymbals. Like the heartbeat (and, perhaps, perspiration rate) of the audience, the tempo of the music increases in time with the pace of the match. If you are a Thai who can't get into these stadiums, you can participate by betting your hard-earned *bhat* (Thai currency) on matches you watch on television. This pastime appears to be as popular as the sport itself!

oblivious to the historical significance of this match. Proud contestants in the ring, like their ancestors before them, battle their opponents, using only empty-hand skills and a well-developed strategy that would rival those employed by even the greatest chess masters. To understand the significance of this form of martial entertainment, you have to examine the roots of Thai Boxing.

King Naresuen, a.k.a. "The Spunky Royal"

The expertise of the brave warriors of Siam was born of the need for self-preservation, rather than box office sales. Their Chinese descendants married members of the Mon and Khmer tribes. This union resulted in what became known as the Siamese State. Their soldiers rode elephants and wore armor, crafted from bamboo or metal, and helmets. They also carried shields and were armed with an impressive array of weapons.

Although the fifteenth century marked the advent of cannons and firearms, Siamese warriors continued to revere empty-hand combative skills. Legend has it that in 1560 King Naresuen of Siam was imprisoned by the Burmese. In an "offer he couldn't refuse," he was told that if he defeated his captors' champion, he would be freed. The fiery royal used his pugilistic skills to win this all-important match and, from that day forward, boxing was Thailand's national sport.

The "Eight Limbs" of Muay Thai

Muay Thai, also called Thai Boxing, is the "science of eight limbs." This means that if you were practicing this martial art, you would use your two hands, two feet, two elbows and two knees (you do the math). This is a powerful, occasionally brutal, form of combat—in other words, it's not a participatory or spectator activity for the faint of heart.

For example, in traditional contests, combatants would bind their hands in cotton or hemp, smear them with an adhesive and dip their powerful, gift-wrapped knuckles into pots of ground glass—adding new, and deadly, meaning to the phrase "reach out and touch someone." If you are among the minority of moviegoers who saw the "Muscles from Brussels," Jean-Claude Van Damme, in *Bloodsport,* you get the picture!

Rated PG

More modern, and seemingly humanized, incarnations of these contests are conducted in accordance with the following rules:

➤ You can use any of your "eight limbs" to strike your opponent.

➤ You wear leather, padded gloves but your feet are bare.

➤ Your ankle is reinforced with support wraps and your groin is covered with protective gear.

➤ Matches are usually three, five or seven 3-minute rounds, which are balanced with a 2-minute rest period between rounds.

➤ A center referee, positioned inside the ring, orchestrates the bout while two judges outside this area select a winner.

➤ The 12 weight classes range from under 112 pounds to 175 pounds and over, with each category spanning 3 to 5 pounds.

➤ Head butting (striking your opponent using your head), spitting, biting or hitting a downed opponent constitutes a foul.

Risky Moves

Please pass the aspirin! A favorite technique used by Thai boxers is pulling their opponent's head toward their knee and striking it repeatedly, leaving the unlucky recipient to wonder if perhaps ballroom dancing or macrobiotic cooking would be a more rewarding pastime.

Master Speaks

Be "well armed." An excellent way for you to develop coordination and power, if you are practicing Muay Thai, is to strike your partner's forearms, which are protected by special pads. Your techniques can, thereby, be performed safely from a variety of angles.

Fit to Fight

While the defensive value of Thai Boxing, with its devastating elbow and hand strikes and lethal knee and foot techniques, is evident, Muay Thai is clearly *not* an activity for everyone. What *has* become popular among fitness buffs today is the conditioning aspect of this sport, and for good reason. As a Thai boxer, you may be bruised and battered but you are also a lean, mean human machine, with sharply chiseled muscles, sculpted abdominals and superb cardiovascular endurance. Combine hundreds of crunches, push-ups, kicks and punches with countless rounds of rope skipping, and what you get is the formula for martial fitness classes featured in progressive gyms and health clubs from coast to coast. Additionally, with the risk of injury minimized, as a boxing "wannabe," you can enjoy the pleasure (?) of sweating and straining Siamese-style, with DKNY sportswear and big-buck Nikes still intact!

Indonesia and Malaysia Export Silat

Indonesia and Malaysia enjoy many similarities. While they are, for the most part, populated by Malaysians, they also include numerous ethnic groups, which are somewhat compartmentalized by language, religion and custom. Hindus, Muslims and Buddhists, coupled with the Dutch and English, have left their imprint. Geographic factors, in the form of the more than 3000 islands that make up these countries, have also contributed to the cultural diversity of these people. In excess of 200 martial arts styles, all under the umbrella of Silat, are practiced in this region.

No Way to Treat a Lady

Popular folklore tells the story of Bersilat, a peasant woman, who set out one morning to fetch some water. Upon arriving at the stream, she watched a battle between a tiger and a large bird that lasted for several hours, with both animals dying at the end of the fight. A short while after, several drunken villagers appeared and attacked the woman. Copying the movements of the bird and tiger, she skillfully evaded her assailants. Later, when the alcohol and displaced aggression of her attackers had worn off, she began instructing the sober villagers in her newfound defensive art. Interestingly, young Indonesian and Malaysian women are encouraged to begin martial training at an early age—living tribute to the impact this legendary female founder of Silat had on the introduction of combative arts in the region.

Take Me to Your Guru

As noted, Silat encompasses more than 200 martial arts styles. Each has its own unique training methods and secret combat strategies. The mecca of Silat is on the islands of Java and Sumatra, home to more than 25 styles and hundreds of gurus, or teachers.

Getting Strategic

Rather than categorizing Silat's styles (or "schools") by region, you should examine them in terms of their core combative strategies. There are seven such strategies:

1. You use open palm techniques (striking with the flat surface of your hand).

2. You employ ground fighting (defensive and offensive techniques performed from a reclining position).

3. You place special emphasis on locking and grappling (restraining your opponent's limbs).

4. You rely on kicking, sweeping (off-balancing) and leg trapping (seizing and controlling your opponent's legs).

5. You depend on natural breathing (a regular breathing pattern) and quick movements.

6. You use deep breathing (extended inhalation and exhalation) and strong, deliberate strikes.

7. You employ weapons like the *kris* (a long knife), *toya* (wooden staff) and the *pedang* (machete).

> **Master Speaks**
>
> One unique element of Silat training is its acrobatic ground-fighting techniques. A fighter executes traps, sweeps and takedowns. One popular exercise for cultivating this skill is performing a push-up, rolling onto your back, followed by a "kip-up" (tuck your knees to your chest and spring up to a standing position). This exercise can enhance your dexterity from the ground.

Guru Gift Shopping

Historically, if you were interested in becoming a Silat student, you would have had to complete an interview in order to qualify to train. Additionally, you might have been required to bring small gifts to your prospective teacher. In response to the pressing question of what to buy the guru-who-has-everything, you might consider tobacco, packets of money or a small knife (symbolizing the "sharpness" of your abilities).

Furthermore, before beginning your training, you and other new students would have to place your hand on a holy book (usually the

> **Martial Smarts**
>
> Ketchup anyone? During the "swearing-in" ceremony performed by new Silat students, the blood of a chicken was sprinkled on the ground. This use of the unfortunate poultry's vital fluid represented the desire that no *real* blood would ever be spilled. Good news for the student, bad news for the chicken!

219

Warrior Words

What to wear? Silat students wear no special uniform for the first 6 months of training. Then you wear a white belt or sash *(bengkong)* for approximately one year, followed by a green one at the intermediate level. As an advanced student, you wear a yellow or red belt or sash. It can take 7 to 10 years to achieve a black belt or sash.

Risky Moves

Hiding behind your skirt? Don't underestimate the defensive value of sarongs worn by Silat practitioners. These garments are not simply a bold fashion statement. They are wrapped around the midsection to protect the abdomen and lower back—like a weight lifter's belt. Employing a swinging motion, practitioners also use sarongs to strike an attacker or to divert his or her attention.

Koran) and swear an oath of allegiance to your teacher and fellow practitioners—promising to be "blood relatives" from that day forward.

Let's Get Physical

With necessary formalities completed, your physical training would begin. Initially, you and other new students would focus on formal etiquette, postures, footwork and fundamental hand and foot techniques. This would be followed by preset form exercises, which incorporate a study of the body's vital points.

At the intermediate level, you would likely begin sparring (contact activity against another student or several students). Additionally, you might start to use a variety of weapons.

The advanced stage of your study will encompass *kebatinan,* or "spiritual training." This will include self-hypnosis designed to enable you to withstand painful locks, punches or kicks and even to not bleed if you're cut! (Imagine the number of Band-Aids used in practice sessions.)

Walk Softly and Carry a Short Stick

Today in Manila, where bright neon lights celebrate popular brands of cigarettes or names of beer, it is difficult to fully appreciate the role martial arts played in the evolution of this country's culture. This is especially true in light of the fact that, for more than 300 years, Spanish colonial officials outlawed the practice of martial systems. Defiant Filipinos continued to use them to defend their families and homes. In fact, martial arts were also an important means of expressing a unique Filipino identity, which is linked to the country's fighting traditions.

I Scream-a, You Scream-a, We All Scream-a for Escrima

Arnis, derived from the Spanish word *arnes,* which means "harnessing" or "trapping," is the principal form of martial expression used by Filipino practitioners.

A popular type of Arnis training, Escrima involves use of two wood sticks (called *bastons* or *mutons)* 31 inches (78 centimeters) in length. They are employed individually, or in pairs, to block and counter attacks. While this type of short-stick combat is certainly at the heart of the style's curriculum, Arnis training also includes boxing, grappling and trapping techniques, use of daggers and short swords, and unarmed defensive drills versus armed attacks.

Unlike many other martial arts systems in which you progress from unarmed to armed training, Arnis is unusual in that you begin by understanding how to use the short stick and, at a more advanced level, learn empty-hand (unarmed) techniques.

Warrior Words

The famous Portuguese explorer and navigator Ferdinand Magellan (1480–1521) came to "permanent" rest in the Philippines. Magellan, armed with a dagger and sword, faced the tribal chief Lapulapu. The chief, a martial arts expert, selected a *baston* (a hardwood short stick) to defend himself and killed the explorer.

Getting a "Handle" on Escrima

As a novice *Escrimador* (student of stick fighting), you can expect to practice:

> ➤ *pandalaga* – repetition drills that stress swinging and striking

> ➤ *sanga at patama* – blocking, parrying (deflecting) and thrusting routines

> ➤ *larga muton* – free-style (spontaneous) exchanges using evasion and countering tactics

Traditional versus Modern

Traditionally, you would wear no protective gear and strikes could be targeted to any part of the body (ouch). This method of rigorous training is still carried on in traditional schools, where emphasis is placed on the self-defense aspect of the style. In addition to using the shield, sword, dagger and spear, you would condition your hands, elbows, knees and feet, as these "weapons" are as essential as those constructed of wood or metal.

Master Speaks

You never learned *this* in high school woodworking class! The Filipino word *sinawali* refers to bamboo carved to resemble lace. In Escrima terminology, this same word is used to describe continuous blocking and countering drills, performed unarmed or armed with short sticks. In order to practice this exercise, block your opponent's attack and immediately counter using a flowing, unbroken pattern.

In sharp contrast, at modern Arnis schools, training takes a more sporting approach. You would wear a padded shirt and a helmet, resembling that worn by fencers. This

Martial Smarts

The modern sport of Arnis is catching on. The first World Arnis Championship was held in Cebu, Philippines, in August 1989. In the early 1990s, the Philippine Olympic Committee recognized Arnis as a sport.

equipment is used to minimize the impact of each blow. Additionally, matches are conducted in much the same way as other martial sports. They are overseen by judges positioned in the center and corner of the ring, and if you are the player who has the highest score (number of strikes) at the culmination of the bout, you win.

Like other Indonesian and Malaysian arts, Arnis wears both a combative and a celebratory face. Although it is a formidable fighting system, its dancelike defensive routines are performed at weddings and other festive events. Called *Sayawa* or *Sinulong,* these entertainment forms feature performers demonstrating postures, using weapons and trapping and unbalancing one another.

What Does the Future Hold?

In 1960, a national Arnis association, called Samahan sa Arnis ng Pilipinas, or Arnis Association of the Philippines, was established to promote Arnis as a sport. While this was still a relatively obscure martial art, with the recent influx of Filipino immigrants to North America, Arnis is quickly becoming popular across the continent.

The Least You Need to Know

➤ Thailand, Indonesia, Malaysia and the Philippines have exported popular martial systems, including Muay Thai (Thai Boxing), Silat and Arnis.

➤ Thai Boxing matches in Bangkok are an extremely popular form of entertainment. The rigorous training employed by its practitioners (minus the risk of contact) is gaining growing acceptance in the form of popular martial fitness programs featured in North American gyms.

➤ The Silat system, which, legend has it, was founded by a peasant woman, includes defensive and offensive movements that mimic animals. It boasts more than 200 styles.

➤ Arnis is a Filipino martial art that includes the study of "short sticks," called Escrima.

➤ These systems feature both unarmed and armed techniques. Schools that teach these styles are either traditional, emphasizing the self-defense aspect, or more sport-oriented, training students for competition.

Getting Technical

The photographs below and on the next page illustrate the kinds of techniques you would perform when practicing a Southeast Asian martial art, Muay Thai.

Figure 19–1 (a, b, and c)

Figure 19–2 (a, b, and c)

Chapter 20

Tae Kwon Do's Spectacular "Feets"

In This Chapter

➤ Discovering Korea's ancient martial arts

➤ Learning about the debut of modern Tae Kwon Do

➤ Tae Kwon Do as a self-improvement tool

➤ Understanding Tae Kwon Do's competition rules and the ranking system

➤ Looking at typical techniques

Sandwiched between China, Japan, Manchuria and Russia, the "Hermit Kingdom" of Korea has attempted to close its doors to foreign invaders for more than 2000 years.

As a result, this country boasts an interesting martial history spanning two millennia and running the gamut from defensive art to popular sport.

This chapter will help you understand Korea's martial art of Tae Kwon Do, from its earliest beginnings to its Olympic success, and the benefits it offers you.

Martial Smarts

It takes no time at all to know something, but it takes a lifetime to gain wisdom. Knowledge without wisdom is a load of books on the back of an ass.

—Korean proverb

The Grandfather of Modern Tae Kwon Do

In 100 B.C., Korea was divided into three sections or kingdoms: Paekche and Silla in the south, and Koguryo in the north. It is in Koguryo that we find the earliest evidence of a formalized indigenous martial art, called Sobak.

The warring classes of Koguryo combined the striking techniques of Chinese martial arts and Mongolian combative methods that relied primarily on grappling, with their own unique kicking art. This amalgamation was called *Sobak*, or "fighting skill." Sobak, often viewed as "the grandfather of modern Tae Kwon Do," is a martial art that relies heavily on kicking using the ball, heel and instep of the foot, aimed at your opponent's legs, ribs and head.

If you lived in the Koguryo Kingdom (between 37 B.C. and A.D. 668) and you were a member of the upper class, you would probably have subscribed to the popular belief that you should use your hands for only artistic endeavors, like painting, composing poetry or writing calligraphy. Therefore, in the event of physical confrontation, you would use your feet to ward off an attacker.

Warrior Words

Cave dwellers "kick butt"! Statues, cave paintings and decorative murals depicting martial arts practice and dating as far back as the sixth century have been found in Korea.

Martial Smarts

Another popular Korean martial art is Hapkido, a combative system that focuses on grappling, throwing and restraining one's opponent. Hapkido synthesized indigenous Korean defensive methodologies with the Japanese martial art of *Aiki–jitsu*. The founder of Hapkido, Choi Yong Sul, perfected his martial skill by studying in Korea and Japan.

Korea's Ancient Warriors

In southern Korea, the Silla State (57 B.C. to A.D. 935) was under constant attack from its western rival, the Kingdom of Paekche, as well as international enemies like Japan. Both had coveted Silla's valuable trading ports and fertile farming lands.

In response to these relentless assaults, a socioreligious organization, the Hwa-rang, meaning "flower boy" or "flowering manhood," arose. Most of this organization's recruits came from the aristocracy, whose youth embraced the ideals of patriotism and chivalry. Philosophy, arts and science, horse-riding skills, archery and empty-hand martial arts formed the basis of their training curriculum (summer camp gone wild!).

Arts 'n' Crafts Replace Martial Arts

Mongolian invaders brought to Korea their unique expertise: shooting arrows from horseback—a skill that seemed infinitely more practical than engaging your opponent hand-to-hand.

Under Yi dynasty rule (1392–1910), civilians gradually replaced the military at the political helm of their country. Ultimately, however, their lack of training led to the deterioration of Korea's martial forces. As these unskilled leaders came to embrace neo-Confucian philosophy, which espoused a doctrine of nonviolence, the complexion of the political state softened—to what might be called a marshmallowlike consistency. This further compromised military and martial traditions. This shift in fighting philosophy is clearly illustrated in a popular Yi slogan of the period, "We Favor the Arts and Despise the Arms."

If you were a Buddhist living in Korea during this period and had embraced an austere form of this religion, you would have discovered the benefits of martial arts study. You would likely have viewed your practice as a means of training and fortifying your body, while strengthening your mind, rather than utilizing your skills for combat purposes. As a result, you would have enjoyed a strong, healthy body and clarity of concentration. You, like other practitioners, would have been able to devote your mind completely to advanced thinking that would lead to enlightenment.

Master Speaks

If you are a Tae Kwon Do student, you should understand the meaning of the names of forms (individual practice exercises) you perform. Many can be traced back to Silla and Hwa-rang warriors. For example, *Moon-moo* honors the 13th King of Silla, and *Ul-ji* is named after a formidable seventh-century general.

Martial Smarts

At the dawn of the twentieth century, most martial arts experts received the bulk of their training in Buddhist monasteries. Conversely, as we approach the end of this century, most practitioners now get theirs at storefront schools in their local mini-mall!

Japan's Impact on Korean Martial Arts

In 1884, a period called the "Quiet Existence" of the Korean people ended with the Japanese takeover. If you were living in Korea at this time, your new rulers would have forced you to abandon your native tongue, and instead, speak Japanese. Furthermore,

Warrior Words

Because Korea was occupied by various military forces for centuries, many displays of cultural identity were suppressed. Now, however, the country's flag, called a *kukggi*, is proudly featured in most Tae Kwon Do schools, or *dojang*. Additionally, if you were practicing this martial art, you would likely wear a crest depicting this flag on the sleeve of your white training uniform, or *dobok*.

Risky Moves

As the martial art of Tae Kwon Do has gone through several stages of development, its focus has shifted away from traditional values and self-defense practice, to sport competition and cultivating potential medal-winning champions. Be cautious when looking for a school. Make sure it's a martial arts institution that shares your philosophy about training.

you would not have been permitted to practice Korean martial arts. Your combative systems would have been replaced by the Japanese martial sports of Judo and Kendo, which were integrated into the Korean educational system. Later, the Japanese martial arts of Aikido, Jiu-jitsu and Karate would be introduced to the Korean population as a means of further indoctrinating you into the Japanese way of life.

If you had remained fiercely nationalistic, however, these acts of repression would have simply reinforced your resolve to resist your country's oppressors. You and like-minded compatriots would have engaged in the clandestine practice of Korean martial arts, while plotting the overthrow of the Japanese imperial forces.

The Birth of Modern Tae Kwon Do

With the country's liberation in 1945, indigenous martial arts again became popular in Korea. This resulted in the creation of hybrid systems like *Tang Soo Do,* which blended Sobak and *Kwonbop* (meaning "fist art") with Japanese Karate.

The need for establishing a curriculum and further evolving these combative systems was of paramount concern among martial artists. This goal was championed by the Korean government. Then-president Syngman Rhee encouraged the unification of various martial arts under one banner. On April 11, 1955, following several committee meetings chaired by General Choi Hong Hi, it was agreed that this new art would be baptized *Tae Kwon Do*. The new name was translated as "foot" or "kicking" *(tae)*, "hand" or "punching" *(kwon)* and "path" or "way" *(do)*, in other words, "foot hand way."

Tae Kwon Do, Westward Ho!

In the late 1950s, Korean instructors brought Tae Kwon Do to North America. Among these first pioneers was Jhoon Rhee. Grand Master Rhee established the first Tae Kwon

Do school in Texas in 1959. Six years later, Master Chung Lee opened Canada's first Tae Kwon Do school in Montreal, Quebec.

Furthermore, many members of the American armed forces (like Chuck Norris, a.k.a. "Walker: Texas Ranger") were stationed in Korea in the 1950s and 1960s. They studied Tae Kwon Do and helped popularize this martial art in the United States.

Tae Kwon Do's "24"

General Choi and his colleagues developed the first set of 24 Tae Kwon Do forms or patterns:

1. *Chon-ji*
2. *Dan-gun*
3. *Do-san*
4. *Woh-hyo*
5. *Yul-gok*
6. *Joong-gun*
7. *Toi-gye*
8. *Hwa-rang*
9. *Choong-moo*
10. *Gwang-gae*
11. *Do-eun*
12. *Ge-baek*
13. *Eui-am*
14. *Choong-jang*
15. *Ko-dang*
16. *Sam-il*
17. *Yoo-sin*
18. *Choi-yong*
19. *Yong-ge*
20. *Ul-ji*

Martial Smarts

It is the philosophy of non-aggression that makes our art unique. Without it, we merely teach street fighting.

—Grand Master Jhoon Rhee

This quote is indicative of Master Rhee's wisdom about the real value of martial arts training. In addition to his tireless efforts in propagating the martial arts, he is famous for creating modern, foam-dipped safety equipment used by practitioners around the world. In tribute to his genius in this area, Master Rhee's protective equipment is displayed at the Museum of Modern Art in New York City.

21. *Moon-moo*

22. *So-san*

23. *Se-jong*

24. *Tong-il*

These names celebrate historical military figures and national accomplishments.

Minding Your Manners

Although the idea of bowing and then kicking or punching someone is understandably strange to people who don't study martial arts, it makes abundant sense to folks who practice this stuff. It's also puzzling to nonpractitioners that anything that's "martial" can help you become a better human being.

There is more to Tae Kwon Do etiquette than a quick bow at the beginning and end of a class. The aim of this and other martial arts is to develop the student beyond the physical level—an important point that is often lost in the sea of sport Tae Kwon Do.

Tae Kwon Do's etiquette guidelines are summarized in its tenets, written by Choi Hong Hi in the early 1960s. Often posted in Tae Kwon Do schools around the world, they serve as a training guide for teachers and students. These tenets emphasize the need for every serious practitioner to develop courtesy, integrity, perseverance, self-control and an indomitable spirit. They outline Tae Kwon Do's positive message of self-improvement.

Risky Moves

"Warm up" to the idea of avoiding injury. To minimize your risk of injury and extend your kicks as high as possible, be sure to warm up and stretch thoroughly before attempting these techniques.

Jumping, Flying and Spinning

As Tae Kwon Do continues to evolve, punching, blocking and parrying techniques, coupled with impressive kicking skills, remain at the heart of this martial art. As a Tae Kwon Do practitioner, you can learn kicks executed from a multitude of stationary positions (or "stances"), or at a more advanced level, performed while jumping. Dynamic kicks are the trademark of Tae Kwon Do and are frequently the highlight of exhibitions designed to showcase this martial art.

The following section describes two levels of kicking: 1) basic and 2) intermediate and advanced.

Basic Tae Kwon Do Kicks

The following are the types of kicks you could expect to learn during the first 6 months of training:

➤ kicks using the ball, heel and instep or edge of your foot, which you perform while standing

➤ kicks you perform from a kneeling position

➤ kicks you perform while turning your body from left to right or right to left

Intermediate and Advanced Tae Kwon Do Kicks

The following are the types of kicks you could expect to learn as an intermediate or advanced student:

➤ kicks you perform while spinning 270 degrees or more

➤ skipping kicks where you jump and one foot remains in contact with the ground

➤ flying kicks with one or both feet where both feet leave the floor

You can perform these basic, intermediate and advanced kicks individually, in multiples or in combination with other kicks or hand techniques. You can execute them in the air, on a target (for example, a bag or pad) or against wood or other solid objects for the purpose of testing your power, or you can direct them at a partner.

The Long Road to the Olympics

Although there are two global Tae Kwon Do organizations, the International Tae Kwon Do Federation (ITF) and the World Tae Kwon Do Federation (WTF), the latter, established in 1973, is the driving force behind this martial art's acceptance into international competition. It was the WTF that was largely responsible for the inclusion of Tae Kwon Do as an Olympic sport. Tae Kwon Do debuted as a demonstration sport in the 1988 Olympics in Seoul and, thanks in large part to the efforts of the WTF, has since attained medal status.

Master Speaks

A simple, inexpensive and effective method of improving your leaping ability is the "box step." Begin by jumping from the floor onto a box. Then reverse this process by jumping from the box back to the floor. Eventually, begin jumping over the box. Gradually increase the height of the box and, in no time, you could be soaring through the air like Michael Jordan.

Risky Moves

Some practitioners routinely perform jump kicks by running 10 to 15 feet (3 to 5 meters) before taking off. This method is not realistic in the sense that it is unlikely you would be able to duplicate it in the competition ring or in a street defense situation. Therefore, it is unrealistic to practice using this method. Instead, perform your jump kicks from a stationary position.

Risky Moves

Spectacular kicking demonstrations have included vaulting over a moving motorcycle to break a roof tile, jumping over 10 people and breaking two boards, and leaping 10 feet (3 meters) in the air, breaking two boards, à la Evel Knievel. But remember, these incredible feats are only accomplished after years of dedicated practice.

Martial Smarts

Leaping Limas! The first person to win an Olympic medal in Tae Kwon Do was Arlene Limas. Representing the USA at the 1988 Olympic Games in Seoul, Ms Limas received the gold medal in the Women's Heavyweight Sparring division.

Master Speaks

If you want to develop high, powerful kicks, your regimen should include drills designed to stretch and strengthen your legs. Progressive stretching exercises, coupled with weight training or resistance drills, can result in impressive gains. Running, using long strides, can also help you cultivate endurance and kicking "explosiveness."

Command Central

The WTF's headquarters or central gym (the Kukki-won) is located in Seoul, Korea. The federation boasts membership of 12 million practitioners in 108 countries, under the auspices of Un Yong Kim, WTF president and a former executive board member of the International Olympic Committee.

Rules of the Game

If you are interested in international competition, the WTF rules outlined in this section will help you understand how the "game" is played.

If you are competing in a sparring division, most of your bouts (contact competition between two contenders) will consist of three 3-minute rounds. Your matches are overseen by five referees: one in each of four corners and a fifth positioned in the center of the ring, or the competition area, which measures 7 by 7 meters (23 by 23 feet).

You will be outfitted in protective body wear called *hogoo* (sounds sticky but it's not), which covers your torso, as well as head gear. Your hands and feet will be bare.

As kicks are at the heart of every Tae Kwon Do practitioner's repertoire, so, too, do they play a key role in competition. For example, although you would receive points for both punches and kicks, only the latter can be scored to the head. In recognition of their more advanced level of difficulty, kicks to the head will give you more points than those directed to the body.

In order for referees to recognize your points, each technique must be accurately aimed at your opponent.

At the culmination of each match, the center referee will confer with the judges in each corner and, upon determining a winner, will raise the hand of the victor (so don't forget to wear your antiperspirant!).

In addition to its position as an Olympic sport, Tae Kwon Do, like most other martial arts, is viewed as an excellent tool for perfection of one's character.

Risky Moves

Although it is essential for you to practice kicks, it is a mistake not to develop skillful hand strikes. It's not uncommon to see incredible punching exhibitions performed at international events, for example, breaking 15 roof tiles with a single punch and smashing 2 bricks using the edge of the hand (which, undoubtedly, had to be followed by the ever-popular broom-sweeping or Hoover-vacuum demonstration).

Baby Steps to Black Belt

As in many other martial arts, your progress as a Tae Kwon Do student would be measured in color belts *gup* that go beyond mere accessory! Generally, you would move from beginner to Black Belt in 11 steps.

1. *Tenth Gup* – White Belt

2. *Ninth Gup* – White Belt with a Yellow Stripe

3. *Eighth Gup* – Yellow or Gold Belt

4. *Seventh Gup* – Yellow or Gold Belt with a Green Stripe

5. *Sixth Gup* – Green Belt

6. *Fifth Gup* – Green Belt with a Blue Stripe

7. *Fourth Gup* – Blue Belt

8. *Third Gup* – Blue Belt with a Red Stripe

9. *Second Gup* – Red Belt

10. *First Gup* – Red Belt with a Black Stripe

11. *First Dan* – Black Belt

Martial Smarts

Tae Kwon Do is a means of developing and enhancing the emotional, perceptual and psychological characteristics that shape the younger generation.

—*General Choi Hong Hi, President, International Tae Kwon Do Federation*

233

The average training time to progress from beginner to Black Belt is between 2 and 4 years. If you become a dedicated practitioner, you will come to realize that achieving Black Belt does not mark the end of the road toward martial arts excellence, but rather signifies a beginning.

There are nine advanced skill or Black Belt levels, called *dan* (loosely translated, this means "degree"). If you achieve a Fourth Dan level, you would generally be classified as a "Teacher," and at the Sixth Dan level, the title of "Master" would likely be bestowed upon you. At Eighth Dan and above, you would be called a "Grand Master."'

The Least You Need to Know

➤ Korea, once called the "Hermit Kingdom," faced numerous invasions by foreign forces resulting in the development of self-defense systems.

➤ The initial focus of Korean martial arts was self-defense and personal preservation, but like many other combative systems, these objectives were later infused with a philosophy of nonviolence.

➤ As with most other martial arts, etiquette plays a major role in the practice of Tae Kwon Do.

➤ Dynamic kicks are an integral part of the Tae Kwon Do student's repertoire.

➤ The World Tae Kwon Do Federation spearheaded this martial arts' bid for Olympic acceptance. The WTF's headquarters, the Kukki-won, is located in Seoul, Korea.

➤ Much like other martial arts, the ranking system in Tae Kwon Do moves from beginner to advanced, with dedicated practitioners recognizing that receiving their Black Belt represents a new beginning in, rather than the end of, their study.

➤ Tae Kwon Do is an Olympic sport, a means of improving your physical fitness and a tool that can be employed to improve your character.

Getting Technical

The photographs on the following pages illustrate the types of techniques you will perform as a Tae Kwon Do student.

Figure 20–1 (a, b, and c)

Figure 20–2 (a, b, and c)

Chapter 21

Choose Your Weapons: Kendo, Kyudo and Kobudo

> **In This Chapter**
>
> ➤ Discovering the sword art of Kendo
>
> ➤ Understanding Kyudo, the way of archery
>
> ➤ Examining Kobudo, Okinawan armed defense
>
> ➤ Typical training techniques

In this computer-obsessed era, with every imaginable electronic gadget at your fingertips, its puzzling why so many people devote so much time to seemingly antiquated martial arts skills of weaponry. After all, isn't your cellular telephone, with its speed dial connection to 911 or your local security company, the only "weapon" you'll need in this day and age?

The big answer to this big question is a big, fat *No*, and this chapter will help you understand why. It will also show you what you can gain from practicing the martial arts of Kendo, Kyudo and Kobudo.

Kendo's Way of the Sword

Kendo is a martial sport created in the Meiji period (1868–1912). It is based on the classical techniques of *Ken-jitsu* (sword skills). Its genesis can be traced to the early days of the Heian period (A.D. 794), when sword exercises were considered a common part of each noble son's education. With the unification of Japan in the sixteenth century and subsequent periods of peace, the need for sword skills was dramatically diminished.

Martial Smarts

Will fight for food! As a result of extended periods of peace in the sixteenth and seventeenth centuries, hordes of *ronin,* masterless samurai, wandered the countryside, looking for work. Many of these displaced warriors—victims of medieval downsizing—turned to other professions including religion, farming and even banditry.

Since the early 1920s, Kendo has been enormously popular in Japan, primarily because it was a highly valued extracurricular activity in middle and high schools, as well as universities.

During the American occupation of Japan after the Second World War, all martial disciplines, including Kendo, were banned. This moratorium came to an end in 1952, the same year the All Japan Kendo Federation was established. In 1970, a new governing body, the International Kendo Federation (IKF), was created. It conducted the first World Kendo Championship, in Tokyo. The primary goal of the federation is the unification and promotion of this martial sport at the international level. Thanks largely to the aggressive efforts of the IKF, it is estimated that approximately two million Kendo-*ka* (Kendo students) practice this martial art worldwide.

Making the "Cut" at a Kendo Dojo

As a Kendo-*ka,* you will begin a typical class seated in rank order for a brief meditation period called *mokuso*. Following a short warm-up, the *sensei* (teacher) will lead you through a series of eight basic cuts and thrusts using a Japanese sword. These techniques are as follows:

1. *oshomen* – downward cut aimed at the center of your opponent's forehead

2. *hidarimen* – diagonal cut aimed at the left side of the mask

3. *migimen* – diagonal cut aimed at the right side of the mask

4. *migido* – diagonal cut aimed at the right side of the breastplate

Warrior Words

Gear up! Kendo-*ka* wear a white or navy blue *dogi* (martial arts uniform) and *hakama* (wide, pleated trousers). They are outfitted with armor called *bogu*. This protective gear consists of a metal and cloth face mask *(men)*, laminated wood breastplate *(do)*, thickly padded fencing gloves *(kote)* and canvas hip shields *(tare)*. Kendo-*ka* are armed with practice swords made of bamboo, called *shinai*.

5. *gyakudo* – diagonal cut aimed at the left side of the breastplate

6. *kote* – downward cut to the right wrist

7. *hidarikote* – downward cut to the left wrist

8. *tsuki* – thrust aimed at the throat

After practicing these movements in the air or trading them with a partner, students progress to *shiai* (contest practice).

Looking for a "Match"?

The *shiai*, or match, is generally a three-point contest, 3 to 5 minutes in duration. As a participant, you would begin with a formal bow *(rei)*, after which you'd raise your *shinai* (wood sword), held in both hands, aiming the tip toward your partner's throat. A torrent of blows and deafening *kiai* (yell of spirit) follow. If you are the first Kendo-*ka* to score three points, you'll be declared the winner of the match. In the event of a tie, the match is continued until either you or your partner scores another point.

You should repeat each Kendo cut or strike thousands of times before learning a new technique. The purpose of this practice, and indeed Kendo itself, is not simply the acquisition of skill, but the building of good character and achievement of a sense of harmony in each student.

Risky Moves

When practicing Kendo, it's unsafe to engage in partner work until you can perform all techniques smoothly and with optimum control in the air alone. Once you've mastered use of a wooden sword you might progress to *Iai*, which involves drawing and cutting with a sharp blade, or *Batto-jitsu* where one test of your skills would be slicing bundles of straw.

Staying on Target with Japanese Archery

Kyudo is the "way of archery." Like other aspects of Japanese culture, its origins are Chinese. The first records of archery in China can be traced back to the Shang dynasty (1766–1045 B.C.). If you were a member of the court during the Chou dynasty (1045–256 B.C.), you would likely have attended sport archery tournaments that were set to music and featured elaborate banquets (perhaps the birth of "dinner theater"?). While the precise date of the first appearance of the bow *(yumi)* and arrow *(ya)* in Japan is unknown, antiquated lacquered versions from the fifth century have been found.

Martial Smarts

In archery, the Japanese bow, which measures 2.2 meters (7 feet), is much longer than Chinese or Korean versions. It's so long, in fact, that an archer has to draw the bow at a position of one-third its length, as opposed to one-half, in order to maintain control of the weapon.

239

Martial Smarts

Everyone needs a hobby. The Yamato school of archery was founded in the middle of the seventeenth century by Morikawa Kozan. This was perhaps the first school to emphasize archery study as a pastime, rather than a military pursuit. In addition to offering instruction of technical skills, the school stressed *shin–mei,* or the development of one's spirit through use of the bow.

Warrior Words

Just horsing around? *Yabusame* refers to archery techniques you perform while on horseback (replace the bow and arrow with a rifle, and the horse with skis, and you've got the modern biathlon). While traveling at breakneck speeds, you shoot small clay targets. Generally demonstrated at festivals and other celebratory activities throughout Japan, *Yabusame* can best be viewed at the Meiji Shrine in Tokyo.

The traditions of Kyudo are firmly rooted in the samurai arts. Archery from standing positions and on horseback was one of the many skills possessed by medieval *bushi* (warriors).

Near the end of the fourteenth century, master archers established a system of Kyudo. In the blink of an eye, several *ryu,* or schools, sprang up and, almost as quickly, disappeared, perhaps because practitioners came to the realization that organized, group sessions were not truly conducive to learning this sport. Instead, they preferred to engage in solitary practice (like singing in the shower and other activities, Kyudo is best done alone, or with one partner!).

➤ **Take Aim at Your Heart**   Like other types of archery, Kyudo focuses on cultivating distance skills and accuracy, but it also transcends mere sport. Hitting the bull's-eye is not the goal. Learning Kyudo is a metaphor for achieving a sense of personal balance, harmony with all things *(wa)* and effortless serenity. As a follower of Kyudo, you would be more concerned with self-development or piercing your *kokoro* ("heart" or "spirit"), than with simply scoring points.

➤ **Filling in the Blanks with Zen**   If you were a Zen devotee, when painting or creating brush calligraphy, you would leave a portion of your creative surface blank. Taking a minimalist approach, you would place only the necessary strokes on the paper, leaving white spaces that can be filled by only the minds of those who look at your work. Viewing these works is at least as interactive as popular video games and Internet sites!

Similarly, when practicing Kyudo, you can achieve a Zenlike state of harmony if you remove the target and instead focus your attention on the actions of the hand, arm and eye in one flowing motion, and then release the arrow with an uncluttered mind.

➤ **More Than Half a Million Served!**   In excess of 500,000 individuals (roughly the number of people crammed into a Tokyo subway car during rush hour!) practice Kyudo in Japan. *Dojo* outside this country have been established in many major cities around the world, and nearly every Japanese cultural center offers Kyudo classes.

➤ **Rank, Uniform and Competition** If you practice Kyudo, you'll notice that its ranking system mirrors that of other Japanese martial disciplines: *kyu,* or color belt steps, from white to brown, and *dan* for Black Belt practitioners. As you advance in rank, flawless form (performing each technique with perfect precision) will take precedence over the number of targets you hit. As a student of this martial discipline, you'll wear a *kimono* (traditional undergarment) and *hakama* (wide trousers).

If you compete at the national and international level, you'll be required to hit targets at a distance of 20, 40 and 60 meters (66, 131 and 197 feet). These tournaments are overseen by the All Japan Kyudo Federation, an organization founded in 1948.

Martial Smarts

What we see depends largely on what we look for.

—*Japanese proverb*

Master Speaks

Unlike Kendo, *Kyudo* and *Kobudo* are not generally practiced in a group class. Instead, if you were to study *Kyudo* or *Kobudo,* you would receive one-to-one coaching from an experienced *sensei* or senior student.

Taking a Swing at Okinawan Weaponry

Karate ("China hand" or "empty hand") was developed primarily to counter unarmed acts of aggression. Kobudo (ancient martial way), Okinawa's "other martial art," came into existence to combat armed attacks.

The *bo,* a 6-foot wood staff, was the mainstay of Okinawa's ancient arsenal in tribal conflicts prior to the Sho clan unification period (1429). As there was a lack of iron ore in the Ryukyu Islands, of which Okinawa is the largest, metal weapons in this country were hard to come by. Those available were generally imported from China and later, Japan, and commanded a high price. Therefore, only the upper classes could afford to purchase these luxuries. As a result, commoners put their trust in the *bo.*

Risky Moves

When you are a beginner, shooting arrows from great distances at targets can lead to frustration and improper technique. Instead, begin by shooting arrows at a close range while paying special attention to minute details of proper form. As you gradually increase the distance of your target, your skills will improve and so will your confidence level.

Martial Smarts

"Musket balls may pierce our bones and sword blades may cut our tendons, but they will never break our spirit," said Janna Eikata, rallying Okinawans against Satsuma invaders in the early seventeenth century. This is clearly not a statement made by the prefecture's Ministry of Travel and Tourism!

Kobudo's "Menu"

In addition to the *bo,* the following weapons have been added to Okinawa's weapons menu:

➤ *sai* – three-pronged metal truncheon

➤ *tonfa* – originally used as a handle in grinding mills, a wood "baton" approximately 45 to 60 centimeters (18 to 24 inches) in length

➤ *nunchaku* – small wood flail or two pieces of wood, each 30 to 45 centimeters (12 to 18 inches) long, connected by a short piece of string

➤ *eku* – boat oar approximately 1.5 meters (5 feet) long

➤ *kama* – long-handled sickle used to cut sugarcane or for woodworking

➤ *tinbei* – shield made of metal, tortoise shell or bamboo, reconfigured from baskets and cooking pots

➤ *rochin* – long-handled knife or machete

➤ *suruchin* – rope or chain, approximately 2 meters (7 feet) long, with metal objects attached at both ends

➤ *tekko* – brass knuckles made of metal or wood

➤ *nunti* – detachable *sai*-like three-pronged weapon (with one point facing downwards) affixed to a long wood staff

All weapons, some of which were used in pairs, were intended to combat the sword or spear. Many were originally ordinary household tools that were modified to enhance their usefulness as a weapon. It's unlikely that today's cappuccino maker or food processor would have the same combative value.

Warrior Words

There are no fewer than five schools *(ryu)* in Okinawa today. The word *ryu* refers to the lineage of a martial system, or school.

Martial Smarts

In addition to the lack of metal on Okinawa, another contributing factor in the development of *Kobudo,* as well as unarmed combative arts, was the fact that natives were prohibited from possessing arms. The first prohibition edict came at the beginning of the sixteenth century, when King Sho Shin (1477–1526) banned the carrying of all weapons by Ryukyuan gentry. A second edict was issued in 1609 by invading members of the Satsuma clan, when they handed down the Fifteen Laws, which would further subjugate the Okinawan people.

Family Tree of Okinawan Weaponry

There are at least five weapons systems in Okinawa. These include *Matayoshi-ryu* (named for its founder Matayoshi Shinko), *Ryukyu* Kobudo (established by Taira Shinken), *Chinen Yamani-ryu* (also named after its founder, Chinen Saburo), *Ufuchiku Den* (created by Kina Shosei) and *Mura bo* style. Their teachings have been passed from generation to generation. Unlike the first four, which are formalized systems, practice of *Mura bo* is limited to villages throughout the prefecture.

Swing, Thrust and Parry

If you were a Kobudo student, you would have to study various fundamental techniques. These include learning to hold the weapon, developing solid stances, utilizing your weight to increase power, cultivating speed through proper footwork and repeating countless numbers of swinging, slashing and thrusting strikes. Defensive strategies include blocking or parrying using a weapon, arm, hand or leg, or shifting off the line of an attack *(tai sabaki)*. As a seasoned Kobudo-*ka,* you'd also employ distance and timing skills to launch a counterattack before an opponent has an opportunity to reach you. This ability to anticipate an attack is called *sen no sen,* which means, "taking the initiative" (a skill that would likely prove useful even for the most savvy corporate bigwig). After developing a high degree of proficiency with these movements, you would begin practicing more advanced techniques, including the following:

➤ *kata* – You will practice patterns that feature a series of exercises for each weapon in the Okinawan Kobudo system. There are numerous *kata* for each weapon. For example, there are approximately 30 for the *bo,* 10 for the *sai,* and perhaps 2 or 3 for each other weapon. These *kata* are generally named after their place of origin or their creator (for instance, *Chatan Yara no Sai* means "the *sai* form of (Mr.) Yara from Chatan village").

➤ *tamashiwara* – Progressing from basics and *kata* practice, you'll begin striking apparatus like a large rubber tire mounted on a wall or a wooden dummy to develop accuracy and power, and to better understand the strengths and limitations of each weapon.

➤ *yoku soku kumite* – You will engage in choreographed sparring matches or mock combat, which will enable you to improve your reaction time.

Although free sparring (unrehearsed offensive and defensive exchanges with a partner) with weapons while wearing protective gear has been attempted, due to the high risk of injury to participants, this form of training has met with little or no success.

The Least You Need to Know

➤ Kendo, Kyudo and Kobudo are modernized weapons systems based on ancient arms traditions.

➤ Kendo practitioners use a wooden sword called a *shinai* to strike an armor-clad partner.

➤ Kyudo, a form of archery, involves use of a very long bow (*yumi*) to shoot arrows at targets.

➤ Kobudo is the name for Okinawan weapons systems, which use a variety of armaments.

➤ Beyond developing obvious physical skills, as a weapons practitioner, you'll also strive to achieve a Zenlike state of harmony—a balance between body, mind and spirit.

Getting Technical

The photographs on the following pages demonstrate the kinds of weapons drills you would perform as a Kobudo student.

Figure 21–1 (a, b, and c)

Figure 21–2 (a, b, and c)

Chapter 22

Shifting into "Neutral" with Tai Chi Chuan

In This Chapter

➤ Discovering how Tai Chi Chuan styles evolved

➤ Learning what you can gain from Tai Chi practice

➤ Information about uniforms and class structure

➤ A glimpse of Tai Chi Chuan techniques

At sunrise each day, millions of people around the world begin their day with Tai Chi Chuan exercises. In China, these people can be seen in parks, courtyards and public squares, slowly performing circular, graceful, fluid movements characteristic of this martial art. Across the globe, in North America, countless aging baby boomers put their caffe lattes aside, deactivate their cellular telephones and practice Tai Chi each day as a means of getting fit and reducing stress.

So, is Tai Chi Chuan a gentle movement art or a martial system? Is it a way of improving your health or a means of reducing daily stress? Is it an age-old tradition dating back to pre-Christian times or a modern fitness activity?

The answer is that Tai Chi is all these things and more, as you will see by reading this chapter.

The "Skinny" on Tai Chi Chuan

Tai Chi, or Tai Ji (translated as "grand ultimate truth"), can be dated back to the Chou dynasty (1045–256 B.C.). This martial art is based on Taoist laws, which govern the

Martial Smarts

The lust for power is the most flagrant of all passions.

—*Tacitus,*
Annals A.D. 100

Warrior Words

Taoism is both an ancient religion *(Tao Chio)* and a school of philosophy *(Tao Chia)*. It deals with the rightful path or way to ultimate truth. Followers strive to be in harmony with all forces of nature and cosmic laws. Lao Tsu, author of the popular text *Tao Te Ching (Classic of the Way and Virtue),* is the founder of Taoism. Lao Tsu and Kung Fu Tsu (Confucius, of fortune cookie fame) are regarded as two of the outstanding thinkers of medieval China.

universe, including the passive principles of yin and active principles of yang. Basically, Taoist laws say that, in order to preserve all life, you must maintain a balance between yin and yang. This law of nature is especially true when discussing the five elements—not rayon, Teflon, Ban-Lon, Dacron and polyester, but wood, earth, fire, metal and water. Tai Chi is based on this concept of harmony and balance.

The wandering Taoist monk Zhang San Feng (also called Chang San Feng), who had studied a multitude of martial arts, is credited with creating Tai Chi. He based this system on his observation of a fight between a snake and a crane. The snake used relaxed, evasive movements and lightning-fast counterstrikes to win the skirmish. Inspired by the reptile's loose, but controlled, movements, Zhang devised a combative form that relied on natural, reflexive techniques.

The *Other* Temple

Like Studio 54 in the 1970s, the Shaolin Temple was *the* place to be for Buddhists and martial artists who practiced external, or hard, styles. Their internal, or soft, counterpart was the Wu Dang Shan monastery. This monastery consisted of more than 100 buildings along 72 peaks in Hubei province in central China, and was the hot spot for Taoists and followers of internal combative systems. There is considerable debate among martial arts scholars as to whether it was Zhang San Feng or his disciples who brought Tai Chi to the Wu Dang Shan monastery in the mid-fifteenth century. This issue aside, the monastery was the mecca for practitioners of internal systems for three centuries.

"Green" Monks

In a demonstration of less than monastic humility, as the fame of the Shaolin Temple and its martial monks increased, Wu Dang warriors began to suffer from what might be best described as an inferiority complex. They were jealous that their monastery was regarded as the "other" martial temple. The emperor Qian Long (1737–1795) exploited this rift. In fact, most of the army that burned the Shaolin Temple consisted of Taoists from the Wu Dang Shan monastery.

From Combat to Calm

Historically, Tai Chi was more martial in its approach than it is today. Currently, greater emphasis is placed on performing the Tai Chi form, or set. Even the language of this martial art is different. There is a sharp contrast with combative terminology you might encounter in other martial arts or in the frenetic "fitspeak" employed in health clubs. For example, as a Tai Chi student, you would flow from "parting the horse's mane" to "crane spreads its wings" and "jade dragon reaches for the pearl." It could take you 6 to 12 months to learn the Tai Chi form and many years before you can refine its movements. At this point, you could begin practicing partner exchange drills called "pushing hands."

Tui Shou (pushing hands) exercises involve pre-set, and later, spontaneous, blocking and striking drills. Using the palm of the hand, you and your partner will take turns pushing or striking each other. After deflecting, or redirecting, a strike, you and your partner will respond with a counterattack. As you become more proficient, you will increase the speed of each strike, deflection and counterstrike, and begin using your entire body more efficiently and more harmoniously. As you become even more skilled, you will advance to uprooting (shoving) techniques that will enable you to off-balance your partners, sometimes hurtling them across the room!

Warrior Words

Tai Ji Fu Hao, the Tai Chi diagram or yin and yang symbol, is a popular good luck charm in China. You wear it around your neck or attach it to doors. You can even tie it to a baby's crib to protect your children from "things that go bump in the night."

Master Speaks

After learning the Tai Chi Chuan form, you can practice it at a variety of speeds to develop different skills. For example, by performing this form quickly, you can improve your balance and timing skills.

Risky Moves

Harm or heal? The principle of stimulating "meridians," energy lines that run throughout your body, is the basis for Chinese medical practices like acupuncture, whose aim is to ensure good health. With a different purpose in mind, this same principle is at the heart of internal martial arts systems like Tai Chi Chuan, where strikes are directed toward an opponent's "vital points" for the purpose of halting an attack.

Tai Chi's Movers and Shakers

There have been countless numbers of people who have contributed to the evolution of Tai Chi Chuan, but four individuals are among the most famous teachers of this martial art.

Risky Moves

Don't go crashing through crash courses. Tai Chi doesn't use a progressive ranking system like those employed by other martial arts. Furthermore, its movements are fairly complex and difficult to truly master. So, if you are looking for instant gratification or even something that you can grasp in the short term, Tai Chi may not be the right choice for you.

➤ **"Barroom Brawling" Wang** The principal student of Zhang San Feng, sometimes called the "father of Tai Chi Chuan," was Wang Tsung Yueh. Wang had visited the Chen family village, which was located about one hour's ride from the Shaolin monastery. Fortified by a large quantity of rice wine, Wang began discussing martial arts with other barroom patrons, who boasted a strong, proud tradition of Shaolin Kung Fu. Predictably, a brawl ensued, but surprisingly it was the diminutive Wang who sent Chen villagers flying through the air. Impressed by his skill, locals begged Wang to teach them his martial art. In what would be described today as a crash course, Wang, using the villagers' Shaolin combative skills as a foundation, accommodated them. This led to the birth of *Chen*-style Tai Chi Chuan.

➤ **"Invincible" Yang** The Chen family villagers became highly skilled Tai Chi practitioners. In the nineteenth century, a guy by the name of Yang Lu Chan (1799–1872) visited to learn more about martial arts. As he was not a blood relative, the villagers weren't likely to teach him anything about their system of martial arts. The clever Yang devised a scheme: he would pretend to be deaf and mute. This enabled him to quietly observe—and learn—*Chen*-style Tai Chi. Each day, after watching students practice, he would retire to his room, where he would imitate their movements. This clandestine activity would continue for several years until Yang was caught in the act. Surprisingly, rather than banishing him, the villagers, who were undoubtedly impressed by Yang's devotion to training, invited him to join them in studying their martial art. Living and practicing in the Chen village for nearly 20 years, Yang developed his area of expertise, "pushing hands," and his combative skills—both armed and unarmed—were, by all reports, unmatched.

After nearly two decades, Yang left the Chen village and traveled throughout China. He was often called upon to demonstrate his skills—something he did with unparalleled success—thereby earning the name "Yang the Invincible." His teaching method would later be called the *Yang* style of Tai Chi.

➤ **"Sunny" Wu**   Tai Chi Chuan's method of internal boxing has two famous sister arts: *Hsing-I* (shape and mind fist) and *Ba Gua* (eight diagram palm). *Hsing-I* features techniques named after the elements, such as wood, air, fire, earth and so on, like a martial arts version of the popular game "scissors-paper-rock." *Ba Gua* emphasizes circular footwork enabling you to step behind an opponent to avoid an attack.

One of Yang's students, Wu Yu Hsiang, concentrated on close combat techniques. By combining these skills with *Hsing-I* and *Ba Gua,* he created the *Sun* style of Tai Chi.

➤ **"Teacher" Wu**   The fourth of the Tai Chi styles is the *Wu* method, developed by Wu Jien Chuan, which emphasizes old combative values, especially uprooting and throwing your opponent. He was a prolific teacher who spread his style throughout southern China.

To Your Health!

Despite its beginnings as a lethal martial art, the greatest benefit of today's Tai Chi is the therapeutic effect it can have on your body.

Research conducted at the Medical Academy of Shanghai and Bellevue Hospital in New York City shows that Tai Chi Chuan can stimulate your nervous system, lower your blood pressure, help you relieve stress and tone your muscles with minimal strain.

Massaging Your Organs and Balancing Your Energy

Proponents of Tai Chi believe that this martial art's rhythmical movements can massage your internal organs, improving your ability to function.

According to Chinese beliefs, when the energy in your body is obstructed or unbalanced, you can become ill. Practicing this martial art can aid the positive flow of *chi* throughout your body's meridians, or energy lines, to promote good health.

No Pain, All Gain

In the West, most exercise is seen as a means of improving health and retarding the aging process. As you get older, high-impact cardiovascular activities like running can have a detrimental effect on your joints and, Tai Chi practitioners believe, on your organs. As a physical activity that is clearly low impact, Tai Chi can offer you many of the same physical and psychological benefits of other, more strenuous, forms of exercise—with minimal risk of damage to your knees, hips and ankles. For example, the Tai Chi set performed from beginning to end without a break, can take you 20 minutes to complete. As this form features low stances and constant movement of all

Master Speaks

In the West, we tend to measure martial artists by their titles or belt color. Additionally, we place a high premium on youth and agility. Conversely, in the East, martial arts practitioners may, or may not, wear a uniform or belt. Furthermore, those of advanced age are revered for their depth of knowledge and held in high esteem.

limbs of your body, your heart rate can be elevated to the desirable 60 to 80 percent of maximum deemed necessary for cardiovascular gains. With its slow, muscle-elongating movements, you can also use Tai Chi as part of a comprehensive physiotherapy program designed to help you recover from an injury or illness.

A Little "Class"

Before you cross the threshold of the Tai Chi classroom, you probably will have lots of questions. What will you wear? What will the classroom look like? What kinds of exercises will you perform? To find out, read on.

Staying Uniform

The only requirement for a Tai Chi uniform is that it be comfortable and allow you freedom of movement. You and other practitioners might wear a Tai Chi uniform or be clothed in a T-shirt, loose-fitting trousers and soft shoes. Similarly, your instructor, or *sifu*, can be attired in anything from street clothes to a formal Chinese uniform and sash.

Unlike other martial arts, in Tai Chi there is no official ranking system. Distinction is awarded based on time invested in training. While some individuals begin teaching early in their career (perhaps, prematurely), most experts recommend you train for a minimum of 5 years before you lead a class.

Decor-um

As with other martial arts, your Tai Chi classroom should be bright, clean and well ventilated. There are no special requirements with respect to the school's decor, except for the ubiquitous photograph of your chief instructor's teacher and, perhaps, the founder of the style you are practicing. You might also see a simple scroll bearing thought-provoking Chinese calligraphy—think of it as a Tai Chi Chuan "motivational message." Some schools still adhere to the practice of burning incense in a pot near the entrance to the practice area. Others offer you tea throughout your practice session. Sadly, the tea-guzzling tradition is being replaced by the presence of a growing number of soft drink and snack-dispensing vending machines.

You might find the class schedule somewhat unstructured, with flexible start and stop times for each training session. It is also not uncommon for students to meander in and out of a class. The result is an atmosphere that is more informal than that of other martial arts schools.

A Leisurely Lesson

As a novice, intermediate or advanced student, you will begin class with a warm-up and exercises for developing correct form and stimulating your *chi* flow. Generally, this is followed by practice of the Tai Chi unarmed form, which, depending on the style, can have anywhere from 24 to 108 movements and take approximately 5 to 20 minutes to complete.

Master Speaks

To develop effective self-defense skills, you have to understand the physical application of every Tai Chi movement you perform and practice it with a partner.

If you are a novice or intermediate student, you may repeat the set. As a more advanced member, you may shift to weapons forms, which include the straight sword, curved saber, long spear or wooden staff. As a seasoned practitioner, you might then progress to "pushing hands" exercises performed with a partner.

Throughout the class, the *sifu* may reinforce visual and physical instruction with the occasional comment, but the general atmosphere of the session remains relaxed.

The Least You Need to Know

➤ Tai Chi Chuan (grand ultimate fist), practiced by hundreds of millions of people worldwide, is an internal, or soft, Chinese martial art.

➤ The four principal Tai Chi Chuan styles are *Chen, Yang, Sun* and *Wu.*

➤ Tai Chi's curriculum is generally divided into set practice, weapons forms and "pushing hands."

➤ Tai Chi's ranking system is based on tenure of the practitioner. Uniform requirements and class structure are generally informal.

➤ Tai Chi Chuan practice can provide you with many benefits, including improved fitness levels and stress reduction, with minimal impact on your body's delicate joints.

Getting Technical

The photographs on the following pages illustrate typical techniques you would learn as a Tai Chi student.

Figure 22–1 (a, b, and c)

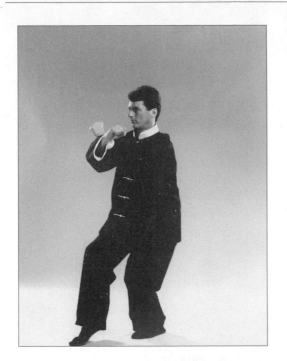

Figure 22–2 (a, b, and c)

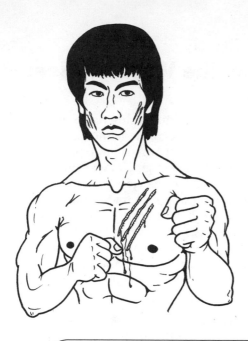

Chapter 23

The Eclectic Approach to Martial Arts

In This Chapter

➤ How Bruce Lee caused a revolution

➤ Eclectic martial arts that pull out all the stops

➤ Learning through seminars and workshops

➤ Discovering how audiovisual aids can help or hinder

➤ Typical eclectic techniques

When you scan your local telephone book or read magazines, you may be dazzled by the number of advertisements you'll see for martial arts schools. Your search will probably be a bit easier if these institutions teach systems that are at least vaguely familiar to you, like Judo, Karate, Tae Kwon Do and Tai Chi.

What do you do, however, when you come across ads for entirely unfamiliar schools or disciplines, like Jeet Kune Do or Sambo or various kinds of commando-style training? How do you learn more about what they teach and whether they'd be appropriate for you? Additionally, if you prefer to study these eclectic martial arts in a noncontact format, what are your options?

This chapter will teach you more about the hands-on—and hands-off—approach to practicing some popular eclectic martial arts.

Martial Smarts

In explaining the importance of economy of motion, Bruce Lee said, "The less effort, the faster and more powerful you'll be."

Lee Leads the Way with Jeet Kune Do

Bruce Lee did much more than bring Asian fighting disciplines to the silver screen. He launched a martial arts renaissance or, perhaps more precisely, revolution. As he was encouraging practitioners to "liberate (themselves) from the classical mess," Lee broke the ties that bound him to traditional combative methods and developed Jeet Kune Do (way of intercepting fist). After years of research, Lee and his followers attempted to incorporate every useful martial arts element into this system. It was "out with the old and in with the new" as they embraced components of various martial arts that they deemed practical and discarded anything they found to be ineffective.

Originally, Bruce Lee studied Wing Chun (a southern Chinese style of Kung Fu). He took components of this martial art and fused it with bits of Karate, Judo, Jiu-jitsu, Western wrestling and boxing. The result was a lethal composite system that served as the precursor for modern eclectic martial arts.

Lee constructed the following curriculum for Jeet Kune Do:

➤ fundamental skills of punching and kicking

➤ concepts of independent motion (moving your limbs independently versus using your entire body)

➤ fainting (faking), body shifting and use of nontelegraphic attacks (techniques launched with no forewarning)

➤ methods of trapping and immobilization (controlling your partner's limbs)

➤ holding, restraining and submission techniques

➤ principles of evading, blocking, destroying, redirecting and intercepting an attack

➤ psychology of attacking and defending

The final level of training intended for practitioners of Jeet Kune Do was the "no limitation" stage, where advanced students were free to explore, change and design their personal fighting style.

As a Jeet Kune Do practitioner, plain and simple is the way you'd go. No elaborate uniforms or belts. No ranking system. And you'd probably spend the same amount for tuition as your buddy who studies Karate, Judo or Tae Kwon Do.

Oh, we should mention here that there are lots of Bruce Lee devotees in their early 20s, who weren't even born at the time of his death. They're often heard debating martial arts philosophy, stating, "Bruce Lee said this" or "Bruce Lee did that." Opportunities for criticism aside, it's encouraging to see the influence of "The Little Dragon" is still alive and well.

Because There Are No Rules

It's difficult to be certain when the first no-holds-barred bouts were conducted. It could have been hundreds, or even thousands, of years ago. What is known is that individuals who engaged in these matches for fortune or fame quickly ascertained what worked—and what didn't. Desperation is, after all, the mother of invention.

There are a variety of modern types of these "extreme" martial arts. Some are more sport oriented, while others take a more combative approach for the sole purpose of survival.

It's Only a Game until Somebody Loses an Eye

Shootboxing, Shootfighting, Trapfighting, Sambo, Vale Tudo, Mu Tau and Luta Livre are names of both combative styles and types of full contact, pulling-out-all-the-stops contests.

With the exception of Sambo (Russian grappling), all of these styles allow you to strike and kick, using any part of your arm or leg. Once your opponent is within arm's reach, you would also have at your disposal any number of takedowns (off-balancing tactics). If you and your partner are on the ground, you can also rely on a wide range of painful restraints applied to the elbow, ankle, shoulder or wrist.

Martial Smarts

Practitioners of these brutal styles who elect to compete often adopt colorful ring names like "King of the Streets," "The Predator" or "Zen Machine." Do these WWF-like monikers make you want to chuckle? Well think twice before you do—these guys are generally the "real deal"!

"Sticking your neck out" takes on all new meaning in these martial arts, where holds applied to this vulnerable part of a practitioner's body are painful, powerful negotiating tools!

As a practitioner of these styles, you'd probably never perform "forms" (routines that resemble dance) and rarely engage in pre-arranged sparring or self-defense drills. Tuition costs are competitive with other martial arts.

While these styles share certain elements, there are some slight differences and they all originated in different countries around the world:

➤ Shootfighting: Shootboxing and Shootwrestling – This "reality" combative style originated in Japan. If you were a Shootboxing practitioner, you'd wear lightweight boxing gloves, as well as padded shin and instep protectors. If you were

Warrior Words

The combat sport of Shootfighting draws its name from a popular maneuver characteristic of this system, called "shooting." This involves rushing in and grabbing your opponent's arms or legs (generally, the latter) for the purpose of off-balancing him or her.

training in Shootwrestling, you'd practice and compete bare-handed and you'd don typical wrestling garb (such as shorts).

➤ Trapfighting – This is an American version of Shootfighting.

➤ Sambo – This is a Russian martial sport based on Mongolian (Sumo-type) wrestling. If you were a practitioner of this sport, you'd likely wear heavy Judo-like jackets, as well as kneepads for protection and shoes to provide better traction.

➤ Vale Tudo – This grappling sport was originally a Brazilian form of street fighting. No fancy uniforms here. If you were a Vale Tudo practitioner, you'd wear street clothes and be bare-chested when competing.

➤ Mu Tau – This sport is a blend of Asian and ancient Greek martial arts such as Pankration. If you were practicing Mu Tau, you'd wear loose-fitting athletic clothing (like sweat pants), boxing gloves and padded headgear.

➤ Luta Livre – This is another form of Brazilian street fighting that has become a martial sport. It relies on striking more than grappling. Head butting (hitting your opponent with your head) and knee and elbow strikes are staples of this sport.

Get Out Your Battle Fatigues

At the other end of the spectrum are combative systems based on military training fused with Asian martial techniques. If you doubt these exist, flip through the pages of any martial arts magazine or your local telephone book. You'll see ads for schools teaching Kravmaga (a system based on Israeli military hand-to-hand combat methodologies), which is the most popular of these types of martial training systems, or techniques employed by the U.S. Navy Seals or by Russia's elite Spetnats troops.

Unlike the hybrid styles noted in the previous section, if you were practicing these martial arts your focus would be on learning interesting and painful ways to subdue an attacker—whether you encountered this individual in the Gulag, in Golan Heights or at your local mini-mall.

Your instructor would likely be a former member of the American or foreign military forces. His or her training would have included hand-to-hand combat, both armed and unarmed.

Entertainment versus Martial Art

We've included Sumo wrestling and Capoeira under this heading for two reasons: 1) they didn't fit anywhere else in this guide and 2) they're viewed more as forms of entertainment than as martial arts.

Hundreds of years ago, Sumo was regarded as a combative art, but its image has since changed drastically. This shift is attributable to the fact that huge guys in diapers who can move with the agility of a gazelle, the power of a top-of-the-line tractor and the flexibility of a ballet dancer are a big audience draw—at both live and televised events. Sumo is big business and serious business. Outside Japan, however, it's unlikely you'll find any amateur Sumo players or commercial schools. So if you've been eating obscene quantities of food and telling your friends that you're in training for the next Sumo grand championship, you might want to put the brakes on your snacking.

If you saw the movie *Only the Strong,* you have a pretty good idea of what Capoeira involves. It is a highly acrobatic, dancelike Brazilian martial art, which is believed to have originated with slaves transported from Africa to South America during the seventeenth century. Legend has it that because their hands were chained, slaves depended on their legs to defend themselves.

A trademark of this physically demanding combative art is its dynamic kicks, cartwheels and break-dance-like movements, which include headspins—this discipline is not for folks who are prone to motion sickness. Static stances are replaced by a flowing opening movement called the *ginga,* which incorporates twisting, bobbing and footwork. If you practice Capoeira, you'll rarely, if ever, use hand strikes.

We're not certain that Capoeira should be classified as entertainment rather than as a defensive form. What we *do* know is finding a commercial school could be pretty expensive when you factor in the cost for round-trip airfare to Rio.

The Quick Fix

The third of these categories consists of systems that come under the heading of crash courses in self-defense, like Defendo and Combato.

These are geared primarily to women looking for a meat-and-potatoes approach to learning a few personal protection techniques. If you were practicing these martial systems, you'd wear street clothes, train in small groups and generally have the opportunity to beat the living "stuffing" out of a heavily padded pseudoattacker. You'd also learn the importance of using your voice as a weapon and executing a steady stream of knee kicks to your assailant's groin. Serious martial artists and dedicated proponents of

Risky Moves

Self-defense programs may be conducted through your local high school, college, community center or religious institution, and tuition for these crash courses varies from market to market. But be warned: unless you practice the techniques you learn in these programs on a regular basis for a reasonable period of time, you may be caught "defenseless."

Master Speaks

One way to reinforce what you've learned in a workshop or seminar is to bring a videocamera or a notebook to record techniques that were taught at the event. Ensure you've obtained the event director's permission prior to videotaping. Additionally, immediately after the workshop or seminar, ask questions and listen attentively to the answers. And don't forget to review this information once you've returned home.

combative systems generally don't have a high opinion of these quick-fix courses.

The World of Workshops and Seminars

A large part of an eclectic martial arts education may be acquired or expanded through workshops and seminars. If you're a student of what might be termed the "composite way" you might look for a specific workshop offering instruction that addresses your developmental areas (for instance, ground fighting or weapons skills). Alternatively, as a means of gaining deeper insight into your martial art, you might attend seminars that feature individuals who have expertise in your particular discipline.

At international events, experts from around the world share their knowledge with beginner, intermediate and advanced students. This free exchange of ideas is similar to trade agreements, wherein all parties benefit, or to global classrooms, where students and instructors from every country can share their passion for the martial arts.

At this point, you may be wondering about the cost of attending these events. This can vary greatly. Here are some examples:

➤ A 2-hour seminar with a renowned practitioner may cost $20 to $40 per person.

➤ An all-day workshop can run anywhere from $40 to $70.

➤ A weekend training camp can cost $60 to $150.

➤ A week of classes (with accommodation and meals) could drive up the price tag from $300 to $700.

In addition to these fees, don't forget to factor in the cost of souvenirs (videotapes, books, T-shirts, crests or photos of renowned martial arts experts and celebrities).

One final note on the topic of workshops and seminars: these events are *not* the exclusive domain of eclectic practitioners. Many martial artists who study classical styles and take an eclectic approach to their training also appreciate this type of learning environment, which intermingles an interesting and diverse mix of combative systems. For example, if you're a Karate student and you attend a seminar that features Jiu-jitsu or Aikido experts, you'll probably learn something new about grappling or throwing an opponent. You might gain an entirely new perspective on kicking from a Tae Kwon Do champion or learn the secrets of cultivating a knockout punch from a world-class kickboxer. And as you continue to train in your chosen martial art, these experiences will assist you in discovering new techniques, and perhaps help you appreciate other styles and disciplines.

Risky Moves

Don't get swept away by guest instructors teaching at your school or featured at international events. Appreciate what they bring to your learning experience, but avoid losing sight of who your *real* instructor is.

Tapes, Web Sites and the Printed Word

For centuries, if you wanted to study martial arts there was only one way to go about it: find a teacher who would accept you as a student. All too frequently, this resulted in a time-consuming and arduous search. And without the aid of a telephone book or access to the Internet, you were in for lots of legwork. Most daunting of all was the fact that this ordeal was merely the beginning! If, at long last, you came across a teacher who would take you under his or her wing, then you'd have to train for years, decades, perhaps even a lifetime, before you were an expert.

Today, however, if you are an individual who prefers to take the hands-off approach to learning eclectic martial arts, then warm up your VCR, plug in your computer or jog down to your local book and magazine shop. Keep in mind, however, that most serious martial artists prefer a flesh-and-blood instructor to one that is electronic. Having a teacher supervise your every move is generally safer and more productive. (It's not, however, as comfortable as working out in your bathrobe.)

Video Master

In this high-tech age, prospective martial artists may pop a cassette into their VCR and bow to a machine which will guide them through a noncontact workout (one that is devoid of personal interaction). What do you do if you don't understand a technique? That's simple: hit the rewind button.

If your local video store doesn't offer a substantial selection of instructional tapes, your city or town probably has one or more martial arts supply stores that may offer a better selection. No video shop and no martial arts store? That's why mail order was created. Simply pick up a copy of a martial arts magazine (most of which run advertisements for companies that specialize in instructional videos for both eclectic and classical combative systems).

The Web Warrior

If you're the sort of person who'd rather cocoon than venture beyond your front door, you may want to put in your class time on the Internet, which is slowly emerging as a resource for martial artists. Without even leaving the comfort of your own home, you can enter any number of "chat rooms" or view video clips of eclectic (and other) martial arts. If you are a Web Warrior, logging on and off will obviously replace the traditional bow at the beginning and end of class.

Alternatively, you can enter the CD-ROM classroom by simply slipping a compact disc into your computer. Many martial arts supply stores, publishing companies and CD-ROM retailers offer a varied menu of martial arts discs.

Spilling Ink, Not Blood

You might prefer to obtain information about eclectic martial arts through books and magazines. If you can't find what you're looking for in your local library or bookstore, there are extensive lists available via the Internet or through publishing companies that specialize in this topic.

Supplementing your classroom training with audiovisual aids isn't a bad idea. In fact, anything that can help you learn more about your own discipline and others should be part of your study.

However, relying exclusively on tapes, the "information autobahn" or print matter to obtain your martial arts education will not provide you with all-important opportunities for personal interaction with a live instructor, as well as with other students.

Credentials, Please

Just who is qualified to teach eclectic martial styles? In these systems, unlike in Karate, Tae Kwon Do, Judo, Jiu-jitsu, Aikido and other classical combative arts, commonly recognized ranking systems are virtually non-existent, as are titles indicating the instructor's level of expertise (such as *Sensei, Sifu,*

Risky Moves

Attempting to learn a martial art without a qualified teacher—one with whom you share a personal bond—is like achieving style without substance.

Master Speaks

If you are interested in exploring the world of martial arts audiovisual aids, consult your instructor. Some of the largest companies that specialize in martial arts videocassettes are Panther Productions, Black Belt Magazine Video and Unique Publication Video.

Sabom or Master). Many eclectic practitioners address their instructor by his or her first name. The title *Coach* is probably as close as you'll get to an indication of the eclectic teacher's rank.

This absence of traditional parchment and title does not necessarily result in a lack of respect on the part of eclectic practitioners for their instructor. Nor is it meant to suggest that these teachers are any less competent than those who are called by a Japanese, Korean or Chinese title. Once many of these eclectic experts begin moving around the training area, it will become abundantly clear that they deserve the same degree of respect as any classical stylist.

As previously noted, certificates and rank don't necessarily translate into competent instruction. But you should apply the same caution in screening these individuals as prospective teachers as you would other martial arts instructors. In gauging their credentials, you may want to check on the length of time they've been training and teaching, as well as other information about their background, along with the number of long-term students they count in their student body. But here's the bottom line: is this instructor the right kind of person to guide you in discovering more about yourself through martial arts training?

Risky Moves

A Jack or Jill of all trades is rarely a master of one area. In the world of martial arts, this means that a well-rounded teacher may incorporate elements of different styles and disciplines. It's unlikely, however, that he or she, at the tender age of 20, 30 or even 40, will have the expertise to teach *all*, or even several, martial arts with the same degree of proficiency.

A Sample Class

Unlike previous chapters that provided sample class plans for classical martial arts, in this chapter, we can provide you with only a general overview of what you might learn in a typical training session, as many eclectic teachers have diverse areas of expertise, and approaches to instruction vary widely.

As a practitioner of eclectic systems, your study generally won't include forms or self-defense and sparring drills. Your class format would likely be spontaneous and you'd rely on an unregimented approach to learn the fundamentals of natural, unrehearsed movements.

Your varied arsenal would include some of the following: striking, kicking, throwing and locking techniques. This might be amplified to include weapons like short sticks, knives and even firearms.

In contrast to training sessions at institutions that feature more conventional systems, your class would probably be smaller (perhaps 4 to 10 students). The atmosphere would be less formal—you'd replace your traditional uniform with a T-shirt and sweat pants or shorts. Handshakes would replace bows. While you might be classified as a

Risky Moves

Why use a $2 word when a $20 one will do? In an effort to distance themselves from Asian-based martial arts, many teachers of eclectic styles use elaborate sounding phrases like "progressive fire mode" (striking until you "connect" with a target) in explaining combative strategies. To avoid making painful mistakes, it might help to learn to read your teacher's "physical" language rather than depending on complex terminology.

beginner, an intermediate or an advanced student, you probably won't use any titles referring to anyone's rank.

Tuition arrangements may be as informal as pay-as-you-go and class schedules may be equally unstructured. For example, if only one or two students show up, the class may be shortened or replaced with a jog in the park. Eclectic schools are flexible in terms of allowing students to drop in or out as they wish.

If you respond better to limited structure and gravitate more freely toward the smorgasbord approach to martial arts training, you might find that eclectic systems can provide many of the same benefits as their more traditional counterparts.

The Least You Need to Know

➤ One of the most famous eclectic martial arts is Jeet Kune Do (way of intercepting fist), a system that was founded by the "The Little Dragon," Bruce Lee.

➤ Shootboxing, Shootwrestling, Trapfighting, Sambo, Vale Tudo, Luta Livre and Mu Tau are some eclectic styles that blend striking, kicking, throwing, grappling and ground wrestling techniques.

➤ Military-based styles include Kravmaga and Spetnats, as well as another that is based on U.S. Navy Seals training.

➤ Some martial arts like Sumo and Capoeira are viewed as forms of entertainment rather than combative systems.

➤ Quick-fix programs are generally short-term courses geared only toward self-defense.

➤ Eclectic practitioners train in schools and at seminars and workshops, or prefer to obtain knowledge through noncontact sources like videotapes, CD-ROMS, the Internet, magazines and books.

➤ Conventional ranking systems, forms and pre-arranged drills, and uniforms are generally not found in schools that teach eclectic styles.

➤ Generally speaking, eclectic styles mix a variety of martial arts. Practicing these styles can provide some of the same (as well as different) benefits as classical systems.

Part 5
Making Your Journey With Confidence

Let's say that for the last few years, you've been kicking, punching and grappling—not in your living room, boardroom or schoolyard, but in a martial arts classroom. You now have a grip on the physical aspect of martial arts practice and maybe even have become a better person as a result of training. Where do you go from here? Reading this chapter will teach you how to take inventory of your physical, mental and spiritual gains as a practitioner. It will also explain the obligation you, as a martial artist, have to your family, friends, school and community, and to the world. In the language of superheroes, you must "use what you've learned to do good!" And if you're a beginner, don't put this book down yet. This is your chance to get a glimpse of what to expect from your martial arts education in the exciting years to come.

Chapter 24

Putting It All Together

In This Chapter

➤ The importance of synchronicity in advanced martial training

➤ Taking a moment to reflect on your accomplishments

➤ Examining old goal plans and constructing new ones

➤ Sharing your gains with family, community and the world

We began this book by telling you why martial arts came into existence—because people needed to protect themselves—and we explained how various cultures throughout history have crafted combative systems in order to survive. Despite the fact that the vast majority of practitioners *never* have to actually defend themselves, this aspect of training may remain your strongest motivator for participating in a martial arts program.

If you haven't skipped any pages between the table of contents and this chapter, then you know that martial arts programs can also help you get or stay physically fit in a challenging and unique way, and maybe *that's* been your goal. Or perhaps you've discovered that many men, women and children today train for other reasons like exploring exotic cultures, entering sporting competitions or making new friends. And from your perspective, these are the most compelling reasons to head down to your local Judo, Karate, Kung Fu or Tae Kwon Do school.

You've also learned that, with the infusion of religio-philosophical teachings, what were once personal *protection* systems became personal *perfection* systems that can help you face and conquer your fears. And perhaps what is attracting you to a study of combative systems is their ability to help people like you become better adjusted, more confident as you achieve goals you never dreamed possible, and less stressed out (as you take a one-hour mini-vacation in each martial arts class).

Or maybe, just maybe, you want it all: self-defense skills and spirituality, fitness and friends, the excitement of discovering new cultures and the challenge of the tournament arena. Whatever your reasons for studying martial arts, you may still be a little unsure how to bring it all together. If so, then this final chapter is for you.

Martial Smarts

The greatest undeveloped territory in the world lies under your hat.

—*Anonymous*

Synchronicity

The dictionary defines *synchronizing* as "making occur at the same time." Whether you're talking about nose-clipped, sequin-capped, modern mermaids performing a swimming routine or about blending sound and image in film, the necessity to hook things up so they work in unison is essential in many activities. And in Eastern thought, *synchronicity,* that is, harmonizing all the elements of life—physical, mental and spiritual—is what makes the world go 'round.

Taking the Holistic Approach

In the Western world, there's a tendency to separate the body, mind and spirit. Eastern traditions, on the other hand, view these aspects of your being as part of a total package. And when these elements are synchronized and inseparable, everything seems to come together in a seemingly effortless, perfect way.

When it comes to martial arts training, for example, there are no exercises that are purely physical. Your mind, and to varying degrees your spirit, must be engaged if you are to perform drills flawlessly. What fortifies your body also strengthens your intellect and satisfies your soul. Blending these elements is the only way to—if you'll pardon the expression—get your juices flowing, and with this unified approach you can strengthen your *chi,* or life force. Perhaps it is this approach that has made holistic medicine more popular in the West. It's becoming increasingly common for families to seek "unorthodox" health care and even for the mainstream medical community to combine "traditional" with "nontraditional" treatments, and provide or recommend services like chiropractic, naturopathy, acupuncture and acupressure, hypnosis and iridology. We've begun to realize the value of treating the *entire* being rather than just opting for quick-fix responses to physical and nonphysical symptoms.

Getting beyond the Physical

In the novice stage of martial training, you were likely preoccupied with your physical development. You concentrated more on getting the hang of learning the basics than on attempting to master complex material. You might have focused, almost exclusively, on acquiring self-defense skills, especially if this was your aim in the first place. Or if physical fitness was at the top of your agenda when you set out on your martial arts journey, you might have wanted to see how many more push-ups and abdominal crunches you could perform, or been somewhat obsessive about how much harder you hit the heavy bag or focus pad or how far you could toss your partner. This approach is natural in the early stages.

After you practiced for a little while, however, you probably became increasingly aware that your body's performance was limited, to say the least, if you didn't involve your brain and soul (or spirit, or whatever you choose to call that indescribable internal force that drives you) in the training process.

Sometimes Less Is More

In most martial arts schools, as you continue to train and are introduced to new, more complicated techniques, you'll probably, in true Eastern educational tradition, begin reexamining your flourishing repertoire and start stripping away things. Skills and strategies that were acceptable at the beginner level are reassessed at the intermediate and advanced stages of training. You may become increasingly less likely to simply accept martial techniques at face value. You may question their validity and look for innovative ways to ensure the efficacy of the drills you're practicing. This reexamination is an important part of the martial learning process.

Warrior Words

Tokui–waza means "favorite technique." A martial arts beginner usually attempts to master everything. A more experienced practitioner, on the other hand, will strive to maintain a degree of competency in all aspects of training, but will generally focus on perfecting a few, well–chosen moves.

Coming into Focus

As your martial study advances, you may come to believe that quality is more important than quantity. Rather than boasting that you know 10, 100 or 1000 techniques, you'll want to pare down to the essentials and, as you continue your journey, travel light. Performing an infinite number of calisthenics won't be as important as doing them properly, ensuring not only that you are getting stronger, fitter and more flexible, but that these gains have a functional application. That is, they'll aid your martial arts progress.

At this stage, you'll likely spend the bulk of your training time on refining what you've learned and looking for new, minute ways of making each movement more effective. In all probability, you'll still challenge yourself by learning new material in the form of more advanced sparring and self-defense drills, or complicated empty-hand and

Warrior Words

Shugyo, meaning "austere training or self-analysis," refers to the practice of personal review and assessment of your skills and abilities, and can result in a sense of rebirth in your martial arts study.

weapons forms. You may also explore fresh methods for making yourself more powerful, energetic and supple. But you'll undoubtedly spend the majority of your time reexamining what you already know and, with the benefit of hindsight and the critical eye of a seasoned practitioner, your training vision might be 20-20!

As you approach the advanced stage of martial arts study and strive to align—or *re*align—your body, mind and spirit, you shouldn't limit yourself to the physical level of learning. We don't mean that, under the guise of becoming more "spiritual," you should begin to cultivate a beer gut and cut back on your sweat time. A healthy body makes a healthy mind—and spirit, for that matter. We *do* mean that, as a more experienced practitioner, although the goals of learning self-defense skills and staying physically fit will remain on your personal training agenda, they'll probably move down your priority list. What will or should move up on this list? Things like appreciating how far you've come (without forgetting how far you still have to travel) and striving to achieve the ultimate goal of a dedicated martial artist—making yourself a better human being and the world a better place.

To look forward to this supreme destination, let's begin by journeying *back*. If you've been practicing for years, this process will be easy to accomplish. But if you haven't yet kicked off your shoes and begun kicking and punching or grappling and throwing, you'll need to use your imagination, or perhaps a crystal ball!

Flashback!

Within the first few years of your martial arts journey, you likely have achieved a couple of things worth celebrating. So, take a moment to rest on your laurels and, without letting your head expand too much, enjoy your accomplishments. Having a hard time? Here are some suggestions…

Your Mom Must Have Been Proud

At this point, you've probably passed several belt examinations. Whether you're a Green, Blue or Brown Belt, or you hold a comparable intermediate rank, you should feel good about the achievement this cloth represents. While the color of your belt is merely a symbol, it serves as a tangible reminder of how hard you've trained and helps you recall the hurdles you've had to clear. Look around. Maybe some of the students who began their martial arts study when you did have fallen by the wayside. But *you* hung in there and now you should be confident about adding the words *achieving Black Belt* to your goal sheet.

Master Speaks

Within the first year, as many as 30 percent of all martial arts students will quit. Between the first and third year, perhaps another 10 to 20 percent will stop. Between the third and fifth year, an additional 10 percent may drop out. Bottom line: if you're going to quit, the odds are you'll do it in the first year, but if you stick to it your chances of achieving your goals improve at each level.

Putting It on the Line

You may remember the first time your instructor asked you to demonstrate a technique or form. Whether this performance was during a training session under the supportive gaze of your classmates or in a more public setting with an audience—of what seemed like millions—you may have felt honored for simply having been asked, but you were probably also terribly nervous. You pushed this feeling aside and performed. Your efforts were rewarded with applause, and a compliment and pat on the back from your teacher. Most importantly, you had the satisfaction of knowing you'd conquered your fears. This single experience, and similar episodes that followed, may have given you smiles that lasted for days or even weeks.

And the Winner Is...

Do you recall the negative thoughts that plagued you the night before your first martial arts tournament? *Will I get hurt? Will I embarrass myself or my teacher? Will my ego and body be so bruised that I may hang up my belt forever?* You may have lost sleep and been too anxious to eat. But rather than fabricating some elaborate excuse ("The president of the United States needs me to lead this morning's space shuttle mission so I don't think I'll be able to attend the competition."), you packed your gym bag and headed off to the tournament. Whether you came home with the hardware or not, you were a winner because the measure of your success was not

Martial Smarts

Whatever task you undertake, do it with all your heart and soul. Do not blame others for your mistakes and failures. The only approval you need is the consciousness of doing your best.

—*Bernard M. Baruch*

limited to the height of a trophy or the weight of a medal but to the fact that you didn't give in to self-doubt and fear.

Since that memorable day, you may have returned to the tournament ring, once, twice or dozens of times. You might even have a few awards to show for your effort. But the image of you standing up before other competitors, the officials and the spectators at your first event and giving it everything you had will remain clear, bright and shiny after the gleam on the trophies and medals fades. While tournaments can be fun and learning to perform under pressure can be an important tool for developing self-confidence, you now have a more realistic view of these events and understand that, while they can serve a useful purpose, they're not the sole reason you should train.

Master Speaks

In tournaments, the real competition occurs between the *you* that existed before you began practicing martial arts and the *you* you're striving to become.

You Like Me...You Really, Really Like Me!

Think back to the earlier stages of your martial arts training. Mentally transport yourself back to the first time a fellow student praised your form and asked you to show him or her how to perform a technique, or to that first demonstration when your ears were warmed by the applause of your classmates. Felt wonderful, didn't it? We all have a need to be appreciated and accepted and to have our efforts recognized and rewarded.

Once you've trained for a few years, you'll undoubtedly become aware that this need can be addressed in the supportive atmosphere of your martial arts school. A kind word from your teacher, who should praise as well as correct your attempts, and the occasional compliment from your *sempai* or *si-hing* (senior students) and *kohai* or *si-di* (junior students) can go a long way in bolstering your sense of self-appreciation.

Furthermore, if you haven't made it a practice to compliment the efforts of your teachers and fellow students—and, for that matter, people you encounter outside the martial

Risky Moves

When a fellow student is performing a technique improperly, your offer to correct his or her form might not be well received. Wait until you're asked for assistance, or offer your services politely by carefully choosing your words. For example, "Would you like to work on that drill together?" is a more welcome phrase than "Ouch—that's awful. Do it like this."

arts classroom—then begin now, as an advanced student, to make others feel good about what they're doing. Receive praise humbly and always find something genuine and positive to say to others.

Feeling good about what you've achieved so far—belts, trophies and the praise of your teachers and fellow students? In the next section, you'll have the opportunity to figure out some of the other ways that martial arts study has influenced your journey along life's path.

Taking Stock

In earlier chapters, we mentioned the importance of establishing your goals and, once you've achieved them, setting new ones. Throughout this book, we've reminded you that this is a good way of improving your chances of success, not just when it comes to martial arts study, but in other areas of your life as well.

Martial Smarts

A journey of a thousand miles begins with a first step.

—*Lao Tsu*

So, at this point, why not dig out your martial arts goal plans and we can check your "score" to date. You won't pass or fail. This is simply an exercise to help you see how much ground you've covered and, more importantly, give you an opportunity to reevaluate your priorities and establish new goals. Remember, what you set out to attain as a beginner may be quite different from what you hope to achieve as an advanced student.

Goal 1: Learning Self-Defense

This may have been your top priority as a beginner and at this stage you probably possess the ability to defend yourself in the unfortunate event of a physical confrontation. But, as noted above, the vast majority of martial artists never have to use their skills in a street fight. So, perhaps it's time to reassess the value of this aspect of training. We don't mean to imply that you should forget that you're practicing a *martial* art. We simply suggest that, as you reconstruct your goal plan, self-defense might be better positioned somewhere lower down the list.

Goal 2: Improving Physical Fitness

You began martial arts training to get into shape, perhaps lose a few pounds and deflate that extra tire that had mysteriously appeared around your midsection. And certainly, since you began practicing, you've sweated, stretched, pushed and pulled, going places your body never thought it would. Although you may not have always liked the process, you have enjoyed the results. You exude energy and have a youthful spring in your step. You're taking fewer sick days at work or school.

277

Martial Smarts

I don't want to achieve immortality by being inducted into the Hall of Fame. I want to achieve immortality by not dying.

—*Leo Durocher, at age 81*

You still recognize the importance of challenging yourself physically, and want to remain healthy and in good shape until you head off to that big martial arts classroom in the sky. But if physical improvement was the single most important goal on your beginner's list, maybe now is the time to ask yourself if that's all there is. Other physical activities can improve your level of fitness, but martial arts training can give you skills and help you stay in shape—on the outside *and* the inside. You may live a life that is not only longer but healthier as well.

So get out your pen and think about where, as an advanced student, you should rank physical fitness as a goal. Place it near the top of your list? Move it to the bottom? Or (perhaps quite wisely) put it somewhere in the middle?

Goal 3: Acquiring Mental Strength

Maybe the driving force behind putting on a martial arts uniform was the desire to achieve mental strength and, as a beginner, you noted stress reduction as your number one goal.

In the highly focused mind of a martial artist, there's little room for stress, self-doubt and other energy-zapping feelings. We're not saying that as an advanced student you won't ever experience anxiety or bouts of self-doubt. Nor do we mean you won't ever be afraid. Fear can be good as long as it doesn't paralyze you. It can function as an internal warning system, cautioning you about impending danger.

But through martial arts study, you've replaced stress with inner calm and self-doubt with self-belief and confidence. While things won't always go your way, you're now more capable of managing even the toughest situations. You've become more disciplined and focused in training and life in general. You're more confident and more positive in thought and action.

This mental strength has likely made you a more disciplined individual and helped you cultivate better study or work habits. As a result, you may be enjoying improved grades or job performance. Additionally, this same mental fortitude has probably assisted you in withstanding negative peer pressure. Thanks to your martial achievements over the last few years, you have a strong sense of who you are and perhaps are experiencing improved relationships with your family and friends, classmates and co-workers.

So, if you are retooling your goal plan, perhaps improved mental strength shouldn't move too far down your personal perfection roster.

Goal 4: Making Friends

Over the last few years of training, you've probably made a number of interesting friends, some of whom may have moved up the rank ladder with you. These relationships may have buoyed you up through difficult times during your training, as well as in other aspects of your life, and these friendships could last a lifetime.

Making friends may have been, and may very well continue to be, an important aspect of your martial arts study.

Goal 5: Competing in Tournaments

Tournaments, on the other hand, might have proved beneficial early on in your martial arts study but, having learned that their real value is helping you face your fears (for example, performing before a crowd), you may now want to reconsider the importance of competing in rewriting your goal plan.

Goal 6: Exploring Exotic Cultures

When the idea of studying martial arts first entered your mind, perhaps you had this image of youself wearing fancy robes and spinning dervishlike. Maybe you saw yourself traveling the world in search of instruction and, along the way, picking up interesting languages and knowledge of a culture very different from your own. Perhaps when you were a novice, this was the most important attraction of martial arts study.

Years later, you may still be interested in the history, culture and terminology related to your chosen martial discipline. In fact, you should be. Learning something about these nonphysical aspects of training will help you better understand your and other combative systems.

So in reevaluating your priorities, this interest may not be number one, but it certainly shouldn't tumble too far down your goal chart.

Goal 7: Becoming Spiritually Fit

Okay. Maybe this aspect of training wasn't at the top of your list when you entered a martial arts school for the first time. If the truth were told, for most beginners, this goal is somewhere near the bottom or isn't even listed at all.

But after practicing for several years, you undoubtedly realize that your spiritual side and your physical and mental side are one and the same. Therefore, at this point, you might reconsider where spirituality should be ranked on your martial arts goal plan. Most experienced practitioners train physically, mentally *and* spiritually. They don't neglect the body, mind or spirit—and neither should you.

Master Speaks

If you give it time, you'll see that studying martial arts has little to do with breaking bones and everything to do with mending your life and the lives of others.

Take a moment to read the goal plan you prepared as a beginner and others that you constructed along the way. Over the years of training, you'll see how much you've changed, not just as a martial artist, but as a person. Perhaps your family and friends who thought you were certifiable when you began punching, kicking and throwing now envy your chiseled physique, welcome your energetic and positive outlook on life and admire the sense of confidence and calm you display.

So, now that you've become a better human being, what's next? Moving toward the ultimate goal of all dedicated martial artists—making the world a better place.

Giving Something Back

After years of training, the joys you've celebrated, accomplishments you've enjoyed and benefits you've gained are wonderful, but what good is all this positive energy if you share it with no one? Many people—your teachers, fellow students, family and friends—helped you arrive at this lovely lofty place. You didn't get here alone. So, maybe it's time to share the wealth. Begin small and go big. Start at home and at your martial arts school, then make your way across your community and perhaps the world.

Martial Smarts

By the time the youngest children have learned to keep the house tidy, the oldest grandchildren are on hand to tear it to pieces.

—*Christopher Morley*

Your Family and Friends

Although your family and friends may be a top priority on your life's goal plan, perhaps you've been so busy practicing martial arts for the last few years (and tending to your career and doing other things) that you haven't spent as much time with them as you should. So arrange a family picnic or a vacation in an exotic locale. Schedule an outing with your buddies and pick up the tab. Share some of the interesting insights you've discovered along your martial path. Invite your spouse, your children, other relatives and your friends to watch you practice martial arts. Better yet, encourage them to begin training and make it a family affair.

Your Martial Arts School

Throughout your years of study, you may have taken much and given little in return. We are not referring to opening your checkbook or wallet. We mean the time-honored tradition in martial arts schools wherein more experienced senior students share the benefit of their learning with less knowledgeable junior students. But giving back shouldn't be restricted to the classroom. It can begin simply. You notice a piece of paper on the locker room floor and pick it up. When you arrive for class, tidy up the reception or viewing areas. Volunteer to assist with a class. Offer to do a warm-up. Help organize inter- and intraschool activities. Share your other talents or skills. For example, if you're a terrific artist, offer your services in conjunction with the next special school project. Don't forget to sprinkle compliments everywhere you go. Be generous in distributing them to your teachers and fellow students.

Warrior Words

Giri is a Japanese word that means "obligation" or "duty." Regardless of which martial art you practice (or even which language you speak!), as a senior student, you have an obligation or duty to give back to your family, friends, school and community.

Your Community

There's an old Chinese expression: "If you can sharpen a sword, you can sharpen a plow." In other words, the skills you've practiced for years that have a "martial" application can be used for noncombat purposes as well. We've mentioned this idea countless times in this guide, but it's especially relevant as we begin talking about what you, as a martial artist, can do for your community.

Why not use your skills and interests to benefit your less fortunate neighbors? Here are some examples.

1. Enjoy board breaking? Organize a fundraiser for a local charity. Begin by asking a wood supply company if it'll sponsor the event by providing boards. Approach a T-shirt supplier and ask the staff if they'll print and donate shirts for all participants. (If your requests are refused, don't forget to factor the cost of these items into your event budget.) Students participate by asking for the support of family, friends and neighbors. For every board students break, a donation is made to a local charity, for example, a children's crisis telephone service, a shelter for battered women or an animal protection agency.

2. If you like to sweat, kick and punch, why not conduct a "power-thon," "spar-a-thon" or "sit-up-a-thon"? Again, participants solicit donations that will be presented to a local charity.

3. Hosting an exam, tournament or seminar? Why not ask participants and spectators to bring a nonperishable donation for food banks or warm clothing that can be distributed to the homeless?

4. Other events? Conduct a "read-a-thon" where you and other students devote a few hours each week to helping people learn to read. Ask a local bookstore

to sponsor the event by donating books and perhaps provide prizes, such as martial arts texts, CD-ROMs or videotapes, which can be awarded to volunteers who achieve the best results. Or organize a recycling program for your neighborhood that begins with your martial arts school. Any neighbor who begins recycling receives free introductory classes or a school T-shirt.

Martial Smarts

Human felicity is produced not so much by great pieces of good fortune that seldom happen, as by little advantages that occur every day.

—*Benjamin Franklin*

The World

Beyond the boundaries of your community lies the world. What can you, an individual, do to improve the global community? Perhaps you can encourage the teachers and students of your martial arts school to jointly adopt a child through organizations like Foster Parents Plan. Or maybe you can take some of the suggestions we offered for helping your community by contacting martial arts schools across the country or around the world, and expanding these activities to the national and international level.

You might be a little impressed at how much you've accomplished since your first martial arts class. Imagine yourself 10 years from now. You could find yourself even more amazed—not simply by your own physical, mental and spiritual achievements, but by the fact that you've used your personal progress to benefit your family, friends, school and community, and the world.

The Least You Need to Know

➤ At the advanced level of training, aligning your body, mind and spirit is essential.

➤ Before moving forward, it's necessary to look back and celebrate your achievements in the areas of rank, public performances, tournaments and friendship.

➤ After you've achieved the goals you established as a beginner, it's time to construct more advanced objectives.

➤ Once martial arts training has helped you become a better individual, you've reached a stage where you can use your skills to have a positive influence on your family, friends, school and community, and the world.

Glossary

The following are some of the more prevalent terms used in this guide. (Including every term would have necessitated writing an entire dictionary!)

Academos   A "school" where ancient Greeks practiced martial arts.

Aerobic   Means "with air" and is a term used to describe cardiovascular exercises involving large muscle groups.

Aikido   "The way of harmonious spirit" is a popular Japanese grappling combative art founded by Ueshiba Morihei.

Anaerobic   Means "without air" and is a term used to describe exercises performed in short, energy-depleting bursts.

Animal systems   Martial arts whose movements mimic those of animals, such as the tiger, snake, monkey and crane.

Arnis   A generic name for Filipino martial arts derived from the Spanish word *arnes,* which means "harnessing" or "trapping."

Ba Gua   Means "eight diagram" and is the name of an internal Chinese martial art.

Bastons (or *Mutons)*   Wood sticks used by Escrima students.

Bengkong   A belt or sash worn by a Silat student.

Black Belt Club   Refers to long-term programs offered by many martial arts schools.

Bodhidharma   An Indian monk credited with creating the Chan (or Zen) sect of Buddhism. Called "Damo" (in Chinese) and "Daruma" (in Japanese), this monk is believed to have brought martial arts to China in the sixth century by creating a fitness regimen designed to strengthen the bodies of Buddhist monks.

Bogu   Protective armor worn by Kendo students. (Note: several schools that teach Japanese Karate have also begun using this protective equipment.)

Bokken   Wood practice sword.

Bokuseki   Zen calligraphy or hanging scroll.

Budo   Means "martial way" and refers to Japanese martial arts employed as self-improvement programs. Called *Mudo* by practitioners of Korean martial arts.

Bugei   A Japanese term used to describe military martial arts.

Bujutsu   A generic term used to describe Japanese combative techniques.

Capoeira   A highly acrobatic and dancelike Brazilian martial art whose origins can be traced back to Africa.

Chen style   One of the four major styles of Tai Chi Chuan. Founded by Wang Tsung Yueh.

Chi (or *Qi*)   A Chinese word used to describe an individual's life force.

Chi Kung   A Chinese exercise system designed to improve the practitioner's health and longevity.

Chuan Fa   Means "use of the fists" and refers to Chinese martial systems that employ striking and kicking techniques. Chuan Fa is now commonly called "Kung Fu."

Daeryon   A Korean martial arts term for sparring.

Dan   Refers to degrees or levels of Black Belt.

Defendo   A crash course designed to teach self-defense skills. Similar to Combato and other "quickie" programs.

Disciple   A student who dedicates him- or herself to martial arts study.

Do (or Tao)   Meaning "path" or "way," this suffix has come to denote the use of martial arts as a self-improvement tool.

Dobok   A martial arts uniform worn by Korean practitioners.

Dojang   Means "place of the way" and refers to a Korean martial arts school.

Dojo   Means "place of the way" and refers to a Japanese martial arts school.

Eclectic martial arts   Hybrid or composite systems that incorporate a mix of combative techniques.

Escrima   A Filipino martial art that revolves around the use of wood sticks called *bastons* or *mutons*. A practitioner of this martial art is called an "escrimador."

Exams   Refers to rank assessments.

Fudoshin   Zenspeak for "immovable spirit" or "total concentration," which describes a practitioner's ability to withstand negative pressure.

Gi (or *Dogi*)   The martial arts uniform worn by Japanese practitioners.

Giri   A Japanese word meaning "duty" or "obligation."

Goju-ryu   Means "hard and soft style" and refers to a type of Okinawan Karate founded by Higaonna Kanryo and further developed by Miyagi Chojun.

Gradings   Refers to rank assessments.

Gup   A term used by practitioners of Korean martial arts to denote ranks below Black Belt.

Guru (or *Goro*)   The Indian, Indonesian and Filipino word for "teacher."

Hakama   Wide trousers worn by martial artists.

Hansoku   Refers to the terminology used by Japanese martial arts tournament officials when cautioning or warning competitors who have committed fouls or violated rules.

Hapkido   A Korean martial art based on Japanese *Aikijitsu* and indigenous combative techniques that was founded by Choi Yong Sul.

Harimau   One of the most popular of the more than 200 styles of Silat.

Hermit Kingdom   The ancient name for Korea.

Hogoo (or *Ho-goo*)   Protective body gear worn by Tae Kwon Do competitors.

Hsing-I   Means "shape and mind fist" and is the name of an internal Chinese boxing system.

Hwa-rang   Korean term meaning "flower boy" or "flowering manhood." Refers to a socioreligious organization that was established in the ancient Korean kingdom of Silla. Members of this organization were trained in philosophy, arts and sciences, horse-riding skills and martial arts.

Hyung   A Korean martial art exercise using choreographed offensive and defensive movements (*kata* in Japanese and *kune* in Chinese).

Introductory programs   Short-term or mini martial arts trial courses.

Ippon   Means "full point" and is used with *wazari* (half-point) in the scoring system used at Judo, Karate and Kendo competitions.

Isshin-ryu   Means "one heart system" and is the name of a style of Okinawan Karate that was created by Shimabuku Tatsuo.

Jeet Kune Do   Means "way of intercepting fist" and is the name of an eclectic combative system founded by Bruce Lee.

Jitsu (or *Jutsu*)   A Japanese suffix used to mean "skill" or "practice."

Jiu-jitsu (or Jujitsu or Jiu-jutsu)   Means "soft/pliable method" or "lighting method" and is the name of a combative system developed in feudal Japan that incorporates striking, throwing and grappling techniques.

Jo   A short wood staff.

Judo   "The gentle (or soft) art (or way)" is a Japanese martial sport founded by Kano Jigoro that relies on leverage to off-balance an attacker.

Jungshin (or *Kun*)   Codes of behavior or rules posted in many martial arts schools.

Ka   A suffix that refers to practitioners of Japanese martial arts, as in Judo-*ka*, Karate-*ka*.

Kalaridpayattu   An Indian martial art characterized by defensive postures, low stances, long strides, high kicks and jumps.

Karate   Means "empty hand," formerly "China hand," and is the name of a Japanese combative system that originated in Okinawa and that uses striking and kicking techniques.

Kat   A curved single-edged dagger used by ancient Egyptian warriors.

Kata   A Japanese martial arts exercise using choreographed offensive and defensive movements. *Kata* also means "example" and is often called moving meditation *(hyung* in Korean and *kune* in Chinese).

Katana   A Japanese long sword worn in your *obi* (belt).

Kebatinan   Refers to a type of spiritual training or form of self-hypnosis employed by advanced *Silat* students.

Kempo (or *Kenpo, Kempoh* or *Kenpoh*)   Means "fist law" and refers to any martial arts based on Chinese combative systems.

Kendo   Means "way of the sword" and is the name of a Japanese martial sport based on ancient samurai sword skills called Ken-jitsu.

Khopish   An axelike weapon carried by warriors in ancient Egypt.

Ki   A Japanese word used to describe an individual's life force.

Kiai   Means "energy harmony" and is the "yell of spirit" used by students of Japanese martial arts.

Kickboxing   A blend of Western boxing and Asian kicking techniques.

Kihap   Means "energy harmony" and is the "yell of spirit" used by students of Korean martial arts.

Koan   A Japanese word used to describe the technique of using riddles or brainteasers to facilitate meditation.

Kobudo   Means "ancient martial way." This name is commonly used to describe a wide range of Okinawan weapons disciplines. The five primary weapons *ryu* (styles) are *Matayoshi-ryu, Ryukyu* Kobudo, *Chinen Yamani-ryu, Ufuchiku Dan* and *Mura bo* style.

Kobudo weapons (or Kobudo *no buki*)   Refers to the numerous weapons used by Kobudo students. Most popular among these armaments is the *bo* (long wood staff), *sai* (three-pronged metal truncheon), *tonfa* (wood handled baton), *nunchaku* (small wood flail) and *kama* (sickle).

Kohai   A Japanese word for a junior (less experienced) student.

Kokoro   A Japanese term meaning "spirit" or "heart."

Korykos   A room within an ancient Greek martial arts school where students practiced boxing.

Koshu   Chinese arts of self-defense.

Kotodama   Means "true word" and refers to an Aikido chant that can be used to heal or harm.

Kravmaga   A military-based Israeli combative style (similar to martial systems derived from the Russian elite forces, or *Spetnats*, and the U.S. Navy Seals).

Kris   A long knife used by *Silat* practitioners.

Krocheirismos   Means "opening moves" and refers to techniques employed by practitioners of the ancient Greek martial art of *Pankration*.

Kukggi   The Korean national flag displayed in most martial arts schools that teach combative systems of this Asian country.

Kumite   A Japanese Karate term for sparring.

Kune   A Chinese martial arts exercise using choreographed offensive and defensive movements *(hyung* in Korean, *kata* in Japanese). *Kune* also means "fist."

Kung Fu   Means "human struggle" or "special skill" and is a term used to describe Chinese combative arts, which served as the foundation of many other martial disciplines.

Kyokushin-kai   Means "ultimate truth" and refers to full-contact Japanese Karate founded by Oyama Masatatsu.

Kyu A term used by practitioners of Japanese martial arts to describe ranks below Black Belt.

Kyudo Means "way of archery" and is a Japanese martial discipline that requires students to use a bow *(yumi)* and arrow *(ya)*.

Luta Livre A form of Brazilian street fighting.

Makiwara (or *machiwara*) A striking post used by practitioners of Japanese martial disciplines to develop power and speed and to condition the student's hand. Similar devices are used by students of Chinese and Korean martial arts.

Mantra An Indian word used to describe an incantation or instrument of thought employed during meditation.

Martial arts A generic term used for self-protection and self-perfection disciplines. The word *martial* comes from the name of the ancient Roman god of war, Mars.

Matsubayashi-ryu A popular style of Okinawan Karate founded by Nagamine Shoshin.

Menkyo (or *menjo*) A Japanese word for certificate of proficiency.

Meridians Energy lines or channels that run throughout the body, transporting *chi* (your life force).

Middle Kingdom The ancient name for China, also called "Zhong Guo."

Mokuso A brief meditation period at the beginning of a Japanese martial arts class. *Hansei* refers to a similar period of reflection at the end of a training session.

Mook Jong A wooden dummy used by students of Chinese martial arts.

Mu Tau A blend of the ancient Greek martial art *Pankration* and Asian combative systems.

Muay Thai Means "Thai Boxing," a form of Kickboxing that originated in Thailand, and refers to "the science of eight limbs."

Mushin Can be translated as "no mind" and is used to describe a state of mental clarity.

Naha One of the three areas of Okinawa where different combative systems were developed.

Ninjitsu Means "art of stealth" and is the name of a Japanese grappling system that incorporates a variety of weapons.

Okinawan Kenpo A popular style of Okinawan Karate that was developed by Nakamura Shigeru. This style uses *bogu*-type gear for full-contact sparring.

Palestra   The ancient Greek name for a gymnasium with a soft clay floor where students practiced wrestling.

Pankration   Means "complete strength" and is the name of an ancient Grecian martial art that combined boxing and wrestling techniques.

Pedang   A machete used by Silat practitioners.

Pneuma   The Greek word used to describe your life force *(ki* in Japanese, *chi* in Chinese).

Pranavayu   The Indian word used to describe your life force.

Pushing hands   Refers to a partner exercise performed by Tai Chi practitioners. Its purpose is to develop defensive and offensive skills and improve a student's coordination.

Randori   The Judo term for free sparring.

Rank (or Ranking System)   A system of assessing a martial arts student's level of ability or expertise.

Rei   A Japanese term meaning "respect," "courtesy" or "veneration." This word also describes the bow performed by students of Japanese martial arts.

Religio-philosophical schools   Systems of thought that had a profound influence on the evolution of martial arts. These schools include Taoism (Daoism), Confucianism, Buddhism, Shintoism, Hinduism, Islam, Catholicism and Tagalog.

Restraints   Controlling techniques wherein you restrict your opponent by means of joint-locking or applying pressure to a vital point, using arm bars or wrist and ankle locks.

Ryu (or *Ryuha)*   Means a "style," "branch" or "school" of a particular martial art.

Ryukyu   The ancient name for Okinawa, also called "Loo Chew" in Chinese.

Sabom   A Korean word for "teacher."

Safety gear   Protective equipment worn by practitioners of many martial arts. One of the chief developers of modern, foam-dipped sparring gear was Tae Kwon Do legend Jhoon Rhee.

Sambo   A Russian martial art based on Mongolian wrestling.

Samurai   Means "one who serves" and is the name of feudal Japanese warriors who were employed by chieftain rulers.

Sanchin   Means "three struggles" and refers to the use of martial arts practice to strengthen your body, mind and spirit. *Sanchin* is also the name of a popular Okinawan Karate *kata.*

Sarong   A skirtlike garment worn by *Silat* practitioners that can be used as a weapon.

Satori   A Japanese word meaning "enlightenment" or "nirvana."

Seft   A long curved sword used by ancient Egyptian warriors.

Sempai   A Japanese word for a senior (more experienced) student.

Sen no sen   Means "taking the initiative" and refers to a martial artist's ability to anticipate an attack.

Sensei   The Japanese word for "teacher."

Shadow boxing   Solo boxing drills.

Shaolin-si   Means "young forest" and is the name of an ancient temple where external Chinese martial arts developed.

Shi Bao Luo Han Shou   "Eighteen movements of the monks" is an ancient martial arts form, or prearranged exercise, believed to be the forerunner of all combative patterns.

Shiai   Judo, Kendo and Karate matches or contests.

Shinai   Wood or bamboo swords used by Kendo practitioners.

Shinkage   One of the most famous Ken-jitsu schools.

Shinshin-kan (or Shinshin School)   Means "mind and body school" and refers to a soft style of Aikido founded by Tohei Koichi.

Shito-ryu   A popular style of Japanese Karate founded by Mabuni Kenwa.

Shootfighting/Shootboxing/Shootwrestling   Eclectic modern combative systems developed in Japan.

Shorin-ryu   Means "young forest style" and refers to a type of Okinawan Karate founded by Matsumura Sokon and further developed by Itosu Anko.

Shotokai   A noncontact system of Japanese Karate that was developed by Egami Shigeru.

Shotokan   Means "house of whispering pines" and refers to a style of Japanese Karate founded by the "Father of Modern Karate," Funakoshi Gichin.

Shugyo   A Japanese term that refers to austere training or self-analysis.

Shuri   One of the three areas of Okinawa where different combative systems were developed.

Si-di   A Chinese word for a junior (less experienced) student.

Sifu   The Chinese word for "teacher."

Si-hing   A Chinese word for a senior (more experienced) student.

Silat (or *Pencak* Silat)   Means "to fend off" and is the name of a martial art that, according to legend, was founded by a peasant woman by the name of Bersilat. This Indonesian and Malaysian martial system includes striking, kicking and evasive tactics.

Sinawali   While this word refers to bamboo carved to resemble lace, it also applies to an exercise employed by Escrima students that involves continuous blocking and countering techniques and that is performed both unarmed and armed with short sticks.

Sobak   Means "fighting skill" and is the name of an ancient Korean martial art that is a forerunner of Tae Kwon Do.

Sparring   Refers to offensive and defensive exchange drills that are either prearranged (one-step sparring) or spontaneous (free sparring).

Style   See *Ryu*.

Sumo   Traditional wrestling that is Japan's national sport and a form of entertainment.

Sun style   One of the four major styles of Tai Chi Chuan. Founded by Wu Yu Hsiang.

Supplex   A Greco-Roman wrestling technique that involves bending your opponent's spine. The term *supplex* is derived from the Latin words *supples* or *sup* (easily bent, pliable) and *plicis* (to bend, also implies submission).

Synchronicity   In martial arts terms, the unification of body, mind and spirit.

System   Refers to a variety of "styles" that fall under the umbrella of a particular martial discipline.

Tae Kwon Do   Means "foot hand way" and is the name of a Korean martial art that employs kicking and striking techniques. General Choi Hong Hi named this martial art and has been one of its staunchest proponents.

Tai Chi Chuan (or *Tai Ji* or *Taijiquan)*   Means "grand ultimate fist" and is the name of a Chinese internal martial art based on circular and flowing movements.

Tai Ji Fu Hao   The popular yin and yang symbol used as a good luck charm.

Tai sabaki   Means "body movement" and refers to the martial arts practice of sidestepping an attack.

Take-ryu   Likely the first *ryu,* or school, of Jiu-jitsu, founded by Takenouchi Hisamori in the seventeenth century.

Tamashiwari (or *tamashiwara)*   Means "to test one's spirit" and is used to describe the Japanese martial arts practice of breaking solid objects. This practice is also employed by students of Chinese and Korean combative systems.

Tan Dien   A point that is located 3 inches (7 centimeters) below your navel and that is generally regarded as the seat or source of your life force.

Tang Soo Do   Means "China hand way" and is the name of a popular Korean martial art that blends the techniques of Sobak and *Kwonbop* with Chinese *Kempo* or Japanese Karate.

Tanto   A short knife.

Target drills   Striking exercises aimed at bags and focus mitts.

Tatami   Mats made of straw.

Te (or *Ti)*   Means "hand" and refers to indigenous self-defense systems that were practiced in Okinawa.

Tjabang   A three-pronged metal truncheon used by Silat practitioners.

Tokui-waza   A Japanese word meaning "favorite technique."

Tomari   One of the three areas of Okinawa where different combative systems were developed.

Tomiki   A competition-oriented style of Aikido.

Toya   A wood staff used by Silat practitioners.

Trapfighting   An American version of Shootfighting.

Uechi-ryu   A popular style of Okinawan Karate founded by Uechi Kambun. This style is based on Chinese *Pan-gai* Kung Fu.

Vajaramusti   An ancient Indian martial art that includes wrestling, striking and weapons practice, as well as the study of vital pressure points called *marman.*

Vale Tudo   A grappling sport based on Brazilian street fighting.

Wado-ryu   Means "way of harmony" and is the name of a style of Japanese Karate founded by Otsuka Hidenori.

Waki-zashi   A Japanese short sword.

Wing Chun   A Southern Chinese combative system developed by a Buddhist nun, Ngh Mui, and popularized by Yip Man, Bruce Lee's instructor.

Wu   A Chinese word that refers to balance or harmony with all things in life. This concept is called *wa* in Japanese.

Wu Dang Shan   An ancient temple where internal Chinese martial arts developed.

Wushu   A word that historically was used to describe Chinese martial arts. The term wushu is now associated with a dynamic, acrobatic martial sport.

Wu style   One of the four major styles of Tai Chi Chuan. Founded by Wu Jien Chuan.

Yabusume   A Japanese martial art that features archery techniques performed while on horseback.

Yang   Believed to be the masculine (hard), light, positive forces that govern the universe.

Yang style   One of the four major styles of Tai Chi Chuan. Founded by Yang Lu Chan.

Yin   Believed to be the feminine (soft), dark, negative forces that govern the universe.

Yoshin-kan (or Yoshin School)   A hard style of Aikido founded by Gozo Shioda.

Zazen   A Japanese word used to describe meditation.

101 People Who Influenced the Martial Arts

In addition to biographical information provided in chapters throughout this guide, the following is an alphabetized list of individuals who have had a profound impact on the development of major martial arts. Finding new and unusual ways to integrate the names of these individuals into daily conversation will undoubtedly impress your family and friends and might rank you among the top-rated "black belts" in the art of name dropping!

As detailed information would necessitate development of a full set of encyclopedia, we have only provided essential highlights, noting any available key dates. An asterisk (*) indicates individuals mentioned in this book.

Anzawa Heijiro (1887-1970)
10th Dan Anzawa Sensei is credited with modernizing Kyudo. Furthermore, he introduced this martial art of Japanese archery to Great Britain, France, Italy and Germany.

Bak Mei
Bak Mei was a rebel in the fight against the Ching Dynasty (1644-1911). He established *Bak Mei* (White Eyebrow) Kung Fu, so named because of its founder's white eyebrows and hair.

*Bersilat
If folklore is correct, Bersilat is a peasant woman who, after observing a fight between a tiger and a large bird, developed a combative system that would bear her name, Silat. It relies on techniques that mimicked these animals' movements.

Bimba
In the early 20th century, Master Bimba played an instrumental role in the popularization of the Afro-Brazilian martial art of Capoeira.

*Bodhidharma (460-534 A.D.)

Bodhidharma, also called Daruma and Damo, was an Indian monk who is credited with bringing Buddhism from India to China in the 6th century A.D. Many legends surround the life of this mysterious monk. For example, it is believed that he meditated for nine years and awoke to create two books. These ancient health guides included exercises that were designed to strengthen the bodies of monks who had grown weak from the rigors of meditation. Bodhidharma also authored a third book, called *The Eighteen Hands of the Lohan*, which was based on his experiences as a member of an Indian warrior caste and included combative routines. Legend has it that this text was the first how-to manual of offensive and defensive martial movements.

Chan Quan Khi (1895-1969)

This Chinese martial arts master fled from his homeland to Vietnam in 1949. He is famous for blending native Vietnamese empty-hand and weapons arts with Chinese Kung Fu to create *Viet Vo Dao* (way of Vietnamese arts).

Chibana Chosin (1887-1969)

Chibana Sensei founded the *Kobayashi-ryu* (old forest style) of Karate and was instrumental in forming Okinawa's first martial arts organization, the Okinawa Karate-Do Renmei, in 1954. This popular and talented teacher produced many skilled Karate-ka including Miyahara Katsuya, Higa Yuchoku and Nakazato Shugaro, all of whom achieved the rank of 10th Degree Black Belt.

*Chinen Saburo (1860-1928)

Founder of *Chinen Yamani-ryu*, this Okinawan Kobudo master was renowned for his superlative *bo* (six-foot staff) skills.

Cho Hee Il (1940–)

This 9th Degree Tae Kwon Do master studied under General Choi Hong Hi. Master Cho is famous for his dynamic kicking ability. He has starred in numerous instructional videotapes, appeared in films and authored several martial arts books. He is also the Director of the International Action Martial Arts Association.

*Choi Hong Hi (1918–)

In the 1950s, General Choi, president of the International Tae Kwon Do Federation (ITF), spearheaded the movement to unify Korean martial arts. In the 1960s, Master Choi authored Tae Kwon Do's "Tenets," etiquette guidelines that emphasize the need for every practitioner to develop courtesy, integrity, perseverance, self-control and an indomitable spirit.

*Choi Yong Sul (1904-1987)

Master Choi, who was also known by the Japanese name Yoshida Tatsuju, was the founder of the Korean martial art Hapkido. Master Choi created this combative system by synthesizing indigenous Korean defensive methodologies with the Japanese martial art of *Aiki-jitsu*.

*Deguchi Onisaburo

Deguchi Onisaburo was the founder of the Omoto-kyo religious movement, which counted among its members Morihei Ueshiba, creator of Aikido.

Dong Naikunon

Dong was a famous Muay Thai Champion who reportedly defeated 10 Burmese fighters, all by knockout, in a single contest that was held in Bangkok in the early 1900s.

Draeger, Donn

Draeger Sensei was both a respected martial arts historian and prolific writer on the topic of combative systems, producing texts that remain on the reading list of every serious martial artist. He held advanced ranking in numerous martial disciplines.

*Estalilla, Ramiro A. Sr.

Estalilla was the first *Arnis* master to bring his martial art to North America when he taught at the Athletic Club of Minneapolis from 1920 to 1929.

Fukuda Keiko (1913 –)

Fukuda Sensei, 7th Dan, is the highest ranked female Judo-ka in the world and the senior teacher of the Kodokan women's section.

*Funakoshi Gichin (1869-1957)

Called "The Father of Modern Karate," Master Funakoshi was a poet who wrote under the pen name Shoto. He was the founder of *Shotokan*, a popular Karate style. His teachers included Itosu Anko, Azato Anko and Matsumura Sokon. During the early 1900s, Funakoshi Sensei was invited to mainland Japan to demonstrate Okinawan martial arts. He became friendly with the founder of Judo, Jigoro Kano, who persuaded Funakoshi to remain in Tokyo where, in 1936, he would establish his first dojo, Shotokan, or "house of the whispering pines." Like his teacher Itosu Anko, Funakoshi Sensei believed that Karate training transcended mere physical technique and could be employed to strengthen practitioners' hearts, minds and spirits. After his death, his students baptized his style *Shotokan*, which is currently practiced by more than six million people around the world.

*Geesnik and Ruska

From 1964 to 1968, these Dutchmen were the two most winning pair of Judo-ka, marking the end of Japan's domination of the sport and paving the way for future non-Japanese champions.

*The Gracie Family

(Carlos, 10th Dan, and Helio, 10th Dan; Carlos' sons: Carlson, 9th Dan; Helio's sons: Rorion, 8th Dan; Rickson, 7th Dan; Royce, 5th Dan and three-time Ultimate Fighting Champion)

Considered the first family of (Octagonal) fighting, the Gracies hail from Brazil. They perfected their brand of rough-and-ready combat on the streets of Rio de Janeiro before moving northward to the United States. Gracie Jiu-jitsu is an amalgamated combative system that incorporates grappling elements of Jiu-jitsu with western-style boxing.

Gye Maung (1933–)

Master Gye is the founder of the American Bando Association and an expert in Burmese Boxing and grappling combative arts.

Han Bong Soo (1931–)

Born in Korea, Master Han is an American Hapkido expert, teacher, lecturer and author. Despite this impressive list of achievements, he is probably best known for his cinematic credits, including choreography and stunt work for the movie *Billy Jack*, which boasts some of the best fight scenes in film history.

*Harrison, E.J.

Harrison Sensei is the British Judo-ka who established the first official Judo school in the U.K., the Budokwai (martial arts group) in 1918.

Hatsumi Masaaki (1931–)

Hatsumi Sensei is the world's foremost Ninjitsu (art of stealth) expert. He is famous for having revived combative techniques employed by the Iga and Koga Ninja, two clans whose formidable skills were used to carry out acts of espionage and guerilla warfare in feudal Japan. Hatsumi Sensei teaches a system that synthesizes classical and modern martial techniques.

Herrigel, Eugen

Herrigel Sensei was the first non-Japanese master of Kyudo (archery) and author of the celebrated text *Zen and the Art of Archery*.

*Higaonna Kanryo (1853-1916)

Higaonna Sensei was born in Naha City in Okinawa. Among his teachers were Arakaki Seisho and the famous Chinese master Ru Ru Ko. Higaonna assembled a variety of Okinawan and Chinese martial teachinques which served as the foundation for Goju-ryu Karate, which was further developed and propagated by one of his most famous students, Miyagi Chojun.

*Hitsui Maedakama

Hitsui Sensei was a great Japanese Jiu-jitsu instructor and fighter who counted the Gracies among his star pupils.

Hwang Kee (1913–)

Master Hwang established Moo Duk Kwan, a classical style of Tae Kwon Do that closely mirrors the ancient Korean combative art of Sobak. He developed this style by incorporating hard Japanese movements with soft Chinese techniques.

Iizasa Choisai Ieno (1347–1488)

Iizasa Sensei was a sword and lance master who created Tenshin Shoden Katori Shinto-ryu, a martial discipline that has produced numerous teachers and champion warriors.

Innosanto, Dan (1936 –)

One of the world's most famous Jeet Kune Do teachers, Master Innosanto received his training under the tutelage of the legendary Bruce Lee, founder of this eclectic style. He is also an expert in Filipino martial arts.

*Itosu Anko (1830–1915)

Itosu Sensei was a student of several celebrated martial arts masters including Matsumura Sokon. Itosu was famous for his impressive striking skills which were the result of a unique training technique that involved hitting stalks of bamboo with his bare hands. As he matured, he began focusing on developing a "safer" brand of Karate that could be introduced into the Okinawan school system. Despite criticism from his peers, Itosu re-tooled several forms (kata), eliminating lethal techniques. He emphasized physical and mental conditioning rather than self-defense and promoted the non-corporal benefits of training, including self-discipline, self-esteem and self-confidence. The result was a kinder, gentler version of martial arts that became part of the Okinawan school curriculum in the early 20th century. One of his most prominent students was Funakoshi Gichin.

*Kano Jigoro (1860–1938)

Kano Jigoro, the founder of Judo, was the son of a sake mill owner and held a doctorate in physical education. Frustrated with the limitations imposed by a rigid class hierarchy, he created the modern belt rank system employed by most martial arts schools today, which rewards the student's ability and commitment. He believed that classical Jiu-jitsu placed too much emphasis on disabling an opponent. Therefore, he set out to create a martial sport that would be called Judo which would feature techniques that would not permanently injure practitioners, but instead would provide them with the opportunity to test their combative skills in a tournament setting. He devoted most of his life to propagating Judo around the globe. His students have continued his work, spreading this martial sport throughout the world. His contribution to the martial arts was recognized in the film *The Judo Saga*, which was the work of Oscar-winning director, Akira Kurosawa.

Kharlampiev, Anatoly

Kharlampiev is founder of *Sambo*, a Russian combative discipline that combines Mongolian and western wrestling with Judo. Although originally intended as a system of self-defense, *Sambo* has since become more sport oriented.

Kim Richard (1917–)

An expert in *Shorinji-ryu* Karate and *Daito-ryu* Aiki-jitsu, Kim Sensei holds the rank of 9th Dan, Hanshi (Polished Master), which was awarded to him by the prestigious Dai

Nippon Butokukai. He has authored numerous books including the best selling *Classical Man.*

*Kim, Un Yong

Dr. Kim is president of the World Tae Kwon Do Federation (WTF), which was established in 1973. Under Dr. Kim's guidance, the WTF was the driving force behind Tae Kwon Do's acceptance into the Olympics.

*Kina Shosei (1883-1980)

This founder of *Ufuchiku Dan* Kobudo was a devout Christian who was famous for his many acts of heroism during World War II.

Kou Tze

Kou Tze was the Chinese martial arts master who founded the Ta Shang Kune (monkey boxing school) in 1900.

*Kung Fu-tsu (551-479 B.C.)

Also called "Confucius," Kung Fu-tsu was one of the great thinkers and philosophers of his time, and his teachings have had a profound impact on the development of the martial arts.

Kyan Chotoku (1870-1945)

Master Kyan, nicknamed "Chan-megwa" (small-eyed Kyan), was a famous Okinawan Shorin-ryu Karate expert. His student roster read like a who's who of Okinawan Karate and included such notable martial figures as Nakazato Joen, Shimabukuro Tatsuo, Shimabukuro Zenryu and Nagamine Shoshin .

*Lao Tsu

Lao Tsu was a famous 6th century B.C. philosopher and author. Additionally, he founded Taoism, a religio-philosophical school that blends Buddhism and Confucianism, whose teachings have had a profound impact on several martial disciplines.

*Lapulapu

Lapulapu was a Filipino tribal chief famous for his impressive and lethal stick fighting skills. He defeated — and killed — the Portuguese explorer and navigator Ferdinand Magellan in the 16th century.

*Lee, Bruce (1940-1973)

Charismatic film star Bruce Lee is credited with causing a martial arts revolution. He studied a variety of combative disciplines and styles. Lee incorporated elements he deemed practical and discarded anything that was, in his opinion, ineffective, to create the *Jeet Kune Do* system.

A partial list of Bruce Lee's film credits include *The Big Boss* (1972), *Fists of Fury* (1973), *Return of the Dragon* (1973), *Enter the Dragon* (1973), and *Game of Death* (1979), which was completed after his death. He also starred as "Kato" in the popular 1960s television series "The Green Hornet."

Lee Deok Moo
In 1790, Master Lee wrote the *Mu Yei Do Bo Tong Il*, the definitive text on the Korean martial art of Sobak.

Lee Haeng Ung (1936–)
Master Lee is the president and founder of one of the world's largest martial arts organizations, the American Tae Kwon Do Association.

*Limas, Arlene (1966–)
Ms. Limas won the Gold Medal in the Women's Heavyweight Sparring division at the 1988 games, making her the first Olympic champion in Tae Kwon Do.

*Mabuni Kenwa (1889-1952)
Mabuni Sensei was credited with combining the circular movements of *Goju-ryu* with the linear techniques of *Shorin-ryu* to create *Shito-ryu* Karate.

*Matayoshi Shinko (1888-1947)
Master Matayoshi was founder of *Matayoshi-ryu* Kobudo, which combines Chinese and indigenous Okinawan weapons disciplines.

*Matsumura Sokon (1809-1899)
Also known as "Bushi (warrior) Matsumura," this martial arts master was a *Kempo*, sword and *bo* (six-foot staff) expert who founded the Shuri-te school of Okinawan Karate.

Mifune Kyuzo (1883-1965)
Considered to have been one of martial sport's premiere instructors, Mifune Sensei was also the author of the *Canon of Judo*. His outstanding work in propagating Judo was rewarded in 1964, when he became the first martial artist to receive the Order of the Rising Sun from the Japanese government.

Minamoto Shigenobu
Minamoto was a 16th century sword master who created the Hojo school of *Iaido* (the art of drawing a sharp blade), which two centuries later was renamed Muso Jiken Eishin-ryu.

*Miyagi Chojun (1888-1953)
Miyagi Sensei modernized Karate and spread the teachings of his renowned instructor, Higaonna Kanryo. Miyagi, like many other martial arts masters, traveled to China where he learned *Kempo* (Chinese Kung Fu). He also journeyed to mainland Japan where he would teach his style of Karate, *Goju-ryu*.

Mochizuki Minoru (1907–)

Mochizuki Sensei launched Yoseikan, an independent school of Aikido in the 1940s. He was a student of Aikido founder Ueshiba Morihei, studied Judo with Kano Jigoro and trained in Karate with Funakoshi Gichin. Mochizuki Minoru's son, Hiroo, changed the name Yoseikan Aikido to Yoseikan Budo (meaning martial ways) in order to better describe the hybrid nature of his father's system.

*Motobu Choki (1871-1944)

Motobu Choki was a colorful Okinawan Karate master who is famous for defeating a European boxing champion in a highly publicized match that was held in Kyoto, Japan, in 1921.

Musashi Miyamoto (1584-1645)

Musashi, creator of the Niten Ichi-ryu (two sword style), was arguably the most famous swordmaster of all time, and after countless battles is believed to have retired undefeated (see Muso Gonnosuke). Musashi was the author of the celebrated text on combative strategy *Go Rin no Sho* (Book of Five Rings), a book that is embraced by martial and Wall Street warriors alike.

Muso Gonnosuke

Legend has it that Muso was the only person who *may* have defeated the great sword expert Musashi Miyamoto, allegedly by using a *jo* (four-foot wood staff). Whether this report is true or not, Muso's superlative weapons skills are preserved today in his style *Shindo Muso-ryu*, which he developed in the late 16th century.

Nagoka Hidekazu

The late Nagoka Sensei was a 10th Dan in Judo who has been described as one of the "fiercest" fighters who ever trained at the Kodokan (Judo's headquarters in Japan). To describe a Judo-ka's techniques as "Nagoka-esque" is considered the highest of compliments.

Nakayama Masatoshi (1913-1987)

Nakayama Sensei was a famous *Shotokan* expert who, with the blessing of his teacher Funakoshi Gichin, launched the Japan Karate Association. Through its innovative teacher training program, the JKA became one the world's most powerful driving forces behind the global popularization of Japanese Karate.

*Naresuen (1535-1605)

King Naresuen was the Siamese royal who, captured by the Burmese in 1560, used his martial arts skills to defeat his captors' champion and was subsequently freed. From that point forward, boxing became Thailand's national sport.

Nishiyama Hidetaka (1928–)

A student of Funakoshi Gichin, Master Nishiyama is an expert in *Shotokan* Karate, president of the International Amateur Karate Federation, and the driving force behind this martial bid for acceptance as an Olympic sport.

Norris, Chuck (1940–)

Chuck Norris is a former professional martial arts champion who has become famous for his film and television roles. He is also an author, teacher and featured lecturer. In addition to his stellar screen performances, he and his association, United Fighting Arts Federation, have played an instrumental role in promoting healthy lifestyles among youth through their "Kick Drugs Out of America" program.

Oetomo, Ki-Ageng Hardjo (1893–?)

Oetomo was one of the greatest teachers of *Penjak* Silat. In 1922, he founded Persaudaraan Seita Hati Tarate (Multi-national Martial Arts Organization).

Okazaki, Henry (1890-1951)

During the roaring twenties, Master Okazaki established the Danzan-ryu school of Jiu-jitsu in Hawaii, whose motto is *Kokua*, a Hawaiian word meaning, "to help one another." Among his most notable students are Jiu-jitsu legends Wally Jay, John Cahill and Richard Richerts.

Okuyama Yoshiji

Okuyama created *Hakko-ryu* Jiu-jitsu. Based on *Daito-ryu* Jiu-jitsu, *Hakko-ryu's* curriculum features striking, throwing and restraining techniques, coupled with the study of Asian medicine.

*Otsuka Hidenori (1892-1982)

Otsuka Sensei trained with Funakoshi Gichin, as well as several Jiu-jitsu teachers, before developing *Wado-ryu* Karate. Otsuka's ultimate goal, to use Karate to stop conflicts in a non-violent way, is reflected in the name of his style that can be translated as "way of harmony."

*Oyama Masatatsu (1923-1994)

Renowned for his ability to subdue bulls, chop stacks of bricks, roof tiles and rocks, and "cut" bottles with his bare hands, Oyama Sensei is also famous for creating Kyokushin-kai, a style of Karate that favors full-contact sparring bouts between practitioners.

Parker, Ed (1931-1990)

Master Parker was a student of K.S. Chow, a famous Hawaiian Kung Fu and Karate teacher. Master Parker established the first commercial Karate school in the United States in 1954, teaching American *Kempo*, a martial art that blended Chinese and Japanese combative disciplines.

*Qian-Long (1737-1795)

Qian-Long was the 18th century emperor who ordered the first destruction of the Shaolin Temple.

*Renaud, Jean-Joseph, and de Montgrillard, Guy

Renaud and de Montgrillard were two French practitioners who became the world's first non-Japanese Judo teachers. They established this martial sport's first Western home in Marseilles, France, in 1889.

*Rhee, Jhoon (1932–)

In the late 1950s Jhoon Rhee was among the first Korean instructors to bring Tae Kwon Do to North America. In 1959, he established the first Tae Kwon Do school in the United States in Texas. Master Rhee also developed modern safety equipment.

*Rhee, Syngman, Dr. (1875-1965)

Dr. Syngman Rhee was the former Korean president who encouraged the unification of various martial arts under one banner. In the 1950s he organized several committee meetings chaired by Tae Kwon Do legend General Choi Hong Hi, and in 1955 it was agreed that this new martial art would be called Tae Kwon Do.

Sakugawa Satonuku Kanga (1733-1815)

Master Sakugawa, a legend in the annals of Okinawan martial arts, was famous for his highly evolved combative skills which earned him the nickname "Tode" (meaning China hand or China fist). Having studied with the famous Chinese *Kempo* expert Kusanku, he later developed the beautiful and infinitely practical *bo* (six-foot wood staff) form Sakugawa no kun.

Sato Shizuya

A 9th Dan in both Judo and Jiu-jitsu, Sato Sensei is president of the International Martial Arts Federation (Kokusai Budoin), one of the largest global organizations dedicated to the propagation of classical Japanese combative disciplines.

Shibata Kanjuru

Shibata was the first bow maker and bow master under appointment by the Ashikaga Shogunate in the 16th century. In tribute to his skills, every bow maker who followed in his steps has adopted the Shibata name. Today, Shibata bows are regarded as the Stradivarius of weapons and are valued in the tens of thousands of dollars.

*Shioda Gozo (1915–)

Shioda Sensei is the founder of *Yoshin* Aikido, a sub-style that employs hard, fast techniques.

Sho Shin (1477-1526)

In an effort to subjugate his people, King Sho Shin issued the first Ryukyuan weapons ban in the early 16th century. This ban resulted in the development of unarmed martial arts, as well as combative techniques that revolved around the use of ordinary implements (e.g., wood staff, oar and sickle).

So Doshin (Nakano Michiomi)

Master So, whose birth name was Nakano Michiomi, was a student of Shaolin Kung Fu and other forms of Chinese martial arts. He developed *Shorinji Kempo*, a system of striking, kicking and throwing that is heavily influenced by the Diamond school of Zen. Practitioners of *Shorinji Kempo* are easy to recognize, dressed in their long, black monk robes that are secured by thick rope belts worn over white *dogi*. Without any male heirs to succeed him, upon his death, his daughter adopted her father's name and assumed the helm of this system.

Su In Hyouk (1939–)

Master Su is the creator of Kuk Sool Won, a Korean martial art that combines both external and internal techniques.

Sun-tzu

Sun-tzu is most famous for his text on warfare, *Sun-tzu Bing Fa* (Art of War). It is interesting to note that despite the fact that this book was written in the 4th century B.C., it can be found in the libraries of most modern corporate leaders — a testament to Sun-tzu's writing and battlefield abilities. The *Art of War*, one of the oldest surviving literary works on martial strategy and ideology, provides guidance on exchanges of both a military and non-military nature, and the principles contained in this text have value on the battlefield, in the boardroom and in daily life.

Sung Duk-ki (1893-1987)

Sung Duk-ki was one of the last masters of *Teakkyon*, a martial game popular among Korean children and youth, which was based on fourteen kicking and off-balancing techniques.

Taira Shinken (1920-1970)

Taira was a student of Yabiku Moden, the creator of Ryukyu Kobudo Kenkyu Hozonkai, a group dedicated to the development and propagation of Okinawan weapon arts. Taira Sensei carried on his instructor's work, teaching Kobudo throughout mainland Japan. His students included prominent martial artists like Akamine Eiryo, Nakamoto Masahiro, Innue Motokatsu and Hayashi Teruo.

Takeda Sokaku (1859-1943)

Takeda Sensei was one of the most well known teachers of Morihei Ueshiba, the founder of Aikido. Sokaku's martial teachings comprised field-tested combative techniques, which were by all accounts extremely realistic and effective.

Takenouchi Hisamoari

Takenouchi Sensei established the *Take-ryu* school of martial arts in the 16th century, the focus of which was grappling and immobilization techniques that could be applied with equal effectiveness to opponents attired in civilian dress and military armor.

*Todd, Walter E. (1927–)

Todd Sensei was one of the first Americans to study at the Kodokan, Judo's headquarters in Japan. In 1949, after receiving his 5th Degree Black Belt in Judo, Todd Sensei established the prestigious Shudokan Martial Arts Association.

*Tohei Koichi

Tohei Sensei is the founder of *Shinshin* Aikido, a sub-style that emphasizes soft, slow movements. A new school established by Tohei Sensei, which focuses on *ki* (internal energy) research, is called "Ki no Kenyukai."

Trias, Robert (1922-1989)

One of North America's most recognized Karate pioneers, Trias Sensei learned *Shuri-te* Karate while stationed in Okinawa during World War II and, upon his return to Arizona, opened one of the first martial arts schools in the United States. He subsequently founded the United States Karate Association. Although the USKA was once one of the largest martial arts organizations in the world, since Trias Sensei's death, it has been divided into several subgroups.

Uechi Kanbun (1877-1948)

Master Uechi studied *Pan-gai* Kung Fu in China with the renowned expert Shu-shi-wa. Upon his return to Okinawa, Uechi taught his students this powerful system, which was based on the movements of the tiger, dragon and crane. After his death, his son Kanei and a group of his senior students changed the name of his system to *Uechi-ryu*, in honor of their great teacher. *Uechi-ryu* is currently one of the most popular Okinawan martial systems in the world.

*Ueshiba Morihei (1883-1969)

Ueshiba Sensei was born in the city of Tanabe, Wakayama Prefecture, Japan, to a family that encouraged him to study the Shignon sect of Buddhism. His religious studies played a major role in his life and, consequently, in the development of the martial discipline he founded, Aikido. Ueshiba was also trained in swordfighting and spent some time in the armed forces. He received additional combative training under the tutelage of the martial arts master Takeda Sokaku who was famous for teaching a particularly realistic combative system that was based on battlefield experience. Ueshiba's training was both corporal and cerebral. He received his physical training from Takeda Sokaku while Deguchi Onisaburo, then leader of the Omoto-kyo religious movement, instructed him from a mental and spiritual standpoint. In an effort to spend his time focusing on refining Aikido, the elder Ueshiba transferred the duties for propagating this martial art to his son Kishomaru. In 1949, with the assistance of the Japanese Ministry of Education, Ueshiba established a *dojo* (school) in Tokyo where Aikido teachers would receive instruction, and, two decades later, he opened Aikido's state-of-the-art *Hombu Dojo* (central headquarters).

Urban, Peter (1934–)
After being denied a rank promotion in Japan in the mid-1950s, Master Urban established his own Karate system, *U.S.A. Goju*, and promoted himself to 10th Dan. His unique views on the martial arts have had an impact on many North American practitioners who, following his lead, have launched their own combative systems. One of Master Urban's most enduring contributions to the martial arts is his popular book *The Karate Dojo*, which was published in the 1960s.

*Wang Tsung Yueh
Wang Tsung Yueh was the principal student of the monk who is sometimes called the "Father of Tai Chi Chuan," Zhang San Feng. Wang demonstrated his combative skills in a barroom free-for-all in the Chen family village, which was located just a stone's throw from the Shaolin Temple, and local residents asked Wang to teach them his martial art. He obliged them, and using their Shaolin fighting skills as a foundation, created what would become the *Chen* style of Tai Chi Chuan.

Wasa Daiichiro (1663–1713)
In a contest held in 1686, this Japanese archery master hit the bull's-eye 33 consecutive times, thereby establishing a record that to date has not been broken.

Wong Long
Master Wong was the founder of *Tan Lan Kune* (praying mantis) Kung Fu. This system, famous for its quick defensive and offensive hand maneuvers, has given birth to several sub-styles including *Seven Star Praying Mantis* and *Northern Mantis*.

Wong Ark Yuey (1900–1987)
This master of Southern Kung Fu, one of the first teachers in North America to accept non-Asian students, was also a Doctor of Holistic Medicine. His martial arts school doubled as a clinic.

*Wu Jien Chuan
Wu Jien Chuan developed the *Wu* style of Tai Chi Chuan, which emphasizes uprooting and throwing an opponent. A prolific teacher, Wu spread his style throughout southern China.

*Wu Yu Hsiang
A student of Yang Lu Chan, Wu Yu Hsiang specialized in close combat (called "small frame") techniques, which he combined with Hsing-I and Ba Gua to create the *Sun* style of Tai Chi Chuan.

Yagu Munemori Tajima no Kami (1571-1646)

This famous martial arts master was a battlefield expert who assisted the 17th century ruler Tokagawa Ieyasu. Yagu also wrote several books about martial strategy and founded the *Yagu-ryu* school of fencing.

*Yamaguchi Gogen (1909-1989)

Nicknamed "The Cat" for his feline-like fighting prowess, Yamaguchi Gogen is famous for popularizing *Goju-ryu* Karate. He was a student of Miyagi Chojun.

Yamamoto Tsunetomo

Yamamoto was the author of the *Hagakure* (Hidden Beneath the Leaves), which described the principles and ethics of the samurai. In an effort to quash the feudal system and replace individual armies with a unified military, this book was banned after the Meiji Restoration in 1868. In 1912, the ban was lifted and the *Hagakure* again became a popular text among martial practitioners.

Yamashita Yoshitaki

Yamashita Sensei was the first Judo teacher sent from Japan to the United States in 1904. His impressive student roster included then-president Theodore Roosevelt, as well as many West Point graduates.

*Yang Lu Chan (1799-1872)

In the 19th century, Yang Lu Chan, also called "Yang the Invincible," traveled to the Chen family village to learn their brand of martial arts. Since he was not a blood relative, villagers were unlikely to teach him their combative system. Therefore, he devised a scheme to bilk them of their knowledge by pretending to be deaf and mute, silently observing their practice sessions, then retiring to his room where he would imitate their movements. When his ruse was uncovered by local folk, they were impressed by his devotion and invited Yang to train with them. He lived and practiced in Chen village for nearly 20 years and became an expert at "pushing hands." Yang then left the village and traveled throughout China, where he was often called upon to demonstrate his skills. His teaching method would later be called *Yang* style Tai Chi Chuan. One of his students was Wu Yu Hsiang, creator of the *Sun* style.

Yim Wing Chun

Yim was the founder of *Wing Chun* (radiant springtime) Kung Fu, based on southern Chinese combative systems, which she learned from Ngh Mui, a Shaolin nun and skilled martial artist. *Wing Chun* relies on close-range unarmed techniques as well as the use of the staff and double knives.

Yip Man (1901-1972)

This diminutive *Wing Chun* master gained stature through the fame and popularity of one of his prize pupils, screen legend Bruce Lee. His other students included members of the Hong Kong Police Department.

Zhang San Feng

Also called Chang San Feng, this wandering Taoist monk, who lived during the Sung Dynasty (960-1279) had studied a variety of martial arts. He developed combative techniques based on the movements of a snake and a crane and is credited with creating Tai Chi Chuan. One of his most famous students was Wang Tsung Yueh, founder of the *Chen* style of Tai Chi Chuan.

Suggested Reading List

In building your martial arts library, you should consult your instructor. You might also want to visit bookstores in your city, as many of the larger ones have excellent sections devoted to the martial arts and to fitness, health, nutrition, philosophy and spirituality. In the interim, we've listed titles for dozens of books that can provide you with additional information about some popular martial arts and related topics. We've listed them by country, or countries, of origin and by related topic.

Chinese Martial Arts

Chinese Boxing Masters and Methods, R.W. Smith
North Atlantic Books

(The) Power of Internal Martial Arts, B.K. Frantzis
North Atlantic Books

Scholar Warrior, D. Ming-dao
Harper San Francisco

Shao-Lin Chuan, The Rhythm and Power of Tan-Tui, S. Kuo
North Atlantic Books

Shaolin White Crane, Yang Jwing-ming
YMAA Publication Center

Japanese Martial Arts

Advanced Karate, M. Oyama
Japan Publications Inc.

Aikido Way of Peace, J. Stevens
Shambhala Publications

Bubishi, The Bible of Karate, P. McCarthy
Charles E. Tuttle Publishing

Classical Bujutsu, D. Draeger
Classical Budo, D. Draeger
Classical Bujutsu and Budo, D. Draeger
Charles E. Tuttle Publishing

Dynamic Aikido, G. Shioda
Kodansha International

(The) Essence of Okinawan Karate-Do, S. Nagamine
Charles E. Tuttle Publishing

(The) History of Karate, M. Higaonna
Dragon Books

Karate-do Kyohan, G. Funakoshi
Kodansha International

Kodokan Judo, J. Kano
Kodansha International

Modern Shotokan Karate, C. Borkowski
Masters Publications

Okinawan Karate, M. Bishop
A.C. Black Publishers

Secrets of the Samurai, O. Ratti and A. Westbrook
Charles E. Tuttle Publishing

(The) Spirit of Aikido, K. Ueshiba
Kodansha International

This Is Karate, M. Oyama
Japan Publications Trading Company

Unlocking the Secrets of Aiki-jujutsu, H.E. Davey
Masters Press

Korean Martial Arts

Hapikido, K. H. Young
Han Do Group Publishing

Kuk Sool Won, I. H. Suk
Kuk Sool Won Association

(The) Making of a Martial Artist, S.K. Shim
TKD Enterprises

Man of Contrast, H. I. Cho
Action International Ma Association

Mastering Taekwondo, T. E. Lee
World Tae Kwon Do Federation

Taekwon-do, The Korean Art of Self-defense, Choi Hong Hi
International Tae Kwon Do Federation

Tae Kwon Do World, Y.K. Kim
Vision U.S.A.

Tang Soo Do, J.C. Shin
World Tang Soo Do Association

Southeast Asian Martial Arts

Asian Fighting Arts, D. Draeger and R.W. Smith
Kodansha International

Filipino Martial Arts, M.V. Wiley
Charles E. Tuttle Publishing

The Weapons and Fighting Arts of Indonesia, D. Draeger
Charles E. Tuttle Publishing

The Wrestlers Body, Identity and Ideology, J. Alter
University of California Press

History, Philosophy and Spirituality

(The) Art of War, Sun-tzu
Barnes & Noble Books

(The) Book of Five Rings, M. Musashi
Overlook Press

(The) Chrysanthemum and the Sword, R. Benedict
Charles E. Tuttle Publishing

(The) Eight Immortals of Taoism, K. M. Ho and J. O'Brien
Penguin Group

Hakagure (The Book of the Samurai), T. Yamamoto
Kodansha Inc.

Kodo, Ancient Ways, K. Furuya
Ohara Publications

(The) Practice of Zen Meditation, H. M. Enomiya-Lassalle
Aquarian Press (Harper Collins)

Spiritual Dimensions of the Martial Arts, M. Maliszewski
Charles E. Tuttle Publishing

Tea Life, Tea Mind, Soshitsu Sen XV
Weather Hill Inc.

Zen and Japanese Culture, D. T. Suzuki
Princeton University Press

Zen Flesh, Zen Bones, P. Reps
Anchor Books (Doubleday)

Fitness, Health and Nutrition

(The) Body in Motion, R. Freeman (ed.)
Time Life Books

Chinese Medicine, T. Williams
Element Books

(The) Complete Idiot's Guide to Eating Smart, J. Bauer
Alpha Books (Simon & Schuster Macmillan Company)

(The) Complete Idiot's Guide to Healthy Stretching, Chris Verna and Steve Hosid
Alpha Books (Simon & Schuster Macmillan Company)

Encyclopedia of Modern Bodybuilding, A. Schwarzenegger
Simon & Schuster Inc.

Mental Toughness Training for Sports, J. E. Loehr
The Penguin Group

Optimum Sports Nutrition, M. Colgan
Advanced Research Press

Power Eating, F. Berkoff, B. J. Lauer and Y. Talbot
Communiplex Marketing Inc.

Stretch and Relax, M. Tobias and M. Stewart
Dorling Kindersley Limited

Additional Resources

In constructing your library, we suggest you give some thought to adding a few magazines about martial arts, as well as magazines about health and fitness. We've provided a few titles that are among our favorites. You might also want to include some videotapes and CD-ROMs, so we've also given you a list of companies that produce these types of audiovisual aids. Many of these organizations also sell martial arts uniforms and equipment. Additionally, shop around your neighborhood. Local magazine, sporting goods, video and computer stores probably offer an interesting selection of martial arts and related publications and other items.

Martial Arts Magazines

Action Martial Arts
P.O. Box 48213
40 Midlake Boulevard S.E.
Calgary, AL
Canada T2X 3C0
Tel: (403) 254-5713

Aikido Journal
50-B Peninsula Center Drive
Suite 317
Rolling Hills Estates, CA
USA 90724
Tel/Fax: (310) 265-0351

Aikido Today
P.O. Box 1060
Claremont, CA
USA 91711-1060
Tel: 1-800-445-AIKI or (909) 624-7770

Black Belt
P.O. Box 16298
North Hollywood, CA
USA 91615-6298
Tel: 1-800-266-4066

Bugeisha
200 Bethlehem Drive
Box 5
Morgantown, PA
USA 19543
Tel: (610) 286-7771

Furyu
Tengu Press
P.O. Box 61637
Honolulu, HI
USA 96839
Tel: (808) 488-5773

Inside Karate
4201 Vanowen Place
Burbank, CA
USA 91505
Tel: (818) 845-2656

Inside Kung-Fu
4201 Vanowen Place
Burbank, CA
USA 91505
Tel: (818) 845-2656

Journal of Asian Martial Arts
Via Media
821 West 24th Street
Erie, PA
USA 16502
Tel: (814) 455-9517
Fax: (814) 838-7811

Karate Kung-Fu Illustrated
P.O. Box 16298
North Hollywood, CA
USA 91615
Tel: 1-800-266-4066

Martial Arts Features and Profiles
3648 Cawthra Road
Mississauga, ON
Canada L5A 2Y6
Tel: (905) 566-5857

Martial Arts Illustrated
19751 Figueroa Street
Carson, CA
USA 90745
Tel: (310) 851-9409

Tae Kwon Do Times
1423-18th Street
Bettendorf, IA
USA 52722
Tel: (319) 359-7202

(The) World of Martial Arts
P.O. Box 4657
Santa Clara, CA
USA 95056
Tel: 1-800-824-2433

Wushu KUNG FU
P.O. Box 4657
Santa Clara, CA
USA 95056
Tel: 1-800-824-2433

General Fitness Magazines

Muscle & Fitness (Weider Publications)
21100 Erwin Street
Woodland Hills, CA
USA 91367
Tel: (818) 595-0478

Shape (Weider Publications)
21100 Erwin Street
Woodland Hills, CA
USA 91367
Tel: (818) 884-6800

Muscle Media
555 Corporate Circle
Golden, CO
USA 80401
Tel: 1-800-615-8500 or (303) 279-3077

Women's Sports & Fitness (Condé Nast)
350 Madison Avenue
New York City, NY
USA 10017
Tel: (212) 880-4530

Oxygen
2505 McKinley Street
Hollywood, FL
USA 33020

Videotapes and Supplies

Asian World of Martial Arts, Inc.
11601 Caroline Road
Philadelphia, PA
USA 19154-2177
Tel: 1-800-345-2962

Century Martial Arts Supply
1705 National Boulevard
Midwest City, OK
USA 73110-7942
Tel: 1-800-626-2787

Black Belt Magazine Video
P.O. Box 918
Santa Clarita, CA
USA 91380-9018
Tel: 1-800-581-5222

Hachi-O-Zan Ltd.
1535 Meyerside Drive
Suite 8
Mississauga, ON
Canada L5T 1M9
Tel: (905) 564-8164

Black & Blue Productions
6354 Arlington Road
Jacksonville, FL
USA 32211
Tel: 1-800-711-9403

Masters Publications
143 Gainsborough Road
Hamilton, ON
Canada L8E 1E4
Tel: (905) 573-1883

Bu Jin Design
2446-30th Street
Bolder, CO
USA 80301
Tel: (303) 444-7663, Ext. 427

Panther Productions
1010 Calle Negocio
San Clemente, CA
USA 92673
Tel: 1-800-332-4442 or (714) 493-7765

Pro-Action Sports
P.O. Box 26657
Los Angeles, CA
USA 90026
Tel: 1-888-567-7789 or (213) 666-7789

Stadion Publishing Co.
P.O. Box 447-D11
Island Pond, VT
USA 05846
Tel: 1-800-873-7117 or (802)723-6175

Via Media
821 West 24th Street
Erie, PA
USA 16502
Tel: (814) 455-9517

YMAA
4354 Washington Street
Rosalindale, MA
USA 02131
Tel: 1-800-669-8892

Martial Arts Organizations

If you'd like information that is specific to a particular martial art, contact the following associations.

International Organizations

Jiu-jitsu

World Kobudo Federation
71 Lancaster Road
Enfield, Middx
EN2 ODW England

Judo

World Judo Federation
Kodokan
16-30, Kasuga
1-Chome Bunkyo-ku
Tokyo, Japan

Karate

World Okinawa Karate
Kobudo Committee
1-2-2 Izumizaki
Naha, Okinawa
Japan 900

Kickboxing

International Sport Karate Association
3501 Southwest Second Avenue
Suite #2200
Gainsville, FL
USA 32607

Karate International Council of
Kickboxing
1251 Ferguson Avenue
St. Louis, MO
USA 63133

Professional Karate Association
3290 Coachman's Way
Roswell, GA
USA 30075

Tae Kwon Do

World Tae Kwon Do Federation
635 Yuksam-Dong
Kangnam-ku, Seoul 135
Korea

United States Organizations

Jiu-jitsu

Jiu-jitsu America
2055 Eagle Avenue
Alameda, CA
USA 94501

Judo

United States Judo Association
19 North Union Boulevard
Colorado Springs, CO
USA 80909

Karate

U.S.A. Karate Federation
1300 Kenmore Boulevard
Akron, OH
USA 44314

Kickboxing

See International Listings

Tae Kwon Do

United States Tae Kwon Do Union
1750 East Boulder Street
Colorado Springs, CO
USA 80909

Canadian Organizations

Jiu-jitsu

Canadian Jiu-jitsu Association
1205 Eighth Line
Oakville, ON
Canada L6H 2H2

Judo

Judo Canada
1600 James Naismith Drive
Gloucester, ON
Canada K1B 5N4

Karate

National Karate Association of Canada
2616-18th Street N.E.
Suite 203
Calgary, AB
Canada T2E 7R1

Tae Kwon Do

Tae Kwon Do Canada
3495 Laird Road
Suite 22
Mississauga, ON
Canada L5L 5S5

International Tournament Divisions

This section provides tournament division information and details for the popular martial arts, which are most actively involved in international competitions.

World Karate Federation

(formerly, World Union of Karate Organizations WUKO)

Required Kata

Bassai-sho, Passai-sho

Bassai-dai, Passai

Kanku-sho, Kushianku-sho

Kanku-dai, Kushianku

Gojushiho-sho, Gojushi-sho

Gojushiho-dai, Gojushi, Useishi

Nijushiho, Niseishi

Gankaku, Chinto

Hangetsu, Seishan

Unsu, Unshu

Seipai

Saifa

Enpi, Wanshu

Seiunchin

Jion

Jitte

Rohai

Suparinpei, Pechurin

Sparring Weight Categories (Male)

Super-lightweight	Under 60 kg
Lightweight	61 to 65 kg
Light-middleweight	66 to 70 kg
Middleweight	71 to 75 kg
Light-heavyweight	76 to 80
Heavyweight	Over 80 kg
Open	Any weight

Sparring Weight Categories (Female)

Under 53 kg

54 to 60 kg

Over 60 kg

World Tae Kwon Do Federation (W.T.F.)

Required Forms

Tae Geuk Chang 1–8

Koryo

Keum Gang

Tae Baek

Pyong Won

Sip Jin

Ji Tae

Cheon Kwon

Han Soo

Sparring Weight Categories (Male)

Finweight	Under 50 kg
Flyweight	51 to 54 kg
Bantamweight	55 to 58 kg
Featherweight	59 to 64 kg
Lightweight	65 to 70 kg
Welterweight	71 to 76 kg
Middleweight	77 to 83 kg
Heavyweight	Over 84 kg

Sparring Weight Categories (Female)

Under 43 kg

44 to 47 kg

48 to 51 kg

52 to 55 kg

56 to 60 kg

61 to 65 kg

66 to 70 kg

Over 71 kg

World Okinawan Karate Kobudo Championship

Required Empty Hand Kata

Seisan	Sanseryu	Kanshiwa
Seryu	Sanchin	Kanshu
Sechin	Gekisai	Saifa
Shisochin	Seipai	Sanseru
Kururunfa	Seienchin	Suparinpe

Fukyugata 1	Fugyugata 2	Pinan
Naihanchi	Ananku	Wankan
Rohai	Wansu	Bassai
Gojushiho	Chinto	Kusanku
Hofa	Chinti	Jitti
Sochin	Niseshi	Jichin
Mutude	Ohan	Bachu
Anan	Baiku	Heiku
Paiho	Sunsu	Jion

Required Kobudo (Weapons) Kata

Bo Kata

Tokumine-no-kun

Sakugawa-no-kun

Urashi-no-kun

Yonegawa-no-kun

Chinen-shikyanaka-no-kun

Sesoko-no-kun

Shukumine-no-kun

Chikin-no-kun

Rufa-no-kun

Shirotoru-no-kun

Katin-no-kun

Hasso-no-kun

Shushi-no-kun

Shoshi-no-kun

Chikin bo

Chatanyara-no-kun

Shishi-no-kun

Shiritoru-no-kun

Ufugushiku-no-kun

Chikin-dai-kun

Shiromatsu-no-kun

Kobo-no-kun

Choun-no-kun

Ufutun bo

Sai Kata

Chatanyara-no-sai

Hamahiga-no-sai

Chikinshitahaku-no-sai

Hantagawa-kurugwa-no-sai

Tawata-no-sai

Kugusoku-no-sai

Yaka-no-sai

Sai ichi

Sai ni

Sai san

Ufuchiku-no-sai

Tokuyama-no-sai

Ishikawaguwa-no-sai

Shinbaru-no-sai

Nicho sai

Sancho sai

Sparring Categories

Junior Male	(under 16 years of age)
Adult	(under 170 cm)
	(over 170 cm)
	(Open, any height)
Female	(All ages)

Kodokan Judo Forms

Two Person Kata Exercises

Nage-no-kata

Katame –no kata

Go-no-sen-no-kata

Kime-no-kata

Ju-no-kata

Koshiki-no –kata

Kodokan-goshijitsu-no-kata

Kokumin-no-kata

Fujoshi-yo-no-kata

Ippan-yo-no-kata

International Judo Federation

Weight Categories (Male)

Super-lightweight	Under 60 kg
Semi-lightweight	61 to 65 kg
Lightweight	66 to 70 kg
Semi-middleweight	71 to 78 kg
Middleweight	79 to 86 kg
Light-heavyweight	87 to 95 kg
Heavyweight	Over 95 kg

Weight Categories (Female)

Under 48 kg

49 to 52 kg

53 to 56 kg

57 to 61 kg

62 to 66 kg

67 to 71 kg

Over 72 kg

International Wushu Federation

Seven Standardized Forms

Long Fist (Changquan)

Southern Fist (Nanquan)

Tai chi (Taijiquan)

Straight Sword

Broadsword

Spear

Staff

Sparring Categories

Two-person Unarmed

Three-person Unarmed

Two-person Armed

Three-person Armed

Japan Sumo Association

(The International Governing Body for the Sport of Sumo)

Rankings

Yokozuna	(Grand Champion)
Ozeki	(Champion)
Sekiwake	(Champion 2nd Class)
Komusubi	(Champion 3rd Class)
Mae-gashiri	(Champion 4th Class)
Juryo	(Competitor 5th Level)
Maku-shita	(Competitor 4th Level)

Sandanme   (Competitor 3rd Level)

Jo-nidan   (Competitor 2nd Level)

Jo-no-kuchi   (Competitor 1st Level)

Mae-zumo   (Beginner)

Kickboxing, Muay Thai and Western Boxing Divisions

Weight Categories

Light-flyweight   Under 110 lb

Flyweight   111 to 118 lb

Bantamweight   119 to 125 lb

Featherweight   126 to 131 lb

Lightweight   132 to 139 lb

Light-welterweight   140 to 146 lb

Welterweight   147 to 156 lb

Light-middleweight   157 to 164 lb

Middleweight   165 to 178 lb

Light-heavyweight   179 to 200 lb

Heavyweight   201 to 210 lb

Super-heavyweight   Over 211 lb

Timetables for Asian Martial Arts

Precise dates for key martial events and the highlights of the lives of some of the combative arts' most prominent figures are often undocumented. This can be attributed to a variety of factors, including a tendency to regard combative techniques as proprietary knowledge and to practice them in secrecy; a reliance on oral tradition in transmitting martial arts information (and misinformation!); and the destruction of numerous written records in Japan, Korea and China during the Second World War.

What is on record is information from the periods when much of the significant activity revolving around the inception and formative years of Asian martial disciplines occurred. Read on and you'll discover dynasties, shogunates, regencies and kingdoms. At the next company cocktail party or family get-together, you'll be able to dazzle friends, relatives and business associates with your seemingly fathomless knowledge about Asian historical timetables.

China

Hsia Dynasty	2200-1766 B.C.
Shang Dynasty	1766-1045 B.C.
Chou Dynasty	1045-256 B.C.
Tung Dynasty	256-221 B.C.
Ch'in Dynasty	221-206 B.C.
Han Dynasty	206 B.C. – 220 A.D.
Six Dynasty Period	220-589 A.D.
Sui Dynasty	589-618 A.D.

Tang Dynasty	618-907 A.D.
Five Dynasty Period	907-960 A.D.
Sung Dynasty	960-1279 A.D.
Yuan Dynasty	1279-1368 A.D.
Ming Dynasty	1368-1644 A.D.
Ch'ing Dynasty	1644-1911 A.D.

Japan

Nara Period	710-794 A.D.
Heian Period	794-857 A.D.
Fujiwara Regency	857-1160 A.D.
Taira Regency	1160-1192 A.D.
Kamakura Shogunate	1192-1337 A.D.
Ashikaga Shogunate	1338-1573 A.D.
Hideyoshi Regime	1573-1598 A.D.
Tokugawa Shogunate	1603-1868 A.D.
Meiji Restoration Period	1868-1945 A.D.

Korea

Era of Three States

Kokuryo	37 B.C.-668 A.D.
Silla	57 B.C.-668 A.D.
Paekche	18 B.C.-668 A.D.
Unified Silla Dynasty	668-935 A.D.
Koryo Dynasty	935-1392 A.D.
Yi Dynasty	1392-1910 A.D.
Japanese Colonial Rule	1910-1945 A.D.

Thailand

Sukhothai Kingdom	1238-1438 A.D.
Ayutthaya Kingdom	1350-1569 A.D.
Unified Sukhothai Dynasty	1569-1629 A.D.

Prasattong Dynasty	1630-1688 A.D.
Ban Plu Luang Dynasty	1688-1767 A.D.
Tak Sin Regency	1767-1782 A.D.
Chakri Dynasty	1782 -

Indonesia

Singosari and Majapahit Rule	1222-1580 A.D.
Mataram Dynasty	1582-1749 A.D.
Bugis Dynasty	1727-1874 A.D.
Surakarta Dynasty	1760-1946 A.D.
Yokyakarta Dynasty	1749-1989 A.D.

Vietnam

Kingdom of Van Lang	2000 B.C.-258 A.D.
Kingdom of Au Lac	258-207 B.C.
Kingdom of Nam Viet	207-111 B.C.
Period of Chinese Rule	111 B.C.-939 A.D.
Ngo Dynasty	939-945 A.D.
Period of Twelve Warlords	965-968 A.D.
Dinh Dynasty	968-980 A.D.
Ly Dynasty	980-1225 A.D.
Tran Dynasty	1225-1400 A.D.
Ho Dynasty	1400-1407 A.D.
Chinese Domination	1407-1428 A.D.
Le Dynasty	1428-1788 A.D.
Tay Son Dynasty	1788-1802 A.D.
Nguyen Dynasty	1802-1945 A.D.

India

Since the time of the Aryan invasion in 1500 B.C., India and the surrounding areas have been a patchwork of principalities and short-lived states. From the southern province of Tamil Nadu to the northern kingdom of Kashmir, rulers have emerged, dynasties were formed and regional governments appeared and, almost as quickly, disappeared. As a result, a historical timetable for India would cover more than 20 pages. Therefore, we could not present this information in the appendix of this guide.

Index